AMAZONIA IN THE ANTHROPOCENE

AMAZONIA IN THE
ANTHROPOCENE

People,
Soils,
Plants,
Forests

NICHOLAS C. KAWA

UNIVERSITY OF TEXAS PRESS
Austin

First edition, 2016

All photographs courtesy of the author

Requests for permission to reproduce material from this work
should be sent to:
    Permissions
    University of Texas Press
    P.O. Box 7819
    Austin, TX 78713-7819
    http://utpress.utexas.edu/index.php/rp-form

♾ The paper used in this book meets the minimum requirements of
ANSI/NISO Z39.48-1992 (R1997) (Permanence of Paper).

LIBRARY OF CONGRESS CATALOGING-IN-PUBLICATION DATA

Kawa, Nicholas C., 1981– author.
    Amazonia in the Anthropocene : people, soils, plants, forests /
Nicholas C. Kawa. — First edition.
        pages   cm
    Includes bibliographical references and index.
        ISBN 978-1-4773-0799-1 (cloth : alk. paper) — ISBN 978-1-4773-
0844-8 (pbk. : alk. paper) — ISBN 978-1-4773-0800-4 (library
e-book) — ISBN 978-1-4773-0801-1 (nonlibrary e-book)
        1. Human ecology—Amazon River Region.   2. Climatic
changes—Amazon River Region.   3. Human beings—Effect of
environment on—Amazon River Region.   4. Human geography—
Amazon River Region.   5. Amazon River Region—Environmental
conditions.   I. Title.
    GF532.A4K39   2016
    304.20981′1—dc23   2015021607

doi: 10.7560/307991

CONTENTS

PREFACE

Amazonia is often seen as a land dominated by nature. A land ruled by biology. A land that erupts in an overwhelming array of flora and fauna, the diversity of which borders on the incomprehensible. A land, to paraphrase Werner Herzog, of overwhelming fornication and the fight for survival (Blank 1982).

Early anthropological research largely upheld this view, depicting the region as a hostile environment to which Amerindians had passively adapted, leaving little more than their footprints in the forest before the arrival of Europeans. More recent studies have challenged this vision, arguing that pre-Columbian indigenous[1] populations transformed large swaths of Amazonia, as evidenced in newly discovered geoglyphs, raised agricultural fields, anthropogenic forests, and enriched soils. Prior to European arrival, the region is estimated to have supported as many as nine million people (Denevan 1992a), including large, complex polities on the banks of the Amazon and its major tributaries that even featured extensive road networks (Heckenberger et al. 2003; Nimuendaju 1953). Rather than simply adapting, it seems that indigenous peoples shaped the Amazonian landscape in myriad ways for hundreds and even thousands of years.

After European contact, however, the indigenous population suffered a massive demographic collapse, and the Amazonian forest quickly reclaimed indigenous settlements and their surrounding agricultural landscapes. Shortly thereafter, Europeans began to colonize the region, launching expeditions to collect cacao, sarsaparilla, and clove, among other resources. In the process, Amazonia was integrated into the broader global economic system. By the late nineteenth century, it emerged as the primary center of latex extraction in the world, providing natural rubber for the burgeoning tire and automobile industries in Europe and North America. And today, a wide variety of commodities—from cacao nibs to Microsoft smartphones—are produced by Amazonians for consumers all over the planet.

When I first arrived in the Brazilian Amazon in 2003, I knew very little of its history. I had ventured to the city of Manaus to teach English, and although this wasn't necessarily my ideal vocation, it allowed me to maintain legal residence in Brazil for a year while I worked and learned Portuguese. I also had hoped that it might lead me to other opportunities more closely aligned with my background in anthropology. To paraphrase Carl Sandburg: I was an idealist; I didn't know where I was going, but I felt like I was on the right track.[2]

Luckily, that year I was offered an internship at the National Institute of Amazonian Research (Instituto Nacional de Pesquisas da Amazônia [hereafter INPA]), where I began to study the "anthropogenic" soils of the region, known in Portuguese as *terra preta do índio*, or "Indian black earth." These fertile soils, the product of long-term indigenous occupation and land use, were one example among many of how Amazonian peoples had distinctively altered their surrounding environment. And this led me to wonder: if even Amazonia had been fundamentally shaped by human populations, was there any place on earth that had been left untouched by humanity?

Today, the human influence on the planet has become so pronounced that many researchers and scholars assert that we have entered a distinct epoch in geological time: the Anthropocene, a new age dominated by humanity. Observed changes in global biodiversity, climatic patterns, and even geological processes have led many to support this claim in the hope that it may draw greater attention to the human impact on the planet. However, the "Anthropocene" also introduces a number of paradoxes and contradictions. As humans are implicated in global biological, climatic, and geological processes, maintaining the distinctions between natural and cultural phenomena has grown increasingly problematic. And while humans are seen as independent drivers of global environmental change, hurricanes in New Orleans and New York as well as tsunamis in Java and Japan clearly demonstrate that humanity is not in control of the planet's forces, much less the only force on the planet.

This book draws from seventeen months of ethnographic fieldwork[3] in Brazilian Amazonia and situates it within this broader context of the Anthropocene. It examines the ways in which pre-Columbian Amerindians and contemporary rural Amazonians have shaped their environment, specifically in regard to their use and management of the region's soils, plants, and forests. However, it also highlights the ways in which the Amazonian environment resists human manipulation and control—a vital reminder in this time of perceived human dominance.

Through this examination, I actively question the conceptual foundations of the Anthropocene. Although this new geological epoch is associated with the rise of modern industrialized societies in Europe, I am able to illustrate that it has a much deeper foundation in the emergence of large-scale agricultural societies, including those in Amazonia. In my critique of the latent Eurocentrism of the Anthropocene, I also show that many Amazonian communities trace their roots to the late nineteenth-century "rubber boom," a period in which Amazonians directly fueled modern industrialization through the production of high-quality natural rubber. And while one of the underlying justifications for the formal recognition of the Anthropocene is to call attention to humanity's pervasive impacts on the planet, I contend that this label also perpetuates a deeply anthropocentric view of the world, one which is arguably at the root of the current ecological crisis. By examining the impacts of climate change on Amazonia today, I argue that any discussion of the Anthropocene requires not only a deeper awareness of the human influence on the planet but also greater attention toward planetary responses to human action. In other words, rather than reinforce an anthropocentric view of the world, the recognition of this new geologic epoch should stimulate deeper eco-centric thinking and greater attunement to the lives of others on the planet.

Admittedly, humans are prominent actors throughout this text and as an anthropologist my primary concern has been with human ways of relating to the world and making sense of it. Still, I want to acknowledge the actions of other Amazonian beings and capture some of their worlds. The stories of soils, plants, and forests presented here are really human stories of these things, but they illustrate ways in which the environment acts independently of humans and can even foil the best of human intentions. At the risk of falling into the trap of overemphasizing the place of "nature" in Amazonian societies— a tendency that has long plagued anthropological thinking about the region—I fully acknowledge the shared roles played by humans and "other-than-humans" in everyday life. In that sense, this book approaches the study of Amazonia from an interdisciplinary stance, one that mixes the sciences with the humanities. It is written largely in the format of a personal narrative, but is not designed to privilege interpretive ways of thinking over scientific ones. Instead, I endeavor to include the stories behind the science, and in drawing from my collaborations with ecologists, agronomists, and archaeologists, I also weave in some of the science behind the stories. In doing so, I show that rural Amazonian people and their relationships to the broad array of Amazonian life offer important insights for rethinking the human place on the planet in this new geological epoch known as the Anthropocene.

ACKNOWLEDGMENTS

Writing is a lonely endeavor. Fortunately, many different people made the writing of this book seem a little less lonely. At times, they even made the process a pleasurable one.

This project grew out of research that I undertook as a graduate student at the University of Florida (UF). Augusto Oyuela-Caycedo ("O-C") was an extremely attentive mentor who urged me to take my ideas and make them into a book. Although I'm not sure that he will approve of what it has become, I don't think I could have written this book without him.

Many others offered valuable insights and encouragement during my time at UF. They include Mike Heckenberger, Chris McCarty, Marianne Schmink, Nigel Smith, Ignacio Porzecanski, Florence Babb, Ken Sassaman, Richard Kernaghan, and the late Hugh Popenoe. The research presented here was supported by a Charles Wagley Research Fellowship from the University of Florida's Latin American Studies Program as well as a Fulbright-Hays Doctoral Dissertation Award from the US Department of Education.

Among the many at INPA, I am indebted to Charles Clement, who served as a mentor during my time in Brazil and taught me a good number of things about Amazonia and its agrobiodiversity. I also received support along the way from Newton Falcão, José Francisco Gonçalves, James Fraser, André Junqueira, Joana Maia Salomão, Claide de Paula Moraes, and Anne Rapp Py-Daniel. Ju Lins was kind enough to help update the appendix of botanical species.

In the city of Manaus I have many people to thank. Rafa, Vinicius, Rodrigo, Roberto, and Suzan Padilla opened their home to me and made me feel like part of the family. The same can be said of everyone at the Condomínio Vila do Sol Maior, especially João, Dudu, Daniel, Vanessa, Maria Ivani, Myrna, Myrlena, Marcelo, Augusto, seu Djalma, Francimar, André, Ayrton, Tássia, seu Carlos, dona Graça

(Araújo), Danielzinho, Meire, seu Jorge, dona Graça (Sales), Hugo, and Muema. And I extend a particularly warm thanks to the Campos family—Leo, Elizangela, Junior, Leonardo, Leticia, Nice, and dona Leó—for their continued friendship and invitations to eat *bolo de nega maluca*.

It is fairly certain that I would not have survived in Borba without the help of Denise Barata. Valdo and Jaime were also great friends who made me feel genuinely at home there. The same is true for the Alencar family, especially Tulio, Binho, and their late mother, Mariete.

Among those at the Institute for Sustainable Development of Agriculture and Forestry of the State of Amazonas (IDAM) office in Borba, I thank Tarcisio, Dorinha, Carlos Alberto, Messias, Edilson, Beckenbauer, Xadonga, and João Gato. I also thank all the families in Puruzinho, Auará Grande, Guariba, Vila Gomes, and the Assentamento de Borba. Bidu, Carlinhos, Claudia, Claudio, Decroli, dona Didi, Francimar, Gleice, Hildebrando, Ivete, Joci, Jucimar, Maciel, Magno, Maria Madalena, Neides, Nilinho, seu Jorge, Tamiko, and Xicão were especially generous with their time, patience, and wit.

Several people gave me feedback on early chapters and drafts of the book manuscript. Special thanks go to Amit Baishya, Jen Erickson, Joe Feldman, Jeff Hoelle, and Mason Mathews. Many others lent a hand in varying ways, from conversations over beers to helpful emails and much-needed moral support. They include but are not limited to Johnny Anderpants, Caitlin Baird, Connor Beckley, Stephanie Borios, Jay Bost, Juliana Campuzano Botero, Kate Clark, Pepe Clavijo, Randy Crones, Jackson Frechette, David Garcia, Rachel Grabner, Damion Graves, Lizzy Hare, Hans Heintzelman, Richard Huaranca, Jeff Hubbard, Ana Lima, Ben Lintner, Camee Maddox, Rafa Mendoza, Ryan Morini, Karen Pereira, Rygar Peseckas, Carson Phillips, Rob Phillips, Tim Podkul, Juliana Saraiva, Tiberio Saraiva, Sam Schramski, Brian Tyler, Jim Veteto, Matt Watson, and Deb Wocjik.

I thank everyone in the Department of Anthropology and Classics at the University of Akron, who hosted me as a visiting faculty member in 2011. Tim Matney and Carolyn Behrman were especially supportive colleagues and friends during my time there.

I warmly thank Homes Hogue and the whole Department of Anthropology at Ball State University, who welcomed me as a new faculty member in 2012. My conversations and exchanges with fellow environmental anthropologist Cailín Murray have been particularly helpful. At Ball State, I also thank Dave Concepcion, Melinda Messineo, and the Sustainability Reading Group for providing a great forum for discussion and debate. Charlie Mason, whom I met in that circle, has become a good friend. Juli Thorson has been a very generous faculty mentor as well.

In Gainesville, I thank Marty Liquori and Deb Main for giving me a space to write in the summers of 2012 and 2013. Meredith Main was also an invaluable supporter and confidant during the writing of this book.

My family deserves special recognition. Chris, Nora, Jim, Nate, and Kolleen have put up with many annoyances and tiring stories from my time and work in Brazil. Despite it all, their patience and support have been unwavering.

Sydney Silverstein offered a countless number of useful suggestions that motivated much-needed improvements to the original manuscript. I am especially grateful for her affection, attention, and care. I also thank Theresa May and Casey Kittrell at UT Press for their help as editors and advocates. Lastly, I thank my late uncle, Sandy Davis, who introduced me to the field of anthropology and sparked my fascination with Brazil. This book is dedicated to his memory.

AMAZONIA IN THE ANTHROPOCENE

AMAZONIA FROM THE DECK OF A BOAT

I never learned the proper technique for tying up a hammock. I had observed several variations in method employed by locals, but I never learned to successfully replicate any of them. Instead, as in much of my life in Amazonia, I did my best to improvise. "Dá seu jeito," Brazilians like to say. Find your way to make things work. And so, following their words, I tried to do things my own way.

Making a few awkward and unseemly knots, I tested my bright yellow nylon hammock. It appeared as though it wouldn't fail me, at least not during the eighteen-hour boat ride to Borba. I then sat for a while, observing other fellow passengers as they situated themselves and made last-minute food and beverage purchases. I eyed a man selling popsicles made from cupuaçu (*Theobroma grandiflorum*), a tangy cousin of cacao (*Theobroma cacao*). Rather than fumble with the change in my pockets and struggle to get the man's attention, I opted to pass on what I knew would ultimately be a messy indulgence in the heat of the late afternoon. Instead, I lay back in my hammock, trying to avoid the kicking legs of the young girl next to me, who was ignoring her mother's scolding. I made an attempt to write in my journal but quickly gave up and began to read. Before long, a horn sounded and the itinerant merchants hawking popsicles and plantain chips hurried off the boat. The boat's engine began to quake and spew smoke, and we started to move.

I made my first trip to Borba in July 2003. At the time, I was an English teacher in the city of Manaus and I had decided on a whim to go for a visit with my friend Daniel, who had family there. Initially, I found the trees lining Borba's Madeira River no more interesting than those I might see on a wooded road in my home state of Illinois. The trees were not remarkably tall, and the river, which was wide like the Mississippi, made the forest on its banks seem rather insignificant by

FIGURE 1.1.   A man stares out from the deck of a *recreio* boat as it chugs upstream on the Madeira River (2010).

comparison. It all melted into one endless brown and green backdrop that slowly, begrudgingly, slipped past the boat. I could not admit this to myself at the time, but I did not find the Amazonian forest to be particularly awe-inspiring,[1] at least not from the deck of a boat (figure 1.1). Like the writer Euclides da Cunha (2003), when finally face-to-face with the "real Amazon," I somehow found it falling short of the image I had long held of it.[2]

Yet on my second trip to Borba, in 2007, after I had taken a short course in tropical botany and learned more about the history of human occupation in Amazonia, the seemingly monotonous and unremarkable landscape began to unfold and reveal more about itself. I noticed breadfruit trees (*Artocarpus altilis*), with their broad, distinctly toothed leaves, in seemingly undisturbed tracts of floodplain forest (figure 1.2). These were living artifacts of the "Columbian Exchange" (Crosby 1986; Crosby 2003), having been introduced from the Old World along with mangos, jackfruit, malay apples, and numerous other fruit trees that now dot the contemporary Amazonian landscape.

Originating from New Guinea, breadfruit and breadfruit trees had migrated across the globe before making a home in the Amazonian forest—a simple fact that illuminates the human and historical dimensions of what we call "nature." The story of breadfruit was just one thread of the many tangled and overlapping histories that helped me to see beyond the brown and green monolithic forest. In the process, I developed a new sensitivity to the histories of individual trees, their habits and lineages, and the suites of economic plants that had arrived with Portuguese colonists, immigrants from northeastern Brazil, and even early indigenous groups that had migrated from other reaches of the Americas. Considering the historical movement of people and plants that had helped shape the contemporary Amazonian landscape, I began to turn my attention to the ways that the "cultural" and the "natural" had become blurred or muddied, much like the silty Madeira River itself.

FIGURE I.2.   Silhouette of a breadfruit tree (*Artocarpus altilis*) with its toothed leaves (Vila Gomes, 2010).

Later, as I explored the region by land, tromping around flood-plain forests, farmers' swiddens, and *terra firme* palm stands, I came upon subtle clues of past human occupation and "disturbance," sometimes dating back more than a thousand years. In tracing the deeply enmeshed relationships between humans and the diversity of other beings living in the Amazonian environment, I started tugging at threads, picking at seams, and examining the stitching that bound together the jumble of Amazonian life. In this book I seek to capture and work loose some of the entwined stories of Amazonian people, soils, plants, and forests.

BORBA AND THE MADEIRA RIVER

The Madeira River is the longest tributary of the Amazon and one of the largest rivers in the world. It cuts a large gash across northern South America, descending from the Peruvian Andes in a northeasterly direction and eventually dumping into the Amazon River in the heart of the basin. The Madeira is a "whitewater" river, carrying massive quantities of suspended sediments from the Andes, which give its water a muddy color not unlike that of a cup of coffee with heavy cream. The river is rich with aquatic life, including a great diversity of catfish, from the tiny candiru (*Vandellia cirrhosa*), known for its ability to become lodged in human orifices, to the great jaú (*Zungaro zungaro*), said to be capable of swallowing a man whole.

As suggested by its name (literally "wood" in Portuguese), the Madeira is one of Amazonia's primary arteries for the transport of raw materials and goods. In recent decades, the river has experienced an increasing traffic of barges carrying soy and industrial commodities between Porto Velho, the capital of the neighboring state of Rondônia, and Manaus and Itacoatiara, the largest cities of Amazonas state. Yet such traffic along the Madeira River is by no means a recent development. Before the arrival of Jesuit priests in the area, Amerindians relied on the river as an important fluvial highway, populating its banks in relatively dense communities. Evidence of large, sedentary societies in the pre-Columbian era—once controversial among scholars—has been supported by the findings of early archaeological surveys as well as studies documenting the "anthropogenic" soils found in the area (Nimuendajú 2004; Hilbert 1968; Simões and Lopes 1987). More recent surveys, conducted along the lower and middle Madeira, suggest that prior research had recorded only a fraction of the archaeological

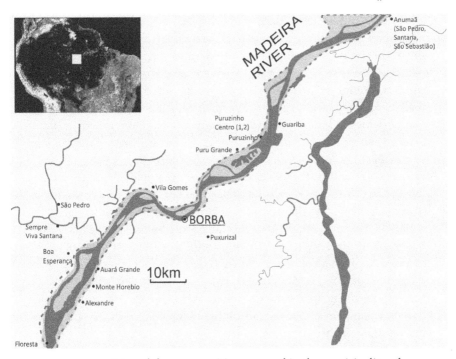

FIGURE 1.3. Map of the communities surveyed in the municipality of Borba, Amazonas state, Brazil.

sites lining the river's banks (Fraser et al. 2011; Moraes 2010; Moraes and Neves 2012).

Borba, located on the lower Madeira River, was one of the earliest colonial settlements established in the central Amazon. First known as Aldeia do Trocano, it was founded as a mission by the Jesuit priest João de Sampaio in 1728 (Comissão de Estudos da Estrada de Ferro do Madeira e Mamoré 1885, 73).[3] After its establishment, however, the mission was moved downstream to escape the threat of malaria as well as frequent incursions by raiding Mura Indians (Keller 1875, 54; Leite 1943, 43; Marcoy 2001, 207; Santos 1999, 78). The Mura were known at the time as the "pirates of the waterways," and surely they referred to colonial Europeans in no less disparaging terms (Harris 2010, 148). As a result of the Mura's frequent attacks, Borba stood as the limit of Portuguese control on the Madeira River in the eighteenth century (Davidson 1970, 12), becoming the first *vila* (i.e., Portuguese town) of the Rio Negro Captaincy, which would later become the state of Amazonas (Leite 1943, 403).

Today, the municipal seat of Borba lies 150 kilometers southeast of the city of Manaus, a distance of 215 kilometers by waterway (figure 1.3). The municipality covers an area of 44,251 km² with a population of 34,961 inhabitants (IBGE 2010).[4] More than two hundred rural communities are distributed throughout the municipality, and their economies are largely oriented around agriculture and extractive activities. Manioc (*Manihot esculenta*), bananas (*Musa* × *paradisiaca*), watermelon (*Citrullus lanatus*), papaya (*Carica papaya*), passion fruit (*Passiflora edulis*), and citrus (*Citrus* spp.) stand out as the primary agricultural products from the area while rubber (*Hevea brasiliensis*), timber, Brazil nuts (*Bertholletia excelsa*), and andiroba (*Carapa guianensis*) oil represent major extractive resources (see the appendix for a comprehensive list of useful botanical species). Fishing and hunting are perennially important subsistence activities, while cattle-ranching has slowly risen in economic importance as well. In the month of June, Borba is also a regional tourist destination, known throughout the central Amazon for its Festa de Santo Antônio, which draws worshipers and revelers from its many communities and neighboring municipalities.

ARRIVING IN BORBA

My friend Daniel's mother had grown up in Borba, and his grandmother and cousin Diana both had houses in the town. On my first visit, I found it to be a bit small, but overall very welcoming. I received invitations to play sand soccer and swim in the cool streams outside of town, and I drank sugarcane rum (*cachaça*) at night with a group of young men, who urged me to play guitar for them. It was a welcome escape from the city of Manaus, its urban anonymity, and its opaque, muggy heat that sometimes made me feel as if I were trapped inside a giant mouth.

On my second visit to Borba, traveling unaccompanied, I arrived in the town's port around noon. I untied my hammock and stuffed it into my backpack, and then gathered the rest of my luggage and started to make my way off the boat. Traversing a wobbly gangplank, I arrived on the floating dock of Borba's port. I was immediately confronted by a group of men offering to carry my bags or provide moto-taxi service. I politely shrugged them off, and began to hike up toward the plaza (figure 1.4).

Almost four years had passed since I visited with Daniel, and al-

FIGURE I.4. The main plaza of the town of Borba (2003).

though I struggled to remember the exact location of Diana's house, I still felt vaguely familiar with the place. I remembered the steep walk up to the main plaza, the plaza's severely manicured trees, the bright blue Catholic church that appeared as if it were melting into the sky, and the enormous statue of Saint Anthony with a halo made of wire that hung over his head as he looked out onto the river.

I walked down the main street that ran perpendicular to the plaza, passing two-story buildings and small businesses, including an Internet café and a general store where men from the port bought cigarettes and choked down shots of sugarcane liquor. Venturing onward, I came upon a series of small, single-story homes, mostly made of brick, with brightly painted stucco facades. The more modest homes were constructed of wood. One house advertised frozen fruit pops (*din din*) for sale with a hand-scrawled cardboard sign. A goat foraged in the grass of the single empty lot on the street.

Soon I came upon Daniel's grandmother's small brick house, which stood at an intersection. I peered in from the street and saw that another family was renting the property. I knew Diana's house was close by, but again I'd forgotten where exactly, so I continued down the road. An old man with a tall tuft of gray hair stood squinting at me fifty feet ahead, and I reasoned he would be a good person to ask. Sure enough, he told me that Diana's house was behind me, on the side street just past Daniel's grandmother's old home. I backtracked and turned down the street, asking a couple of boys if they could point out which house was Diana's. Without knowing it, I had already arrived. "It's here," they told me.

Diana, whom I knew I would instantly recognize because she looked just like her daughters who lived in Manaus, came out and gave me a hug. "I didn't think you were coming anymore," she said. In my semi-stuttering gringo way, I explained why it had taken me longer than I had expected to return. She showed me the room that I would stay in while I was in town, the same one I had slept in a little less than four years earlier.

Over lunch, I got caught up with Diana while we ate rice and beans, *farofa*, a salad of cucumbers and tomatoes, and fried jaraqui[5] (*Semaprochilodus* sp.), a popular regional fish. She told me about her grandmother's health and her younger daughter's new job. I talked to her about school and the research that I intended to do in Borba, a study on smallholder agriculture. I explained that I'd be spending much of my time outside of the town, visiting the rural communities of the municipality. In an expression of motherly concern, she urged me to beware of small-time drug traffickers and mosquitoes, and demanded that I go out to buy a mosquito net for my hammock that very day.

RURAL SMALLHOLDERS OF THE *INTERIOR*

During my first week back in Borba, rather than venturing off alone I befriended the local agricultural extension agents, who kindly took me on trips to the agricultural settlement just outside of town. In the late 1990s, INCRA (the Brazilian National Institute of Colonization and Agrarian Reform) undertook the project of opening roads into the periphery of Borba's municipal center to provide landless families with properties for agricultural production. Of these, the primary project was that of the Assentamento do Puxurizal (Puxurizal Settlement), named after a stream that runs through the forests just outside of town.[6] Within Puxurizal, 110 lots of varying sizes (from around 60 to 100 hectares) were defined and allocated to families; some of these ended up being exploited strictly for their timber resources while others were traded and sold. Most, however, were eventually occupied by rural farming families.

In the *assentamento*, I became familiar with Amazonian smallholder agriculture. I saw mixed agroforestry projects of açaí (*Euterpe oleracea*), cupuaçu, and other Amazonian fruit trees along with the ubiquitous swiddens of manioc, a woody shrub with starchy roots that serves as the region's primary staple crop. Some farmers also experimented with growing pineapple (*Ananas cosmos*), but many of the plants were suffering from wilt caused by a virus introduced by the pineapple mealy bug, known in Portuguese as *cochonilha*. Although extension agents tried to help farmers fend off these pests and the associated viral wilt, this seemed to require an unfortunate reliance on chemicals that were not easily accessible to the majority of farmers.

It quickly became apparent to me during these visits that while many outsiders, far removed from the reality of Amazonia, were concerned with the destructive force that agriculture represented to the Amazonian environment, many rural smallholder farmers in the region saw themselves as fighting a losing battle against the relentless attack of pests, fungi, weeds, and disease that threatened their crops, and subsequently their livelihoods. Even as extension agents and farmers gained access to agro-chemicals and other modern scientific methods for contending with such threats, they seemed to help win only minor battles. For the Amazonian farmers I came to meet, the image of the "fragile forest" was a wildly foreign concept. Instead, what they experienced on a daily basis was an environment of robust, defiant vitality.

As I accompanied the extension agents and learned about the challenges of Amazonian smallholder agriculture, I sought out farmers who cultivated the soils known locally as *terra preta do índio*, or "Indian black earth." I had first read about the *terra preta* phenomenon in an environmental anthropology course I took as an undergraduate. I had found that it is an unusually fertile soil in a land that is often viewed as hostile to agriculture. Compared to the acidic, highly weathered Oxisols and Ultisols[7] of the Amazonian uplands, *terra preta* soils generally have more stable organic matter (SOM), higher pH, and higher concentrations of plant-available phosphorus (Glaser et al. 2001; Sombroek et al. 2002). And what had caught anthropologists' attention was that *terra preta* was believed to have been produced by indigenous groups of the Amazon region prior to European colonization. This stood in direct contradiction to the prevailing notion that the impoverished soils of the Amazonian uplands inhibited cultural development in pre-Columbian Amazonia. *Terra preta*, in other words, demonstrated that indigenous groups had not simply adapted to the poor soil conditions of the region, but rather altered them in ways that expanded their productive potential (Glaser and Woods 2004; Lehmann, Kern, et al. 2003). Although the process by which the soil had been produced was not entirely understood, fantastic claims had been made about it, including the possibility that it could "grow" like any other living organism (Woods and McCann 1999). Some scholars had even suggested they could represent a model of sustainable agriculture for the future (Glaser et al. 2001; see also Kawa and Oyuela-Caycedo 2008).

Although there were only a few relatively small areas of *terra preta* in the Puxurizal settlement, I found two properties with the dark soils characteristic of such indigenous habitation sites. One of these was situated beside the Puxurizal stream. A man from town lived on the property part-time, planting açaí, manioc, and a mix of fruit trees. He also cultivated sugarcane (*Saccharum officinarum*) and corn (*Zea mays*), which were believed to grow best on the rich *terra preta* soils. A polished stone axe head had been found on the property as well, adding further credence to the idea that it had once been an indigenous habitation site.

The other property with *terra preta* that I encountered in the settlement had been leased by a municipal lawmaker. He had contracted a man to plant eight hectares of watermelon, which he intended to sell in Manaus. In this case, the rich soils of old Indian villages were exploited for the seasonal cultivation of an Old World crop that was then shipped on boats out of Borba to urban consumers in the state capital. The unexpected articulation of Amazonian indigenous history with modern capitalist production initially surprised me, but as I spent more time in rural Amazonia, this case proved to be far from unique. In fact, much of the contemporary Amazonian landscape and its "natural" resources are linked to long histories of human activity and are often opportunistically seized by modern entrepreneurs.

Following a week of visits with farmers in the Assentamento do Puxurizal, I wanted to make contact with longer-established rural communities outside of town to find more examples of agricultural activity on *terra preta* soils. The head of the agricultural extension agency, Tarcisio, invited me on a trip with representatives of the Banco do Brasil to visit communities on the Madeira River that had undertaken bank-financed agricultural projects. On the morning of the trip, however, the bank representatives didn't appear, and Tarcisio was forced to delay the excursion. Rather than wait around another day or two,

I decided to head out on my own. Just a few days before I had met a man named Carlos, who was the president of a community with large stretches of *terra preta* that overlooked a floodplain lake in an area known as Puruzinho. I reasoned that a trip to visit him would serve as a good introduction to life in the *interior*.

PURUZINHO

That same morning, unperturbed by a "stomach bug" that had left me feeling somewhat ill, I went down to the port and found the boat *São Joaquim de Autazes*. I asked Zeca, the captain, if I could catch a ride downstream. He said he could drop me off on the floodplain in Puruzinho and from there I would have to ask someone to motor me across the floodplain lake to where Carlos lived. I wasn't entirely sure how the logistics of the trip would work out, but rather than fret over the details, I picked up some last-minute supplies and hurried back to the boat. Shortly thereafter, we left town.

Around two and a half hours after leaving the port, we neared Puruzinho. I hopped off the *recreio* into a smaller boat, known as a *voadeira*, with a forty-five-horsepower engine tethered to its side. One of the deckhands got the engine started and with the engine gunned, we were untied. Bouncing over the larger boat's wake, we made a beeline for the shore. The deckhand manning the *voadeira* dropped me off on a small mudflat in the floodplain and I thanked him as I tried to make sense of my surroundings. An acute sense of isolation crept over me as the *voadeira* motored off. I was standing all alone on a fat slab of mud on the banks of the Madeira River. Strapping on my backpack, I looked out at the massive river as the *voadeira* and *recreio* began to shrink from view, looking like nothing more than miniature figurines or toy boats, slowly becoming enveloped by water.

I crawled up the slick clay and then slowly, self-consciously traversed two long trees that had been chopped down to give access to the relatively stable ground where the floodplain community resided. A group of people in front of a small house that looked something like a local general store stared out at me. Thankfully, I was welcomed by Jucila, a skinny young woman with long, yellow-orange dyed hair. I told her that I wanted to visit Carlos in the community across the floodplain lake. She said her brother could take me over in his canoe by *rabeta* (a small five-horsepower motor with an extended "tail" and prop) if I just paid for the gas, which she sold out of her house for

R$3.50 (about US$2) a liter. I bought a liter, and within a few minutes her brother Zé, a short fellow with a small, muscular frame, was leading me down a path to his canoe.

The canoe sat in a muddy little shallow at the edge of the flooded forest that opened into the floodplain lake. I soon realized that the Nike tennis shoes I was wearing were not going to fare well as they began to stick in the thick, oozing mud. I then understood why nearly everyone wore rubber flip-flops—it was the only footwear well adapted to the amphibious life of the rural Amazon. I slipped off my shoes and socks, dropped them into the canoe, and stuck my bare feet into the water and mud. After a few attempts to push the canoe off, we made it out of the shallows and into the lake.

Four small communities stood on the north end of the lake, two on the floodplain and two on *terra firme*. People from nearly every household fished. In the lake, they caught a wide diversity of fishes, from peacock bass (*Cichla* spp.) and piranhas (various genera in the Characidae family) to the beloved staple jaraqui, a silver fish with black- and yellow-striped fins. Sometimes fishermen even caught the coveted but increasingly rare pirarucu (*Arapaima gigas*)—a bony-tongued fish that breathes air and can reach several hundred pounds in weight and more than six feet in length. Although many families fished year-round, fishing was most productive in the dry season, when the lake shrank and the fish became concentrated in a much smaller volume of water. The residents of the communities relied on gill nets (*malhadeiras*), hand lines (*linhas*), and spears (*zagaias*) for fishing. Some even fished with bows.

Passing the canoes of morning fishermen, we crossed the lake and arrived at Carlos's home. It stood amidst a collection of wooden houses in a small clearing that gently rose above the lake. I wondered how many other communities were tucked away on similar lakes in Amazonia's interior, just outside of view.

At the time, Carlos was out working at his *rancho*, processing and toasting *farinha*, or manioc flour. His neighbor and son were out in the *casa de palha*, an open-air palm thatch house that sat beside Carlos's home and had a small, worn billiards table in its center. A young boy named Kleberson played in the dirt, stopping occasionally to stare at me. Pigs and chickens hunted and pecked their way around the yard.

After twenty minutes or so, Carlos arrived, shirtless and in cuffed pants, his tanned body dusted with manioc flour. He greeted me in a friendly manner and asked if I had come for the INCRA meeting; that governmental agency was instituting a program to provide assistance for the construction of new homes in rural communities of Borba. I explained that I had just come to see some of the *terra preta*. Clearly needing time to relax after a long morning of work, he invited me into his home.

We chatted for an hour while sitting on the wooden floor of his house, drinking sweet black coffee. When Carlos seemed properly rested, we took a stroll around the area to check out the *terra preta*. He explained that *terra preta* was often used for the cultivation of watermelon in the community. In fact, an inlet (*furo*) had been built so that the boats of middlemen from Manaus could gain access from the Madeira River to the floodplain lake for easier loading of the watermelon during the height of the season. In decades past, they had planted thirty, forty, even fifty hectares of watermelon that were sold in the markets of Manaus, he said. Although many community residents' complained that the soil had begun to grow "tired," the *terra preta* still held special value for production, just as I had witnessed in the Assentamento do Puxurizal, outside of the town of Borba.

Walking through watermelon fields and secondary forests, I occasionally stopped to pick up handfuls of soil for inspection. Most forested areas in Amazonia maintain a thin layer of organic matter from decomposing leaf litter that collects on the forest floor, but such rich topsoil usually only extends to a depth of twenty centimeters. In *terra preta* soils, the dark organic matter can extend as far as a meter or even two meters below the soil's surface. Carlos estimated that it reached a depth of at least sixty to eighty centimeters in the area that we surveyed.

Surrounding the watermelon fields stood thick stands of palms, dominated largely by caiauê (*Elaeis oleifera*) and urucuri (*Attalea phalerata*), both commonly found in association with *terra preta* and considered "indicator species" of the soil (Junqueira et al. 2010). Caiauê is used by indigenous groups for the valuable oil produced by its small orange fruits while urucuri has been used for thatching roofs and continues to be used for that end. Throughout the fields, Carlos and I also came across ceramic potsherds littering the dark soil. Near his home, Carlos told me, they had even unearthed a "Buddha." I was fairly certain that what he had found was in fact an anthropomorphic burial urn, common to central Amazonian archaeological sites. His inclination to associate the artifact with Eastern religion reminded me of how little we actually knew about the people who had left behind such traces of their existence. And still, their actions continued to reverberate up to the present, although with little enduring human form, manifested in the soils and palm stands that we examined that day.

Walking back from the watermelon fields, we returned to Carlos's place and found that the community meeting concerning the INCRA housing project was about to begin. Everyone had to come to sign the agreement for the project. During the meeting, Carlos, who had served as president of the community, officially stepped down. With misty eyes, he handed the presidency over to his brother. Carlos's brother, a wide, soft-spoken man, then proceeded to talk about the schematics of the new houses, and after thirty minutes, almost everyone's interest had waned. Around that time, Jucila appeared and told me she had come to take me back to the floodplain. I thanked Carlos for his generosity and time and then said goodbye.

I spent the night on the floodplain of Puruzinho with Zé's family. Zé had told me that he would take me back to town by *rabeta* early in the morning. I drank coconut water and ate a large watermelon that Carlos had given me, sharing it with Zé, his wife, Cândida, and their four children. The community's generator was broken, but I found it pleasant to spend a night without electricity, that is, until the mosquitoes began to descend upon us. "The visitors are coming," Zé announced wryly.

Inside, in the dim candlelight, Zé's children played several spirited rounds of dominoes with me. They emphatically slammed the domino played at each turn while directing provocations at the opposing team ("Hey look, I just killed your deuce!"). Meanwhile, their pet paca, Bebel, which was named after a character in the latest primetime telenovela, *Paraiso Tropical*, crawled around on the wooden floor, occasionally butting in on the game.

As I tried to sleep that night, mosquitoes slipped through cracks in the ceiling and floor of the house and found their way over to my hammock. The situation was made worse, I was told, by the lack of working electricity. Even with my mosquito net, their insistent buzzing sounded as if they were flying deep in my inner ear. I tried to block them and the thoughts of dengue fever out of my head, and somehow at some point I fell asleep.

Around 5:00 a.m., Zé woke me up in the dark. We had a quick coffee "to warm the belly," as he liked to say, and then headed down toward the canoe with his neighbor, who was coming along for the ride. I ambled across a large tree to get to the mud flat where the canoe waited for us, but before I made it there, I lost my balance and my right leg ended up falling into the shallow muddy water below. Slick mud covered my entire pantleg, though I was relieved to realize that was the extent of the damage. Embarrassed by the fall and my distinctively foreign clumsiness, I laughed to save face and then clambered into the canoe.

Zé got the small *rabeta* motor running, and dipping the long prop into the water of the Madeira, we started the trip back to town in the dark of the early morning. Within a half hour of departure, however, the "stomach bug" that had been bothering me the day before forced me out of the canoe and into someone's front yard. Zé and his neighbor chuckled as I bent over in a mix of pain and relief, thankfully masked in the darkness of the pre-dawn. We arrived in town a few hours later without me having suffered any further incidents.

I hiked up the road to Borba's plaza, my pants half-covered in mud, and my stomach on edge. I had made it through my first trip to the *interior*.[8] I was then faced with the task of making sense of what I had experienced there. I would return many more times to see Zé, Carlos, and the others in hopes of better understanding rural Amazonia, its past and present, its soils and plants, and of course, its people.

THE *CABOCLO*

In Brazil, rural Amazonian people are commonly referred to as *caboclos*. The term *caboclo* is derived from the Tupi language, but its precise meaning and origin are debated. Costa Pereira (1975) proposed that it comes from the term "caa-boc," meaning "one who came from the forest." An alternative interpretation suggests that it is derived from the phrase "kari'boka," which translates as "children of the white men" (Buarque de Holanda Ferreira 1971; also cited by Parker 1985 and Ioris 2005). Although the term *caboclo/a* is generally applied to an individual coming from the *interior* or a rural area of the Amazon, its historical emergence was tied to racial classification in the colonial period. The first appearance of the word in dictionaries describes *caboclos* as "civilized Brazilian Indians of pure blood" while later definitions refer to *caboclos* as individuals of mixed Portuguese and indigenous descent (Parker 1985). Following the colonial period, literate urbanites and white-collar workers applied the term *caboclo* to the illiterate and semiliterate agriculturalists and collectors of the rural zones (Wagley 1976, 289). In this manner, *caboclo* became not only a racial category, but a term used by elite classes to establish social differentiation from the Amazonian peasantry.

Charles Wagley's *Amazon Town* is the first full-length ethnography describing "*caboclo* culture," an important departure from the otherwise dominant focus of Amazonian anthropology on indigenous peoples. In his classic text, Wagley first describes the term *caboclo* as how "city people in the Amazon refer to inhabitants of small towns and the rural population" (Wagley 1976, 31). In his discussion of stereotypes associated with the *caboclo*, Wagley writes that they are perceived as excellent hunters and fishermen with a keen sensitivity to the habits of animals. Yet he also acknowledges the pejorative nature of the term, stating: "Still caboclo and tapuia are used in a sense of dispraisal; people do not use them when speaking directly to people of Indian physical characteristics." When he directly inquired about the usage of the term, an informant shared: "'It's not a hard word . . . but it makes a person sad'" (Wagley 1976, 140; see also Pace 1997).

In my personal interactions with rural Amazonians, I avoided usage of the word *caboclo* because of my own uneasiness with it.[9] Over time, however, I became acquainted with its varied uses, meanings, and ambiguities. What did it really mean to be *caboclo*?[10] In some isolated instances, I heard people use the term with a sense of self-irony, as in "Hell, what do I know? I'm just a *caboclo*." Others occasionally used it in defiant expression of rural pride ("Damn right I'm a *caboclo*!").[11] But in these rare cases the term was largely employed in the form of a reactionary or defensive quip. It seemed that no one I came across actively identified as a *caboclo*.

The image of the *caboclo* is rooted in ambiguity. A *caboclo* is considered to be neither Amerindian nor of European descent, not fully rooted in Amazonian tradition nor completely integrated into "modern" industrial society. Superficial observation might suggest that rural Amazonian or *caboclo* communities live up to the image of traditional Amazonian livelihoods, crafting their own wooden canoes, fishing with bows, planting manioc with little more than a machete, and hunting pacas (*Agouti paca*) and peccaries (*Pecari tajacu*; *Tayassu pecari*). The majority of households I visited engaged in these activities, but many also had TVs with satellite dishes and DVD players, tuning in nightly to the primetime Brazilian *novelas*, soccer matches, and sometimes even Hollywood films or Thai martial arts flicks. Many households also had sound systems that blasted the latest hits in the popular musical genres of *forró* and *tecno-brega*. Others bought refrigerators and freezers on credit from department stores in Manaus to allow themselves to enjoy cold soda or to freeze fish and wild game.

Like most people across the world, rural Amazonians lead lives that are in many ways both seemingly traditional and exceedingly modern. And while they live in a place that appears to be surrounded by untamed nature, I saw with time that Amazonian nature was in many ways quite thoroughly socialized and enculturated. In this place, all the simple binaries that classic social theory once relied upon seemed to collapse before me.

THE ANTHROPOCENE

Early anthropological research portrayed Amazonia as an unforgiving environment that imposed severe constraints on human populations and their development. Under the "tropical forest model"[12] presented in the *Handbook of South American Indians* (Steward 1946–1959), it was asserted that small, impermanent settlements were characteristic of the majority of Amazonian indigenous societies through time. The late Betty Meggers, a North American archaeologist, emerged as the leading proponent of this model, arguing that the broad upland forests of the basin severely limited socioeconomic development because of their infertile soils, lack of wild food resources, and generally inhospitable conditions (Meggers 1996). Although Meggers recognized that prehistoric indigenous groups like the Tapajó had maintained dense populations with defined social complexity, she attributed this to the exploitation of rich fluvial sediments of the floodplains and stressed that they had reached the "maximum level of cultural elaboration" for their given environment (1996, 149). In the title of her most influential book, Meggers even went as far as to condemn Amazonia as a "counterfeit paradise." Recently, a small group of scholars has reinvigorated her arguments in a slightly more nuanced fashion, claiming that interfluvial areas of the region—those isolated from the region's major rivers—were largely unoccupied in pre-Columbian times and experienced only minimal human influence from the activities of hunter-gatherers (Barlow et al. 2012; Bush and Silman 2009; McMichael et al. 2012; Peres et al. 2010).

Yet in my research examining *terra preta* sites in rural communities of central Amazonia, I witnessed the deep, enduring impacts humans had left on the landscape, which were clearly, though sometimes very subtly, manifested in the region's soils and forests. My observations have been reinforced by a wave of recent anthropological and archaeological research that contends that humans altered large swaths of Amazonia and its forests—both along major riverways *and* in interfluvial areas—long before the arrival of Europeans (Balée 1994; Balée and Erickson 2006; Denevan 1992b; Erickson 2005; Heckenberger et al. 2007; Heckenberger et al. 2008; Roosevelt 1991). Evidence supporting this argument has been documented in various forms: enriched "anthropogenic" soils (Glaser and Woods 2004; Lehmann, Kern, et al. 2003); geoglyphs (Ranzi et al. 2007; Schaan et al. 2007); earthen mounds (Roosevelt 1991; Schaan 2004; Schaan 2008); raised agricultural fields (Erickson 2005; Rostain 2008; Rostain 2010; Walker 2008); cultivated forest islands (Posey 1985); and concentrated stands of useful tree and palm species (Balée 1989; Balée 1994; Levis et al. 2012; Shepard and Ramirez 2011). More than simply adapting to the environment, it seems, indigenous societies actively shaped the Amazonian landscape in countless ways for hundreds and even thousands of years.

Today this area of scholarship is gaining greater acceptance as it becomes more and more clear that humans have fundamentally altered the planet, even in places once viewed as pristine wilderness. Ongoing scientific research demonstrates that human activity—mostly in the past few hundred years, but especially in the past few decades—has had considerable impact on global biodiversity, climatic patterns, and even geological processes (Dirzo and Raven 2003; Ellis 2010; Steffen et al. 2007). Drawing from this growing body of evidence, the atmospheric chemist and Nobel laureate Paul Crutzen has declared that we now live in a new epoch in geological time: the Anthropocene, a period defined by humanity's presence on the planet (Crutzen and Stoermer 2000; see also Crutzen 2002; Zalaciewicz et al. 2010).

Many have come to support this claim in the hope that it may draw greater attention to the human impact on the earth. However, the conception of the Anthropocene brings with it a number of challenges and contradictions. While some researchers suggest that humans have essentially overcome "the great forces of nature" (Steffen et al. 2007), humanity's ability to alter the biophysical environment also reflects our embeddedness within ecological systems and should remind us of our dependence upon them (see Latour 2012 and Crist 2013 for more critical discussion). The Anthropocene thus presents a fundamental paradox: with the increased recognition of humanity's capacity to change the environment, the separation between the human and the nonhuman, or people and the environment, has grown increasingly fuzzy, to the point that it is rendered almost meaningless.

The nature–culture divide that has served as the foundation for much of Western thought is slowly dissolving, or at least, as scholars like Bruno Latour have been arguing for some time now, is being fundamentally reevaluated[13] (Latour 1993; Latour 2006; see also Descola 2013 and Santos 1992). This has numerous consequences for our understanding of humanity and the human relationship to the world. To begin, it challenges long-established disciplinary boundaries and divides, particularly those between the sciences and the humanities. The historian Dipesh Chakrabarty (2009) points out, for example, that the tendency to differentiate between natural history and human history— or "Species History" and the "History of Capital" as he puts it—is becoming increasingly problematic, and has begun to push the limits of historical understanding (see also Serres 1995, 4). To frame it in different disciplinary terms, this would suggest that any study of present-day ecology requires a consideration of humans, and conversely that the contemporary study of humanity requires thoughtful examination of human relationships to a broad array of other life-forms and forces.

In this way, and despite its name, this designation of the Anthropocene is starting to encourage broader ecological thinking, at least for theorists who have grown concerned with the latent anthropocentrism that dominates much of modern thought. Actor-network theory (Latour 2007), posthumanist philosophy (e.g., Franklin 2008; Pickering 2008), and the writings of Gilles Deleuze (e.g., Deleuze and Guattari 1985), among others, have inspired new currents in ethnography that seek a "decentered" perspective—one that recognizes the actions of both humans and nonhumans without necessarily privileging one over the other. Within this milieu, social theorists like Donna Haraway have explored the limits of "the human" by directing attention to human relationships with "companion species" (Haraway 2003; see also Tsing 2012) while also raising questions about the boundaries between *Homo sapiens* and other species, given that humans are composed of a wide diversity of symbionts (Haraway 2008; see also Sagan 2013, 17–32; Dunn 2013). Cultural anthropologists inspired by Haraway's work have begun a movement toward "multispecies ethnography" (Kirksey and Helmreich 2010; see also Kohn 2007, Ogden 2012, Raffles 2010), and scholars like Deborah Bird Rose (2009) have discussed the need to write and think within the realities of the Anthropocene, encouraging ethnography that accounts for the rich diversity of relationships and agents that make up human lives and lifeworlds.

In this book, I take up the call to write in the Anthropocene while I explore this new geological epoch from the vantage point of the rural Brazilian Amazon. Recognizing that humans have transformed the Amazonian environment in many notable ways, I show that pre-Columbian Amerindians and contemporary rural Amazonians have left lasting signatures on the landscape through their use and management of the region's soils, plants, and forests. However, I also consider some of the ways in which the Amazonian environment resists human manipulation and control, and I describe how Amazonian peoples recognize the agency of their environment as expressed through their folktales and beliefs.

In the chapters that follow, I also highlight many of the problems underlying thinking about the term "Anthropocene." To begin, chapter 2 ("People") considers the latent *Eurocentrism* that plagues the characterization of this new geological epoch. Since the origins of the Anthropocene[14] are often traced to Europe's industrial revolution, people of northern industrialized regions are identified as the primary actors on the planet while those of rural areas are largely ignored or portrayed as helpless victims. In contradiction to this view, I review how Amazonia has been integrated into global capitalist markets since the colonial period, and I contend that Amazonians even directly fueled modern industrialization with the production of high-quality natural rubber during the so-called rubber boom. In recognizing rural Amazonians' marginalization, I also highlight their resiliency in the face of environmental and economic change.

In chapter 3 ("Soils"), I examine the *terra preta* phenomenon, which serves as prime evidence of human alteration of the Amazonian environment long before industrialization, provoking questions about the *presentism* inherent to the conceptualization of the "Anthropocene." Through my engagement with contemporary rural farmers, I look into both the benefits and challenges farmers face in cultivating such soils while problematizing *terra preta* as a model of "sustainable agriculture." Although *terra preta* is inspiring new agricultural technologies to curb climate change, I show that it reinforces a problematic *fantasy of control* characteristic of the Anthropocene: the idea that with the "right" techno-scientific knowledge humanity can reengineer the world's ecosystems and work them to full advantage.

Chapter 4 ("Plants") explores the social lives of plants in rural Amazonian communities, detailing their various powers and capacities. This chapter opens discussion about the possibilities of *nonhuman agency* that runs counter to the undergirding belief of the Anthropocene that humans are the only consequential actors on the planet. In a related manner, chapter 5 ("Forests") examines recent debates over prehistoric human alteration of Amazonian forests, highlighting the problematics inherent to classifying forests strictly in relation to human action. In doing so, I point to the *anthropocentrism* of the Anthropocene while relying on the folkloric figure of the "Big Snake" to question human dominance in the landscape.

Finally, the concluding chapter of the book examines the impacts of climate change on Amazonia as well as the problems of global biodiversity loss. My analysis raises questions about the politics of conservation and the responsibilities of global environmental management in Amazonia and the developing tropics. I argue that living in the Anthropocene not only requires deeper awareness of the human influence on the planet, but also greater attention toward planetary responses to human action. Ultimately, I contend that an increased awareness of humanity's precarious position on the planet should be used to push for a more inclusive vision of ecology for the future.

Chapter 2 | PEOPLE

THE "ANTHROPOS" IN THE ANTHROPOCENE

Since the Anthropocene era is defined by the widespread human influence on the planet, it seems only appropriate to start here with people. The purpose of this chapter, however, is not to reinforce anthropocentric thinking but rather to question how this new geological epoch frames human history and human relationships to the environment. When we look at the Anthropocene from the vantage point of rural Amazonia, many of the problematic assumptions that undergird this geological epoch are thrown into sharp relief.

One of the crucial problems with the conceptualization of the Anthropocene is that it identifies humans as the primary actors of consequence on the planet while nearly all other forms of life are portrayed as slaves to humanity's whims. A less obvious but no less concerning issue is the latent Eurocentrism that is embedded within this point of view. Since most scholars trace its origin to Europe's industrial revolution (e.g., Crutzen and Stroemer 2000; Steffen et al. 2007; cf. Certini and Scalenghe 2011), the people of industrialized nations stand on center stage while legions of others in nonindustrialized societies are either ignored or portrayed as hapless victims, even though they arguably have just as much bearing on the planet's future. To put things bluntly, the conceptual framework of the Anthropocene insinuates that there are two types of people in the world: those who have the power to ruin the planet and those who are powerless to stop its ruin.

This problematic framing of humanity and human–environmental relationships can be found in most depictions of Amazonia's inhabitants too. The two most common stereotypes of Amazonians are those who destroy the forest and those who serve as its venerable yet vulnerable custodians. Among the former are usually illegal loggers, miners, ranchers, and agro-industrialists while the latter are typically imagined to be indigenous peoples living in isolated reaches of the region.

The vast majority of Amazonians living in the rural countryside, however, do not easily align with either of these depictions, nor can their livelihoods be placed into clear-cut categories of those who "wreak ecological havoc" and those who "promote environmental conservation." Instead, the lives of most rural Amazonians defy such simplistic binaries as they engage in the basic subsistence activities of fishing, hunting, and agriculture but are also well acquainted with the market economy and consume an increasing number of goods coming from the region's city centers.

In this chapter I delve into the contradictions and conflicting images surrounding rural Amazonians and their livelihoods. I begin by examining fishing practices to illustrate the ways in which rural Amazonians use experiential and embodied knowledge to secure their subsistence from the local environment. However, I also point to the ways in which their livelihoods are defined by entrepreneurialism and articulation with the broader regional and global market economy through contemporary trade with river barges. While Amazonia is typically viewed as peripheral to the rise of modern industrial capitalism, I show that many contemporary rural Amazonian families are descended from migrants who came to the region to collect rubber either during the "rubber boom" of the late nineteenth century or during World War II to support the Allied Powers, and are thus directly tied to the industrial origins of the Anthropocene. To conclude, I discuss some of the fallacies in the characterization of rural Amazonians as *caboclos*, which in turn reveal some of the deeper problems with the Anthropocene.

In short, I present here a view of the Anthropocene that is distinctly rooted in rural Amazonia, a world that is populated by people and shaped by them but also resistant to their desires. It is a world that is made up of rivers and rubber trees and fish but also modern electronics and the seductive allure of money. It is a world of many competing actors and interests that have been implicated in modern industrialism since its inception. And it is a world in which rural Amazonians have carved out their own distinctive niche despite being marginalized and labeled as "backwards" *caboclos*—in essence, the overlooked *anthropos* of the Anthropocene.

FISHING

I learned to fish by hand line, the way that many Amazonians fish, especially children. Initially, Zé teased me about the 0.4 millimeter nylon line that I had bought in town, picking it up and asking incredulously, "Is this the line you're going to fish with?" He was accustomed to using lines that were at least twice as thick. I thought such teasing was a display of macho Amazonian fisherman talk—"real men fish with thick lines"—but Zé explained to me that he was worried that the line would cut into my hands whenever I "reeled in" a fish of any decent size.

Nonetheless, I decided to give my line a test late one afternoon. Zé had used his cast net to catch some pacu fish (*Metynnis* spp.; *Mylossoma* spp.) and he gave me one for bait. Zé's son, Zezinho, decided to accompany me, picking out one of his dad's lines with a rather sizable hook, and then we all headed down to the river.

I tossed my line out. It didn't extend nearly as far as I had hoped. As I "reeled" it back in by hand, Zé gave me an odd look and asked if that was how I fished. "I guess so," I responded sheepishly. I didn't really know how to fish Amazonian rivers by hand line. I was used to casting with a rod and reel in lakes of the American Midwest. He offered some advice: "Just toss the line out and let it sit and then wait for the fish to come."

While I was getting the hang of things, Zezinho felt a tug. He pulled on the line and it began to zig and zag in the muddy river water. He excitedly gripped the line, stepping a few paces to his left and right as he cajoled the fish ashore, eventually pulling it up onto land. It was a red and yellow catfish known as a pirarara[1] (*Phractocephalus hemioliopterus*). It probably weighed only a kilo or so, but Zezinho was content with his haul.

I still had nothing. Occasionally I felt a nibble, and every once in a while I pulled my line in, to find that my bait had been purloined. Zezinho tried to coach me, saying "Don't let the fish play with your bait" and "You need to set the hook!," but as much as I tried, I couldn't seem to get a fish on. Around 5:30, Zezinho was itching to go play soccer, but I told him that I needed just a little more time. After checking my bait and casting out, I got a bite. I gave the line a swift pull and I felt a fish on the other end as the line dug into my palms. I coaxed it near the bank, deeply worried that it would spit the hook. Before it could do so, I yanked it out of the muddy water and up onto the flat slab of floodplain where I stood. The fish's dorsal side was deep gray, which transitioned to white on its belly, and it had brilliant black lined patterns on its sides and a long shovel mouth. It was a surubim (*Pseudoplatystoma fasciatum*), one of the few prized catfish in the region. Hearing my excitement, Zé, who had gone back to the house, came down and helped

FIGURE 2.1. A man paddles back home after checking his gill nets on Puruzinho Lake (2010).

me unhook it, concerned that it might strike me with one of the jagged spines on its pectoral fins. The fish wasn't very big, but it was large enough to feed a few people for dinner. On those occasions when I caught a surubim with more than enough to share with friends, I felt a rare pleasure that was outshined by few other experiences from my time in rural Amazonia.

Aside from a few exceptions like the surubim, however, catfish, or *peixe liso* (literally "smooth fish"), were generally frowned upon at the dinner table. Most Amazonians gave preference to scaled fish (*peixe de escama*), which I couldn't easily access in the region's lakes without a canoe. Since most families attempted to catch a large quantity of fish to meet their basic needs and also have a little extra for sale or trade, lakes were customarily fished with gill nets, especially in the dry season when fish were in abundance (figure 2.1). In the rainy season, however, fish move into flooded portions of forest, escaping fishermen due to the sheer immensity of area covered by the water in its increased volume. During that time of the year, fish were scarce and needed to be actively hunted down, one by one. For that reason, many men fished by bow.

The idea of fishing with a bow fascinated me, not just because of the allure of indigenous technology and its exoticism but also because of the sheer skill involved in the activity. To successfully catch a fish in this manner, the fisherman typically balances in a tiny hollowed-out canoe while aiming and firing a big arrow with a metal trident tip, known as a *zagaia*, from a bow. To simply view the fish in the waters of a flooded forest was a skill that required years of honing. I could rarely make out any of the fish swimming below the water's surface, much less identify them at the species level. This laid bare the fact that rural Amazonians had forms of embodied and experiential knowledge that were entirely foreign to me—forms of knowledge that I would likely never possess. This was the result not of some innate superiority but rather of lifetimes of direct engagement with the Amazonian environment. And they relied upon that knowledge for the most fundamental aspect of living—their subsistence.

My friend Zico was deadly with a bow and consistently caught many of the most sought-after species of fish, including matrinxã (*Brycon amazonicus*), which he and his wife, Grace, grilled with cilantro, chives, and salt cooked inside the belly. Knowing that I had a fondness for matrinxã, Zico invited me over every time he caught one while I was visiting. To contribute to the meal, I brought over beer or soda, but I often felt obligated in some way to do more. Though I would never learn to catch a matrinxã with a bow and *zagaia*, Zico offered to take me out on Puruzinho Lake to show me how it was done.

ZICO, THE *ZAGAIA*, AND THE BOW

We tied a small hollowed-out canoe, or *casco*, to the back of Zico's larger canoe and then motored, for about twenty-five minutes, to the edge of the flooded forest. From there, we slipped into the *casco*. The edges of the hollowed-out canoe sat only a few centimeters above the water, which left me uneasy since any brusque movement could easily capsize the vessel. I had already learned this the hard way on another occasion with my friend Valdo. So I sat as still as possible, letting Zico guide our way.

We glided through the flooded forest. We were not far from the community, but the sounds and ambiance of the place had a distinct feel in the dappled forest light. The buzz of insects radiated around us. A troop of squirrel monkeys appeared on tree branches above our heads. I had never seen monkeys in Puruzinho before.

Silence fell between us as Zico focused his eyes on the water. His eyes looked through the surface, to the world inside the water. It was a world that I could not honestly see.

I never asked Zico if fishing made him think like a fish.[2] I worried that the question would have seemed asinine if I had asked it in such a way. But I knew that every fisherman has to think about the habits of the fish being pursued, the types of water they prefer, the depths they inhabit, and the places where they like to hang out—whether it be in rocky or sandy bottoms, or around fallen trees or stick-ups. If fishing does not require the fisherman to think like a fish, then at the very least it demands an appreciation of fish habits and perhaps even fish habitus.[3] Although North American anglers who fish for hobby in the summers often talk about their "luck," it seemed to me that the attainments of rural Amazonian fishermen rarely rested on random chance. Instead, their success derived from countless hours on the water: waiting, watching, testing, assessing. Embodied ecological knowledge—the deep physical attunement to the environment and the life that dwells within it—does not easily come from anywhere else.

Scanning the water, Zico came upon his first target. He carefully propped himself up, grabbed his bow, threaded the *zagaia*, and fired it into the water. I waited to see the fish appear on the other end, but instead, the *zagaia* buoyed up and sat on top of the water the same as it had left the bow. With an expression of silent disappointment, Zico pulled the canoe over to pluck the *zagaia* from the water, and we moved on to what we hoped would be a more auspicious spot, gliding back through the amphibious world of trees and water.

Again Zico repeated this performance, but missed another and then another. And then another. My back began to ache from sitting in the canoe for what seemed like hours, trying to remain focused, trying to remain silent. On the fifth attempt, Zico targeted a caparari (*Pseudoplatystoma tigrinum*), a catfish similar to the surubim, with brilliant black and white lines running on its sides. He fired the *zagaia* and within an instant the water exploded. The caparari thrashed with the trident tip deep in its side. We had our first fish.

Zico retrieved the *zagaia* and then lopped the fish on the head with the butt of a machete and tossed it into the canoe. With his confidence restored, he was prepared for more. Before long, Zico had three additional fish, including a matrinxã. As we headed back to the larger canoe, ready to make the trip home, Zico confessed, "I thought I wasn't going to get one for you." In friendly deflection I told him, "I was worried that I was bad luck."[4]

The image of Zico in the hollowed-out canoe with the *zagaia* and the bow hangs in the back of my memory. For me, it continues to be a valuable illustration of rural Amazonian livelihood practice—an impressive display of embodied knowledge and performative skill derived from years of patient training. However, this portrayal of Zico projects a very narrow, perhaps even skewed, view of rural Amazonian life. It is the version of Amazonia that I had wanted to see, one that I naively associated with a romanticized indigenous Amazonia of the past. But that perspective offers only limited insight into the broader panorama of rural livelihoods and productive strategies, including some that align poorly with sentimentalized stereotypes of the region and its people. Zico, for example, also cultivated a variety of Hawaiian Solo papayas on *terra preta*, which he sold weekly to boats that traveled to Manaus. He was the soccer star of the community too, and played in weekend tournaments throughout Borba. On several occasions, he pulled in large sums of cash, not unlike a successful weekend gambler. He had even saved up money from his papaya sales and soccer tournament winnings to buy a freezer for his family so they could enjoy cold drinks in the evening as they watched their favorite soccer team, Flamengo, play on TV.

Zico, like all people in the world, observed traditions of heterogeneous origins. He fished and farmed, played soccer and gambled on some games, drank Coca-Cola, and bought big-ticket consumer items. In no way did he, or anyone else I encountered, live in an isolated sphere of existence that was of discretely Amazonian "tradition."

In his own reflections on Amazonia, the anthropologist Stephen Nugent once wrote, "The compulsive interest in the exoticism of Amazonian naturalism and primitivism obscures the invisible armies of the region . . . people who are Amazonian because they live there, not because they embody other people's expectations of 'real' Amazonian qualities" (1990, 18). And I admit that I too suffered under the illusion of what I sometimes thought were "real" Amazonian qualities while finding myself strangely disturbed by their juxtaposition with other elements that seemed out of place, like on the afternoons I spent eating fish with *farinha* while listening to European techno dance music.

Such "hybridized" forms of living, however, are not the product of the last few decades of economic globalization. Instead, they are the predictable extensions of a much longer history of economic integration extending back to the colonial period, when Amazonia began sourcing Europe with a wide number of natural resources and products. And of all the extractive resources that have shaped the history of Amazonia and its relations to the world beyond it, none was more transformative than rubber.

OS SOLDADADOS DA BORRACHA/ THE RUBBER SOLDIERS

When the price of rubber skyrocketed in the late 1800s with the expansion of the North American and European tire and automobile industries, migrants flooded Amazonia in hopes of making it big. The boom sparked a major repopulation of the region following the demographic collapse of the contact period and the devastation of indigenous populations (Hecht 2013, 396–397). The search for rubber also led to a penetration of the most isolated areas of the Amazon basin, resulting in conflicts with surviving indigenous groups, and in some cases leading to forced indigenous labor. Horror stories abound in northwestern Amazonia in particular, where the torture of indigenous workers in the rubber trade took on dimensions of the surreal in what Michael Taussing (1984) has described as a "culture of terror" (see also Stanfield 1998).

At the height of the rubber boom, the Madeira River valley attracted a large number of immigrants from northeastern Brazil[5] who were seeking out the quality rubber obtained from the species *Hevea brasiliensis*, found in the region (Weinstein 1983, 53). Maria Mitouso de Melo, onetime resident of Borba and mother of the acclaimed Amazonian poet Thiago de Mello, tells the story of how her father came to the region: "In the year 1899, my father sold several houses that were inherited by Mother. . . . At the time my father was a salesman in Fortaleza-Ceara, where we resided. With the news that in Amazonas, rubber was making lots of money, he sold everything he had and came to do business in Amazonas" (de Melo 1983, 9; translation mine). Unlike de Melo's family, however, most of the northeasterners originated from arid countryside (*sertão*), which suffered from notorious droughts and poverty. Rather than venturing to the Amazon with hopes of getting rich, many of these migrants[6] may have been simply looking to make a modest living (Weinstein 1985, 96).

The rubber that was tapped along the Madeira River came from wild stands of rubber trees, or *seringais*. Typically, the extraction of rubber occurred under a patron–client system, known in Portuguese as *aviamento* (Aramburu 1994; Little 2001, 27–31; Teixeira 2009). The *patrão*, or the landowner, provided supplies on credit to the rubber-tappers, who were granted access to tap trees that were linked through a network of paths in the *seringal*. Under this system, rubber-tappers had to agree to deliver all their rubber to the patron and to buy their supplies exclusively from him (Dean 1987, 40). This relationship was highly exploitative since the *patrão* could manipulate the price of goods given on credit. The rubber-tappers, however, were afforded some degree of independence, as latex extraction was seasonal[7] and they could determine "their own work rhythms and production schedules" (Weinstein 1985, 93). Nonetheless, Barbara Weinstein points out that rubber-tappers "did not enjoy complete autonomy," arguing further that "over the long term, the *caboclos'* low political and social position left them vulnerable to various forms of coercion and deception by members of the rural elite" (92–93). Reflecting on the contradictions of the patron–client system Aramburu (1994) explains: "*aviamento* . . . united the world of the *caboclo*, as isolated as it may have been, to regional and national society, and finally to the world market. Paradoxically, it introduced the *caboclo* to the international division of labor and the modernity of the world market, and at the same time, [it presented] the primary obstacle to development and modernization of life and social relations in Amazonia" (83; translation mine).

The rubber boom led to an unparalleled concentration of wealth in the city of Manaus, rivaling even some of the European and North American centers of commerce (Garfield 2013, 17; Grandin 2009, 26–28; Hemming 2008, 179–182; Mann 2011, 325–326). Manaus was the first Brazilian city to install electric lights and a trolley system, which was heralded as one of the most advanced streetcar networks in the world. It is said that men lit cigars in the city's streets with large denomination bills and took baths in champagne while women had their laundry sent to Europe. Opera stars from Italy even traveled across the Atlantic and up the Amazon River to perform at the famed Teatro Amazonas, as depicted in the opening scene of Werner Herzog's film

Fitzcarraldo. The theater house also served as one of several examples that inspired the anthropologically trained novelist Amitav Ghosh to write: "On the banks of every river you'll find a monument to excess" (2000, 20).

The Amazonian "Belle Epoque" did not last for long, however. Its undoing began in 1876, when Henry Wickham, a native of Britain, smuggled Brazilian rubber tree seeds to Kew Gardens in London.[8] The seeds were successfully propagated in their greenhouses, and the seedlings were transferred to Ceylon (Sri Lanka) and then later Malaysia. Unlike Amazonia, where leaf blight prevented the establishment of a plantation system, South and Southeast Asia proved to be excellent regions for planting rubber trees in high densities (Dean 1987; see also Mann 2011, 340–341). By the 1920s, most of the world's production of natural rubber had shifted to Southeast Asia, and the rubber boom went bust, leading to a splintering of the Amazonian economy (Schmink and Wood 1992, 46–50).

During World War II, however, rubber production experienced a resurgence in Amazonia. As the plantations in Malaysia came under control of the Japanese, the Allied Forces suffered a rubber shortage, leading to demand for Brazilian rubber once again. At that time, a second wave of migrants swept through the Amazon region. Like before, they were largely men from the Brazilian Northeast who became known as the *soldados de borracha*, or the "rubber soldiers" (Garfield 2013, 86–126). A large number of them moved to the lower and middle Madeira given the region's "fame" for rubber, as one old-timer in Borba named Nini had put it. Many people whom I encountered in the rural countryside mentioned that their father or grandfather had been a "rubber soldier" and several of the rural communities I visited in Borba, including Puruzinho, traced their roots back to the period.

In addition to "Brazilian rubber" extracted from trees of the genus *Hevea*, other forms of latex known as "sorva" and "balata" were collected in Borba and along the course of the Madeira River and its tributaries. Balata (also known in Brazil as *maçaranduba*) was the name given in the British market to latex derived from several species of the genus *Manilkara* (Dean 1987, 38). Compared to *Hevea*, it yielded durable and less elastic latex that was used for machine belting. The term "balata," however, was also applied more generally by locals. Seu Hernando (or "Mr. Hernando"), an elder Puruzinho resident, explained to me that the latex of several different trees (garrote [*Brosimum rubescens*], parajuba [*Dialium guianense*], rosada [*Micropholis* spp.], and sorva [*Couma utilis*]; Grandtner and Chevrette 2013) were mixed together to make "balata," which was later shipped abroad.

Oral histories shed much light on this period when balata and rubber were widely collected on the lower Madeira. In my conversations with dona Célia ("Mrs. Célia"), an eighty-one-year-old woman from Puruzinho, I learned that her husband and other men from the area made trips into the *centro*, or the deep isolated reaches of the forest, spending up to four or five months collecting latex. The men (I heard no stories of women collecting balata) carried only the most basic provisions, which consisted mostly of manioc flour and munitions for hunting game for their subsistence. Seu Laudelino, another Puruzinho resident, plainly summarized the time, saying: "We suffered a lot."[9] On one memorable trip he and his crew lost their manioc flour when their canoe capsized and they were forced to rely strictly on hard, dried meat. "*Só carne assada, bem torradinho.*" But, he contended, "working with latex [*goma elástica*] was the way [back then] . . . that's all there was."[10]

Despite their suffering, men who worked with rubber sometimes recall the era with a bittersweet nostalgia. They were tough times, but times they were proud to have lived through. They paddled to the far reaches of the municipality of Borba that today in an era of motorboats still seem distant, far-removed, isolated. They went up the Sucunduri, Igapó-Açu, Tupana, Acari, and Abacaxi Rivers, which all ran far from the Madeira, the main artery of the region. Unlike the *centro* of Brazil's urban areas today, which serves as the center of commerce and activity, the *centro* in rural Amazonia lies deep in the forest, or the *mata* (Raffles 2002, 222–223). Stories of hardship and near scrapes with death are often recounted from this period, and many legends and oral traditions are told in the context of this time when men would get lost in the woods, encountering Curupira, Juma, and other creatures of Amazonian myth.[11]

As was the case during the rubber boom, the rubber soldiers collected latex under a patron–client system. Before men would leave for the *centro*, their *patrão* would provide them with provisions for their trip and for their families during the period they would be absent from home. On return from their trips, men paid the debts they owed to the *patrão*. Those who could not collect sufficient latex remained in debt. Those who were able to collect beyond what they owed were paid the difference by the *patrão*. At times, competition among men collecting latex could be fierce.

While I was eating a dinner of fried jaraqui (*Semaprochilodus* spp.) with Sapo one evening, he shared with me a story that his grandfather's brother had told him about his days working with balata. The story illustrates the perils, both physical and psychological, real and imagined, of balata extraction at the time:

> My grandfather's brother who lived in Trocanã told me this story before he passed away. He had worked with balata in Borba and had reached the point where he was pretty well off, but he was worried that the men working with him were jealous of his success. One night he dreamt of a vulture picking away at his bones and when he woke the next day, he was afraid that they would come to kill him. He decided to take off for Mapiá [a river east of Borba], but just as he suspected, a group of men that worked with balata followed him out of town and surrounded him. He was worried they were going to kill him, but they said they would let him escape with his life since they had been friends. Still they demanded that he leave town and all of his possessions behind. He then took off into the woods of Mapiá and spent six months living off fruits and other foods he could find in the forest. Every day he prayed and recited the "Pai Nosso" [Lord's Prayer] and "Creio em Deus Pai." After several months in the forest, he realized that he was being accompanied by a small man all in white who told him that he was entering hell. There he saw the souls of people who he had known in Borba, but who were still alive. He saw his sister, Zuza, on all fours with a dog in her mouth. The man in white said she had sinned by aborting unwanted children. And then the man in white escorted him away from hell and told him that it wasn't his time to die, but that he had to repent for his sins since he had had relations with his adoptive father's woman. He was told that he would have to return to his body on earth, which then appeared before him like an animal and it disgusted him. Shortly thereafter, he said, he was found on the banks of a small river and brought back to the city and was given clothes. Only then did he realize he was completely naked.[12]

Stories of treachery and backstabbing among latex collectors and rubber-tappers are often heard when Borba's residents talk of this era. Of course, most of the crimes committed against rubber-tappers and extractivists occurred on the orders of local rubber barons. Some residents of Borba recall the stories of their parents and grandparents, who claimed that when individuals had been too successful at repaying their *patrão*, and were able to profit off rubber or balata extraction, they would be threatened or, in other cases, murdered. Seu Laudelino, for example, explained that his *patrão* in Borba treated him fairly, but men in the neighboring municipality of Nova Aripuanã, just upriver, were not always so fortunate. If a man tried to make more than what he owed his *patrão*, "he'd get paid with a bullet," seu Laudelino told me matter-of-factly.

Some died at the hands of their patrons and others narrowly escaped. In Maria Mitouso de Melo's autobiography, she recounts her father's flight from the *seringal*, following the advice of a friend, who told him: "'Mr. Mitouso, go, run away, because the *patrão* is going to kill you, since that's his way, when an employee has a balance like you have, he has you killed so he doesn't have to pay'" (de Melo 1983, 52; translation mine). De Melo goes on to write,

> That was how many rubber-tappers and workers died in the distant *seringais* of our Amazonas! They came from the Northeast full of hope and delusion, thinking about making lots of money, but what awaited them was death, either from malaria or from the crimes committed by their patrons. How they suffered, these poor Brazilians who came to brave our forests in search of rubber! And how much evil was in the hearts of some men of this time, and how many crimes went unpunished! (de Melo 1983, 53; translation mine)

Many of the older residents of communities in Borba said that local patrons paid fairly, however, and so it is possible that violence and extortion were the exception rather than the rule, at least for Borba's residents along the Madeira River between the 1920s and 1960s. Manoel Saraiva, from the community of Caiçara, was the main patron in Borba at the time, and many interviewees spoke highly of him, as a good and decent *patrão*. Seu Hernando, seu Laudelino, and other residents of Puruzinho all agreed that he paid them when they returned after their months of labor in the *centro*. Their balances were never denied, and they said that despite the hard work, the money was usually enough to buy several months of provisions for their families when they returned home.

In the off-season, when men were not collecting latex, they engaged in other extractive and agricultural activities. Some cut firewood for the steamships that stopped at Manoel Saraiva's *barracão* (general store or depot) in the community of Caiçara, before it chugged upstream to the town of Borba. They also collected Brazil nuts (*Berthol-*

FIGURE 2.2.   Canoeing on Puruzinho Lake (2010).

letia excelsa) and andiroba nuts (*Carapa guianensis*), which they sold to Saraiva. And, of course, they helped out in their own families' fields, planting manioc (*Manihot esculenta*), bananas (*Musa* × *paradisiaca*) citrus (*Citrus* spp.), and tobacco (*Nicotiana tabacum*) along with watermelon (*Citrullus lanatus*), corn (*Zea mays*), and beans (*Vigna unguiculata*). "Now people just work for money," dona Célia explained to me, "but at that time there were few families [in Puruzinho], and we helped each other out."[13]

In the 1960s and 1970s, the price of latex fell once more, and the market for Amazonian rubber and balata virtually disappeared. This was a cycle just like any other that the Amazonian peasantry has experienced in its centuries of existence. And as before, the diminished dependence on latex resulted in an increase in agricultural production as well as a generalized diversification of rural livelihoods in the region (Fraser et al. 2009, 232–233; Nugent 1993, 182). The patron-client system, or at least some iteration of it, also remained "despite many theorists' consignment of it to the dustbin of pre-capitalism," as remarked by Hugh Raffles (2002, 191). Rather than being replaced, Richard Pace points out, the patron–client system was simply retooled to more effectively articulate with market capitalism (1998, 113–134).

If we accept modern industrial capitalism to be the engine of the Anthropocene, then we can affirm that contemporary Amazonia is populated by the descendants of people who were responsible for fueling that engine—or perhaps more accurately, supplying some of its most critical parts, including tires, machine belting, valves, and numerous other rubber components. In the wake of the rubber years, however, rural Amazonians held a position that was ambiguous in its economic articulation. Clearly they did not live in isolation from the world economic system, but they remained marginalized by it in many ways. Their negotiation within the system continues in a similar manner today: most people engage the market but still maintain subsistence practices that can ensure their survival independent of it. It is precisely this ambivalent relationship with markets and "modern" industrial society that defines rural Amazonian livelihoods. And in one of its most recent forms—the burgeoning barge economy—I witnessed the evolution of this negotiation up close.

ZÉ AND THE BARGE ECONOMY

Before I ever went fishing with Zico, I had spent many mornings and afternoons on Puruzinho Lake with Zé (figure 2.2). On occasion we trolled for peacock bass (*Cichla moculus*) with a hand line and lure (*currico*), but usually Zé fished with gill nets he had purchased in Manaus. Depending on the mesh size of the net, one could catch a range of fishes, from two-pound jaraqui to two-hundred-pound pirarucu (*Arapaima gigas*; see table 2.1). I looked forward to our excursions to check the nets out on the lake and it was my impression that Zé enjoyed such trips too, though his motivations were clearly different from mine. Not only did he fish for his family, and the occasional friend who showed up for dinner after drinking *cachaça* for lunch, but Zé also relied on fishing as a vital source of supplementary income.

During an early stay in the community of Puruzinho, I encountered Zé late one morning as he returned from a successful fishing trip on the lake. In his hand he carried six fat fish strung up on a reed. I had secretly hoped that he would prepare a fish stew for lunch that afternoon, but instead he walked briskly past me toward his canoe, which was tied up on the river. Concealing my disappointment, I inquired as to where he was going with the fish. He pointed to the slow-moving barge across the river, as he balanced his *rabeta* motor on one shoulder with the fish in his opposite hand, and told me he was going to try

TABLE 2.1. COMMONLY IDENTIFIED FISH SPECIES IN BORBA, AMAZONAS, BRAZIL

Family	Species Name	Common Name	English Name
Arapaimatidae	*Arapaima gigas*	pirarucu	arapaima
Callichthyidae	*Hoplosternum littorale*	tamuatá	
Characidae	*Serrasalums rhombeus*	piranha-preta	black piranha
Characidae	*Pygocentrus nattereri*	piranha-caju	cashew piranha
Characidae	*Serrasalmus serrulatus*	piranha-branca	white piranha
Characidae	*Serrasalmus spilopleura*	piranha-amarela	yellow piranha
Characidae	*Tiportheus albus*	sardinha	
Characidae	*Brycon amazonicus*	matrinxã	
Characidae	*Colossoma macropomum*	tambaqui	
Characidae	*Metynnis* spp.; *Mylossoma* spp.	pacu	
Characidae	*Piaractus brachypomus*	pirapitinga	
Cichlidae	*Astronotus* spp.	acará-açu	oscar
Cichlidae	Various genera	acará; cará	oscar
Cichlidae	*Cichla moculus*	tucunaré	peacock bass
Cichlidae	*Cichla ocellaris*	tucunaré-açu	peacock bass
Cichlidae	*Cichla temensis*	tucunaré-paca	peacock bass
Curimatidae	*Curimata* spp.	branquinha	
Doradidae	*Oxydoras niger*	cuiu-cuiu	
Erythrindidae	*Hoplias malbaricus*	traíra	
Hemiodontidae	*Hemiodus* spp.	charuto	
Loricariidae	*Pterygoplichthys pardalis*	bodó	leopard pleco
Osteoglossidae	*Osteoglossum bicirrhosum*	aruanã; sulamba	monkey fish; Aruana
Pimelodidae	*Phractocephalus hemioliopterus*	pirarara	redtail catfish
Pimelodidae	*Pseudoplatystoma tigrinum*	caparari	tiger shovelnose catfish

(*continued*)

TABLE 2.1. (*CONTINUED*)

Family	Species Name	Common Name	English Name
Pimelodidae	*Pseudoplatystoma fasciatum*	surubim	tiger shovelnose catfish
Pimelodidae	*Calophysus macropterus*	piracatinga	
Pimelodidae	*Hypophthalmus* spp.	mapará	
Pimelodidae	*Pimelodus blochii*	mandi	
Pimelodidae	*Pinirampus pirinampu*	piranambu	
Prochilodontidae	*Prochilodus ngricans*	curimata	
Prochilodontidae	*Semaprochilodus* spp.	jaraqui	
Sciaenidae	*Plagioscion* spp.	pescada	

to sell them. His body language projected a modest determination as he arranged the motor on the canoe, and in his eyes I thought I caught a look that reflected a fixation on that allure of possibility, a look that you see in the eyes of a man who senses that he is about to make some money.

Every day as many as a dozen massive river barges pass through the municipality of Borba on the Madeira River as they transport soy and industrial goods between Porto Velho, the capital of the neighboring state of Rondônia, and Manaus and Itacoatiara, the largest cities of Amazonas state (figures 2.3 and 2.4). With such traffic, new economic opportunities have arisen for the inhabitants of communities along the Madeira River's banks. Many households living on or near the river sell fresh fish, agricultural produce, bushmeat, wild honey, and sometimes even drugs to the barge operators, or *balseiros*. The *balseiros* occasionally purchase these products with cash, but more often than not they trade diesel or sometimes industrialized foods, like frozen chickens, in exchange for the fresh produce and goods. Diesel is a particularly valuable commodity because it provides energy for community generators, allowing rural families to watch television in the evenings and, for those households that have freezers, to preserve fish or enjoy cold drinks.

Barges represent new market opportunities while also creating

FIGURE 2.3. A small canoe motors out to meet an oncoming barge as another barge passes by on the Madeira River (2010).

FIGURE 2.4. A man waits for a barge on the banks of the Madeira River (2009).

economic arrangements different from what was seen in the past. Before the arrival of the barge economy, households sold goods either to a middleman or to a local *patrão*, since the patron–client system of the rubber era had remained largely in place. In other cases, rural producers traveled to the city to negotiate the sale of their products, which created both the extra costs of transport and vulnerability in negotiation when market prices were lower than anticipated. Furthermore, households usually had to focus on the production of one or two agricultural items so these could be sold in the relatively large quantities necessary to make such ventures profitable. This was because production of crops destined for regional centers, including watermelon and papayas, often required a relatively high degree of capital investment for seeds, agrochemical amendments, and labor.

With the barge economy, however, households now have the opportunity to sell or trade small quantities of a wider variety of products. They can also sell delicate fruits, like biribá (*Rollinia mucosa*) or graviola (*Annona muricata*), which ripen quickly or become damaged easily in transit to the city. And I witnessed both men and women selling goods on the barges, including women that I suspect might have been previously isolated from market opportunities because of domestic responsibilities that restricted their mobility. Now, the market comes right to them.

On only one occasion did I venture out to the barges with Zé. He had purchased a large slab of pirarucu fish from his friend and wanted to take it out to trade for diesel. I asked if I could make the trip with him and Zé was more than willing to oblige me. I brought my camera along with the intention of visually capturing some activity of this new rural Amazonian economy.

When we arrived we found that Cândida's brother Sapo was already there selling fish. Zé and I climbed aboard, and he began negotiating with the *balseiros*. The *balseiros* made no attempts to make me feel welcome, doing little more than grunting in my direction.

While Zé negotiated, I went up on the flat of the barge to take a look at where the containers and semi-trucks stood. As I snapped a few photos, one of the truckers on board spotted me and moved in my direction. I sensed the distrust behind his dark sunglasses. "Tudo bem?" I asked. He responded with a frigid "Tudo bom." Other men on the barge gave me looks that ranged between stares and glares. In an attempt to defuse the tension, I told the trucker that I was just visiting with a friend. The trucker interjected, "Yeah, well, I saw you taking photos and I was thinking that if you're spying on us then we're gonna have to kill you." I laughed nervously and said I was just "hanging out." "That's exactly what I'm worried about," he shot back. I tried to explain further that I was a researcher, and that I was simply accompanying my friend Zé. I placed my hand on the trucker's shoulder in a forced attempt to establish a friendly rapport with him. He quickly shrugged me off.

I went back down to the control room of the boat, where Zé was still talking with the *balseiros*. They eventually agreed to give him two drums of diesel in exchange for half of the pirarucu. With the deal done, we got back into the canoe and pushed off. I was relieved to put the barge behind me as we made our way back to shore.

"Those guys really didn't like me being there," I shouted to Zé over the din of the *rabeta* as we motored back. Zé laughed and told me that one of the *balseiros* had called him aside and asked why he had brought me along. He said he explained to the *balseiro* that I was *gente fina*, good people, and that I wasn't "doing anything he was thinking about." Still I was concerned that I might have compromised Zé's business with them, but he told me not to worry. I couldn't tell if Zé, the ever-confident entrepreneur, had concerns of his own. If he did, he never revealed them to me.

I learned later that the *balseiros* usually siphoned diesel directly from the barge's fuel tank and traded it for the fish, fruit, and other products that they consumed. In essence, they were swindling their bosses, the barge owners. Many barges also ran drugs, weapons, and other contraband between Manaus and Porto Velho. People said it was especially dangerous to approach them at night since the *balseiros* lived in fear of getting hijacked and most of them were armed. Only after all these details were made available to me did it become clear how imprudent it had been to take pictures or even make the trip out to the barge at all. I also understood why my presence on the barge had left nearly everyone uneasy.

Weeks later, Zé went to see the same *balseiros* to trade more fish for diesel. Apparently their suspicions about me had passed. He said that they had even inquired about me: "Hey, where's the gringo? When's he coming back?" To which they added, "We hope we didn't scare him away."

Though I spent little time on the barges themselves, I witnessed the impact that the barge economy had in many communities in Borba. In some places I visited there were household heads who dedicated themselves solely to the sale and trade of goods on the barges, developing a defined sense of the *balseiros'* desires while also gauging which goods turned the best profit. They sold fresh honey and limes and even beer they had purchased in the town of Borba to meet the demand. Occasionally, the *balseiros* gave CDs and DVDs in exchange, circulating new forms of popular culture in rural communities, including a memorable documentary on the first Brazilian soccer team composed of men with dwarfism, which I watched on my birthday.

The swarm of economic activity surrounding the barges directly contradicted the stereotypical depictions of rural Amazonians that I heard reproduced in Manaus and other urban centers of Brazil. To many urbanites, *caboclos* were lazy dolts, living a hand-to-mouth existence, fishing just enough to fill their bellies for the day and then retiring to their hammocks for a nap. It was clear to me, however, that people in the rural countryside actively carved out a living, always looking for new opportunities that might appear on the horizon. Their *jeitinho*—their way of making things work, their way of getting by, their hustle—was on constant display. As Zé frequently reminded me, "Hey, you know we don't stop."

This gritty entrepreneurship and catch-as-catch-can attitude[14] exhibited by Zé and many other rural Amazonians I met is derived from a legacy of resilience in the face of social and economic constraints. For centuries, Amazonians toiled in lakes, rivers, forests, and fields to secure their subsistence while also attempting to meet the demands of others. From the recent boom of river barges back to early colonial collecting expeditions,[15] Amazonia's rural inhabitants have always been the mediators between the region's resources and the broader world that covets them. They occupy the liminal space between isolated indigenous groups and (European-descendant) city slickers, between raw Amazonian nature and the modern urban centers, between "local" resources and "global" capital. And despite this, rural Amazonians are frequently denigrated and written off by urbanites as "backwards" *caboclos*. Yet what it means to be a *caboclo* is not easy to pin down. In fact, it is still very much up for debate.

SO WHAT IS A *CABOCLO*?

When I arrived in Manaus in 2003, my travel guidebook informed me that I could take an excursion outside of the city to visit a "*caboclo* village." According to the guide, *caboclos* were simply "river people."[16] Yet upon arrival, I soon heard the term—almost universally pronounced "caboco," without the "l"—popping up in conversation among urban residents. At times the term seemed rather benign, as when used, for example, as a form of address among friends or acquaintances: "Hey, how's it going, my *caboclo*?" In many other instances, however, I heard middle- and upper-class urbanites using the word in an unequivocally disparaging manner. When something was tacky or in poor taste or "below them," they told me, "Oh, that's so *caboclo*."[17] Unsurprisingly, there was more to the *caboclo* than my guidebook had let on.

Some anthropologists who study the region continue to employ the term *caboclo* in reference to rural inhabitants despite its pejorative nature.[18] Deborah Lima (1999) has argued that the word has two uses: one as an academic "fixed category" referring to the Amazonian peasantry and the other as a relational term, often used colloquially to establish social distance. Lima notes, however, that little consensus exists on how *caboclo* is defined anthropologically, and she questions whether its academic usage should be considered appropriate at all.[19]

Some social scientists have defined *caboclos* in racialized terms, as people of mixed Amerindian, European, and African descent[20] (e.g., Wagley 1976). Others have described *caboclos* as the historical Amazonian peasantry (Nugent 1993; Harris 1998), tied to the patron–client system that developed during the rubber boom (Weinstein 1983; Weinstein 1985). *Caboclos* have also been considered a "quasi-ethnic group" (Chibnik 1991) as well as a "cultural type" that developed in adaptation to the Amazonian environment (Moran 1974; see also Moran 1993a). But as Pace (1997) rightly argues, few individuals in the rural Amazonian countryside willingly self-identify as *caboclo* since the term is largely a derogatory one. So why then, he asks, do anthropologists insist on a label that people themselves largely reject or rarely self-apply?

Pace contends that anthropologists have adopted their usage of the term from middle-class Amazonian urbanites. The reason for this, he speculates, is "possibly because the colleagues and peers of the researchers are inevitably members of the Brazilian urban middle class and most dialogue and collaboration in research occurs with them, not the rural inhabitant. The researcher adopts the world view and vocabulary of the urban middle class peer to interpret the rural inhabitants. Only in this way can the abusiveness of the term possibly be ignored or rationalized" (1997, 86). Although many of Amazonia's urban dwellers acknowledge that their family originated from the *interior*, or that perhaps even they themselves had once been rural denizens, most middle- and upper-class individuals distance themselves from what they see as the "backwardness" of rural Amazonians (Boyer 1999). In the eyes of many urbanites, *caboclos* are backwoods hicks who do the bare minimum of work to secure their subsistence and then spend the rest of their day swinging in a hammock. The *caboclo* stands as a foil to the modern, urban industrial worker and his or her disciplined march toward "progress."

The high mobility of Amazonians coming from the *interior*, however, thoroughly complicates urbanites' attempts to distance themselves from the rural population. It is common for rural families with resources to send their children to the towns and cities of the region to acquire secondary education. Others leave the *interior* to seek out employment, living with urban relatives or settling at the urban periphery in squatter settlements, known as areas of *invasão*—literally "invasion." These migrants to the city thus attempt to separate themselves from the image of *caboclo* as they move to join the ranks of "modern" urban Amazonians. Boyer explains that "some people affirm that they 'were caboclos' before arriving and adapting to urban life, while others mention that their family still is [caboclo]" (1999, 31; translation mine). However, some maintain a shifting identity as they trade their time between urban and rural settings over the course of their lives. Although many settle down in the city, others return to their rural communities after years of urban struggle. Still others grow up in the city but harbor affection for the countryside, seeking solace in it later in life. Ironically, most middle- and upper-class urbanites in Manaus aspire to own a *sítio*, or rural landholding, where they can go on the weekends to host barbeques and escape the pollution, crime, and overcrowding of the city.

Among rural farmers whom I met in communities on the lower Rio Madeira, many men and women had lived in Manaus and other cities for extended periods. Some of them worked selling popsicles (*picolé*) and other foods in the streets of the city, trying their best to survive in the informal economy. Seu Gestolino of Puruzinho, for example, told me that he was raised in the countryside but spent much of his young adulthood working on fishing boats departing from the port of Manaus. After a decade of toiling on boats, he eventually "retired" back to the countryside, where he managed cacao, manioc, and even a few cattle. Across the river from Gestolino lived a man named Careca ("Baldy") with a very different story. He made his career in the army, and then after retirement he purchased a small farm on the Madeira River where he cultivated cacao, bananas, and other fruits. Although he still had a house in Manaus and children who lived there, he preferred the relative solitude and good hunting in the *interior*. An urbanite who happens to take the boat to Borba might spot Careca bathing in the river in front of his house in the early morning, mistakenly assuming him to be a poor, illiterate rustic, stagnating at the margins of the modern world. Only in talking to Careca would the boat passenger find out that he is an educated military man from Manaus with multiple landholdings. The stories of many other individuals I met in the countryside were equally disruptive of the inherited narratives about rural inhabitants or the stereotypical *caboclo*.

Some authors argue that *caboclos* have been ignored by the anthropological community because Amazonian ethnographers have focused on indigenous groups and purposely overlooked populations of undefined ethnic identity (Harris 2000; Nugent 1993; see also Adams et al. 2006). In the introduction to his book *Amazonian Caboclo Society*, Nugent clarifies his argument, explaining that "Amazonian peasant societies—*caboclos* in the vernacular—are not literally invisible; rather they have been treated as marginal in relation to an overdetermined naturalism represented by a forest of mythic proportions and marginal in relation to 'proper' Amazonian social formations, Indian societies (and, on the distant horizon, the promise of modernity)." He writes further that

> the caboclo is portrayed—when portrayed at all—as the incomplete other (if not, more brutally, simply polluted or pathological) and is an unsuitable anthropological other because the very existence of caboclo society subverts the formal distinction between the other and the observer. Caboclo societies represent ersatz others and not "real" others both because they are the outcome of conquest and not, as it were, "local society," and because their existence is testimony to the depredations of "civilizing" influence. (Nugent 1993, 43)

For Nugent, the study of *caboclos* requires anthropologists to tackle difficult questions about the relationship of the ethnographer to the ethnographic subject, largely because *caboclos* do not fit into any accepted category of the latter. To expand upon Nugent's point, I would

argue along with Pace (1997) that *caboclos* are "invisible" in the ethnographic literature because the *caboclo* figure itself is a caricature of
the rural population that is drawn by urbanites and members of the
middle and upper classes. The *caboclo* is invisible because no one actively self-identifies as a *caboclo*. Once one goes searching for *caboclos*, they quickly recede into a forested background, just like Curupira or any other Amazonian mythological figure.

On my last visit to Puruzinho in 2010, I called my friend Rafa from
a public phone in Borba to tell him that I was going to the *interior* for
a few days, and that when I returned, I would be on my way to see him
in Manaus. "What do you mean, you're *going* to the *interior*? You're
already in the *interior*," he quipped. "Fine, then, I'm going to the interior of the *interior*," I told him. From his vantage point in the capital, the town of Borba was already the *interior*, so how could I possibly
be going into the *interior* if I was already there? And like a never-
ending sequence of Russian nesting dolls, the people in Puruzinho in
turn told me about those communities that *really* lived out of the way.
Places "where people barely talked to you when they see you, real *caboclos*, you know, almost like Indians." And even when I visited indigenous reserves with agricultural extension agents, I heard about the
places where there were people really isolated from civilization, "real
savages."

Several decades earlier, Charles Wagley had confronted the same
phenomenon when looking to interview *caboclos* in Gurupa in eastern Amazonia:

> In the late 1940s when Eduardo Galvão and I were preparing for re-
> search in Gurupa [Para] . . . our colleagues, government officials,
> and others in the city of Belem exclaimed when we outlined our re-
> search plans, "So you are going to study the caboclos of Gurupa."
> When we reached Gurupa, our informants and friends in the town
> looked puzzled at first when we used the term. Then, they told us
> that the caboclos da beira (riverbank inhabitants) lived on the al-
> luvial islands across the river channel. . . . The caboclo was a rub-
> ber gatherer cultivating only a small plot of quick-growing crops in
> the annually flooded varzea. . . . Later, we spent time on the islands
> coming to know the so-called caboclos only to find that they did
> not identify themselves as such. They pointed to the north toward
> the Brazilian–Guiana border. "There are caboclos there," they ex-
> plained . . . to them the caboclo is the autochthonous Indian. (1985,
> viii; also cited in Pace 1997)

And so the *caboclo* is pushed further and further afield, regardless of how "deep" into the *interior* one goes. It's *caboclos* all the way down.[21]

So what really is a *caboclo* then? A strawman upon which Amazonians project their prejudices? A simple caricature of the rural population? What urbanites might see as ghosts of their former selves, before they became urbanized, before they became "modern"?

My contention is that the *caboclo* can be understood as all of these things. But perhaps even more, the *caboclo* is a scapegoat for Amazonian society and Brazilian society more generally. Although rural Amazonians have adopted satellite dishes and DVD players, Honda outboard motors and cell phones, their access to the benefits of modern industrial society is still severely limited when compared to the middle- and upper-class urbanites who snidely label them as *caboclos*. *Caboclos* are thus the class of people who never fully gain the benefits of modern industrial capitalism and its technological production or "progress." And in the minds of many middle- and upper-class urbanites, *caboclos* are the people who stand in the way of the "order and progress" (*ordem e progresso*) emblazoned on the Brazilian flag.

The perceived stagnation of rural Amazonians, however, is not the direct cause of the region's underdevelopment but rather an effect of its embrace of modern industrialization. Writing in the context of the rubber boom, Barbara Weinstein argues that "what the local and foreign rubber traders saw as the innate deficiencies of the Amazonian labor force can be seen by the more sympathetic eye as rational, and often courageous, forms of resistance by the rubber-tappers to debt peonage on the one hand, and proletarianization on the other" (1985, 102–103). Precisely because of this balancing act that they are required to perform, rural Amazonians have never, in the words of Stephen Nugent, "been granted full status as integral social forms." Instead, he writes, "they are treated as contingent, incomplete, haphazard meldings of the detritus of aboriginal social formations and the remnants of European commercial experiments" (1993, xxi).

To be sure, the characterization of rural Amazonians as "incomplete" social forms or degenerative *caboclos* speaks more to the failures of modern industrial capitalism and its ability to meaningfully provide for people than the shortcomings of rural peoples themselves. After all, rural Amazonians were the ones who suffered death threats and malaria to collect rubber for the Allied war effort and Henry Ford's automobiles;[22] they are the ones today who continue to feed passing barge operators and the urban professional class with fresh fruits and fish; they might have even been the ones who at some point smuggled your drugs. What they have gained in return is a very small sliver of modern industrial capitalism's promise of prosperity.

CONCLUSION: ON *CABOCLOS* AND THE PROBLEMS OF THE ANTHROPOCENE

The primacy and privilege of urban industrial (and post-industrial) populations over those of the rural countryside is a dominant trend that pervades thinking about the Anthropocene. Humans are seen as dominating the planet, but it is a very specific variety of human that is said to do so—those who live in cities and suburbs who drive cars, work in industry or business offices, and eat processed foods. Meanwhile, people in rural areas who secure their own subsistence by farming and fishing while participating in alternative economic networks are overlooked or considered irrelevant to humanity's future and the future of life more generally on the planet. Their present is seen as something of the past.

In uncertain times such as these, however, it is rural people's capacity to adapt to variable economic and environmental conditions that gives them certain advantages. Rather than pitying or disparaging them, the urban industrial world, it would seem, could learn a great deal from them about contending with precariousness. Although Amazonia has long been integrated into the global capitalist system, rural Amazonians continue to utilize distinctive forms of ecological knowledge honed by direct engagement with their environment through the practice of daily subsistence activities. Through fishing, hunting, collecting, and farming, rural Amazonians are attuned to the movement of fish, the seasonality of forest fruits, and the ebb and flow of the region's rivers. Their forms of local ecological knowledge also encourage a vision of human–environmental relations that differs fundamentally from the worldview that undergirds the Anthropocene. Rather than viewing humanity as the ruler of the earth or its future conqueror, rural Amazonians typically acknowledge the agency of a wide number of nonhuman others that challenge human intentions and desires. Perhaps due in part to their history of marginalization, they seem to both recognize and accept the simple truth that we as humans are not at the center of the universe.

In the chapters that follow, I move to explore human–environmental interactions in further detail, examining specifically human relationships to the region's soils, plants, and forests. As I shift focus increasingly toward the lifeworlds surrounding Amazonian peoples, I show that while humans have long shaped the environment, it is wrong to assume that humanity can exert absolute control over it. Instead, we are embroiled in an endless process of negotiation.

Chapter 3 ‖ SOILS

AN ANTHROPOLOGY OF SOIL

Long before the rubber boom and the construction of Manaus's opera house and even before the Amazon region was named after the warrior women of Greek myth,[1] people had been altering its landscape in subtle and persistent ways—for millennia. Through their subsistence activities, early hunter-gatherers dispersed the seeds of palm fruits, expanding the plants' distribution across the region while shaping their populations through the selection of traits most desirable to humans (Clement 1988). Concentrations of seeds discarded in temporary camps also favored the development of oligarchic forests—those dominated by a select number of species—that proved to be valuable reservoirs of food for humans and animal species alike. And as early as 2,500 years ago and perhaps even much earlier, large indigenous settlements formed, depositing massive amounts of organic materials through everyday food production and subsistence practices. Manioc peels, cacao pods, palm fronds, charred logs and sticks, animal dung and fish bones, and human excrement too, all piled up over years and years of village living. With time, this had a distinctive impact on the landscape, slowly transforming the very ground upon which people walked.

Today, such settlements can still be identified by their dark, fertile soils, known in Brazil as *terra preta do índio*, or Indian black earth.[2] In contradiction to the prevailing notion that Amazonian *terra firme* (upland) soils inhibited the development of complex societies, *terra preta* demonstrates that past human populations changed regional soils in ways that actually increased their agricultural potential. When compared to most other Amazonian upland soils, *terra preta* exhibits higher pH, more stable organic matter, and higher concentrations of plant-available phosphorus, among other key nutrients (Glaser et al. 2001; Glaser et al. 2002; Lehmann, Pereira da Silva, et al. 2003; Sombroek et al. 2002). Large quantities of vegetative charcoal, or "biochar," are also characteristic of the soil, making it an effective carbon sink. For these reasons, *terra preta* has been vaunted as a potential model of "sustainable agriculture" in Amazonia and beyond (Glaser et al. 2001; Kawa and Oyuela-Caycedo 2008).

Although the industrial revolution is typically set as the origin point of the Anthropocene, *terra preta* is one example among many demonstrating that humans had started shaping the world long before Europeans invented the steam engine. But what is perhaps even more concerning than the Anthropocene's presentism and neglect of human history—especially that of the peoples of nonindustrialized regions of the world—is its foundational belief that people are not only changing the earth but coming to dominate it through the use of science and technology. The recent fascination with *terra preta* as a model of sustainable agriculture is symptomatic of this tendency, as it highlights humanity's ongoing commitment to the fantasy that with the "right" technical knowledge, we can reengineer the planet's ecological systems and work them to our full advantage without facing any consequences.

This chapter presents a history of scientific investigation into *terra preta*. Drawing from my collaborations with Brazilian archaeologists, I discuss the insights this soil offers for understanding Amazonian indigenous history and settlement. Shifting focus to contemporary usage of *terra preta*, I look at the benefits and challenges it presents to Amazonian farmers while also considering the obstacles inherent to its implementation as a model of "sustainable agriculture" in other regions of the world. To conclude, I contend that while *terra preta* represents prime evidence of prehistoric human alteration of the Amazonian environment, contemporary farmers' engagement with the soil and the life that it sustains also reveals the many ways in which the environment continually defies human control.

OS CONFEDERADOS AND THE
EARLY INVESTIGATIONS OF *TERRA PRETA*

When the American Civil War ended in 1865, an estimated twenty thousand Southerners chose to move to Brazil rather than be reunionized (Harter 1985, 12). Most of the Confederates, known in Portuguese as "Os Confederados," settled in the south of Brazil, particularly in the state of São Paulo. However, one contingent of Confederates, led by Major Lansford Hastings, ventured north to the Brazilian Amazon. After surveying areas along the lower Amazon River, Hastings was provisionally granted a tract of 60 square leagues of land to the south of the city of Santarém, agreeing to pay 22.5 cents per acre at the end of three years (Griggs 1987, 18). A little more than a year after having procured the land, however, Hastings succumbed to yellow fever on a trip to recruit more settlers from the American South (Harter 1985, 26). Despite the loss of their leader, many of the colonists remained, making their living farming the Amazonian soil and toiling in the equatorial sun.

Shortly after establishing themselves in Santarém, the Confederates began cultivating corn (*Zea mays*), cotton (*Gossypium barbandense*), tobacco (*Nicotiana tabacum*), and sugarcane (*Saccharum officinarum*) (Harter 1985, 30; Smith 1879a, 144). Several families situated their plantations on *terra preta do índio*. The dark, coffee-colored soils, rich in organic matter and especially valuable for the cultivation of sugarcane and corn, stood in strong contrast to the sunset orange and red clays that otherwise dominated much of the Amazonian uplands. These "Indian" soils owed their name to the abundant potsherds typically strewn about their surface, which concealed an even greater wealth of indigenous artifacts lying deeper below. Whether they initially realized it or not, the Confederates were farming on old Amerindian villages.

One Confederate, Romulus J. Rhome, operated a large sugarcane plantation at Taperinha[3] on such a *terra preta* site and took interest in the abundance of buried archaeological artifacts that he encountered in the dark soils. Over time he amassed a significant collection of indigenous cultural material, as noted by the visiting North American geologist Herbert Smith: "We find fragments scattered everywhere, and Mr. Rhome has been making archaeological collections for years. He gets all sorts of curious clay figures: vultures' heads, frogs, a cock with comb and wattles complete, a whistle, and one odd-looking affair punched full of holes, which—so Mr. Rhome laughingly insists—must be a toothpick-stand" (Smith 1879a, 169). Although relatively little literature can be found on Rhome,[4] he unknowingly began what would become a tradition of North American archaeology in the lower Amazon, and today, part of his collection is housed at the Museu Nacional in Rio de Janeiro (Nimuendaju 1953, 59). In an equally significant contribution, Rhome helped draw attention to the relationship between *terra preta* and pre-Columbian indigenous settlement in the Amazon region.

Around the time that the Confederate colony was established in Santarém, a young Canadian geologist named Charles Frederick Hartt was exploring the Amazon basin with Louis Agassiz on the Thayer expedition (1865–1866). As a member of the expedition, Hartt spent fifteen months in Brazil collecting fossils and geological specimens, which Agassiz hoped would yield evidence of Late Pleistocene glaciation at sea level in the tropics, an event that he thought would have destroyed all life on land (Agassiz and Agassiz 1868, 428). Agassiz believed that such a discovery would demonstrate divine re-creation, and thus disprove Darwin's theory of evolution (Brice and Figueiroa 2003). Although Hartt did not agree with Agassiz's case for glaciation, the expedition sparked a deep fascination with Brazilian Amazonia that would guide the rest of his life's work. After returning to the United States and accepting a teaching position at the newly founded Cornell University in 1868, Hartt began preparing for a second trip to Brazil.

Hartt returned in 1870 as the leader of the Morgan expeditions (Hartt 1874, 1). The intended purpose of these expeditions was to study the geology of the Amazon valley, but Hartt and his students also dedicated considerable time to archaeological investigation in the region. On his previous visit, he had the fortunate opportunity of meeting Domingos Soares Ferreira Penna,[5] a Brazilian scholar who had written extensively about the archaeology and ethnology of the Amazon (Barreto and Machado 2001). The two forged an important friendship, and through their correspondences, Penna brought *terra preta* sites and artifacts to Hartt's attention, encouraging him to investigate Amazonia's archaeological wealth (Hartt 1873, 19; Hartt 1874, 3; Hartt 1885, 6, 9; Moraes Bertho 2001, 150).

During the first of the Morgan expeditions, Hartt visited the Confederate colony in Santarém and took the opportunity to see Romulus Rhome's plantation in nearby Taperinha, which also featured a large shell mound (*sambaqui*) on the property (Hartt 1885, 2). After inspecting the mound with Rhome, Hartt suspected that it was not a natural formation, but rather a large midden left by early indigenous inhabitants. He had little time to examine the site on that first visit and was required to return to Santarém. However, during the second of the two expeditions, Hartt received some financial support from Harvard's Peabody Museum (then the Museum of Ethnology), specifically for the collection of artifacts (Hartt 1874, 5). On that second expedition, he revisited the Taperinha site twice. With the assistance of two of Rhome's men,[6] he excavated part of the massive shell midden and collected pottery and bones that were interspersed throughout the mound as well as other artifacts found in the *terra preta* on the overlooking bluff (Hartt 1885, 3). Upon returning from the Morgan expeditions, Hartt remarked in his published preliminary report: "The archaeological material has been so rich that it has been difficult to work out. New collections have constantly been coming in, and what I intended as a short report on the antiquities of the lower Amazonas, has grown to be a large volume on the antiquities of the whole Empire" (Hartt 1874, 7).[7]

The association of *terra preta* with indigenous artifacts led Hartt, Rhome, Penna, and others who surveyed the region to the logical conclusion that these dark earth sites had been former indigenous settlements. However, the relationship between the soil's fertility and indigenous habitation was not entirely understood. Hartt reasoned that indigenous groups had been attracted to what he considered naturally occurring pockets of fertile soil (Hartt 1885, 12). Hartt's student Herbert Smith, however, had an alternative explanation. Drawing from the writings of Pedro Cristoval de Acuña, the Jesuit priest who chronicled the Amazon voyage of Pedro Texeira in 1639 and who had described large indigenous populations found along the banks of the Amazon, Smith offered the following: "At Taperinha, as at Diamantina and Panéma, and far up the Tapajós, the bluff-land owes its richness to the refuse of a thousand kitchens for maybe a thousand years; numberless palm-thatches, which were left to rot on the ground as they were replaced by new ones. For the bluffs were covered with Indian houses, 'so close together,' says Acuña, 'that from one village you can hear the workmen of another'" (Smith 1879a, 168). Inspired by such accounts, Smith attempted to envision Amazonia as early European explorers may have seen it,[8] and in doing so, he provided an early theory for the formation of the *terra preta* soils, contending that they were the product of generations of kitchen middens and accumulated organic refuse. Although some later scholars attempted to refute this theory, suggesting that *terra preta* soils had formed from volcanic ash (Camargo 1941) or dried lake beds (Cunha Franco 1962; de Faria 1944; Falesi 1974), Smith's insights would be largely upheld by the scientific community more than one hundred years after his initial observations (Lehmann, Kern, et al. 2003; Glaser and Woods 2004).

Perhaps unknowingly, Smith and other explorers of his time exposed *terra preta* as part of a larger "domesticated" environment. This evidence would later be used to challenge the view of Amazonia as a land of extreme environmental constraint, suggesting instead that past human action had altered the environment in ways that rendered it more congenial for human habitation, a process described as "landscape domestication" (Clement 1999; see also Posey 1985). But several questions remained. Were *terra preta* sites merely the result of accumulated organic waste from sedentary villages, as Smith hypothesized, or were there other key elements that contributed to their formation? And in developing an understanding of its genesis, could *terra preta* be re-created? Lastly, might *terra preta* serve as a model for more productive or "sustainable" forms of modern agriculture in Amazonia and elsewhere?

ANNE AND CLAIDE

In January 2010 I met the Brazilian archaeologists Anne Rapp Py-Daniel and Claide de Paula Moraes, who at the time were doctoral students at the University of São Paulo. I was also a doctoral student then, nearly halfway through a year of field research in Borba. Although my initial studies in the region in 2003 and 2007 had focused on use and management of *terra preta*, my dissertation research had shifted focus, to explore sociocultural factors that shaped the diversity of plant species managed by smallholder farmers in Borba. When I met Anne and Claide, the initial honeymoon phase of my dissertation research had transitioned into a period tinged by feelings of isolation, doubt, and boredom, mixed in equal parts. I saw their arrival to Borba as a welcome opportunity to exchange new ideas, explore different areas of the municipality, and hopefully, recapture interest in my studies by revisiting the soil that had first sparked my fascination with Amazonia and its history.

For Claide's dissertation project, he was surveying *terra preta* sites along the lower and middle Madeira River. It had long been suspected that there were far more archaeological sites straddling the major riverway than previously documented, but little research had been conducted since the surveys of Simões and Lopes, who had visited the area in the 1980s (Simões and Lopes 1987). Following his survey, Claide intended to excavate a few key sites to test his hypothesis that Tupian peoples had expanded out of southwestern Amazonia and migrated to central Amazonia along the course of the Madeira River between seven hundred and twelve hundred years ago.

Evidence of the first human settlement of Amazonia dates back to approximately ten thousand years ago, but as Eduardo Neves and colleagues point out, much more is known about the beginning and end of the pre-Columbian occupation of the region than what happened in the middle five thousand years of the process (2003, 30). The first occupants to arrive in the region were hunter-gatherers with relatively simple technologies for securing their subsistence. The archaeological evidence suggests that ceramic production began around seven thousand years before present (BP)[9] (Roosevelt et al. 1991; Roosevelt 1995), and by 2,500 BP large horticultural chiefdoms had emerged in the region (Roosevelt 1993). Later, between the fifth and thirteenth centuries, Amazonia experienced a cultural explosion with elaborate pottery manufacture, including massive, highly decorative funerary urns in the Marajoara and Polychrome traditions (Roosevelt 1991). Through his research, Claide intended to fill in some of the gaps in the archaeological record in central Amazonia, specifically looking at the emergence of horticultural societies that were thought to be associated with the development of *terra preta*.

Over five days I accompanied Anne and Claide, motoring up and down the Madeira in a boat that Claide had rented from a butcher in town. I introduced the couple to some of the communities in the municipality that I knew had large stretches of *terra preta*, and we tracked down others that had been previously identified by archaeologists or local residents. During the survey, Claide and Anne combed through the *terra preta* at each site, inspecting an endless number of potsherds and ceramics that shared commonalities with those of the Paredão and Guarita phases found in archaeological sites near Manaus (see Heckenberger et al. 1999). We also found artifacts from the historical period, including ceramic wine bottles from Amsterdam that were widely traded in the seventeenth and eighteenth centuries between Europeans and Amazonia's rural inhabitants. Although Anne and Claide wouldn't speculate as to whether the earliest ceramics we encountered had preceded those of sites along the lower Negro and middle Amazon Rivers, they seemed to fit into the broader framework of ceramic traditions that they had seen in other areas of central Amazonia. I did my best to keep up with the couple, both in terms of assessing the significance of the findings and matching the pace of their work. Anne and Claide rarely stopped for a break, subsisting on little more than crackers and bright orange tucumã palm fruits during our boat rides between survey sites. In just a few days, we had visited more than a dozen communities.

One of the most striking *terra preta* sites we encountered was at the community of Vila Gomes, which consisted of four houses situated on a bluff overlooking the Madeira River, just upstream from the town of Borba. While we were interviewing the community residents, a young couple pointed out to Claide that two large ceramic pots were peeking out from the ground just outside the front door of their home. Due to erosion and years of sweeping the area, the tops of the pots, which were in fact funerary urns, had been dislodged and destroyed.

Claide thought it would be best to salvage what remained, but before doing so, he wanted to ensure that the community understood his work and the significance of such artifacts for understanding the history of the region. On more than one occasion, he had been suspected of searching for gold or other mineral deposits, and he was careful to make certain that his intentions were not misconstrued. Claide thus spent one morning with the community presenting some of his past research from a site near Manaus and then went on to explain the significance of such funerary urns and their role in the mortuary practices of early indigenous inhabitants of the region. The community members seemed genuinely fascinated, but also a little perplexed as to why anyone would dedicate such a great deal of time and resources to study old Indian settlements and burial urns.

Following his presentation, Claide asked the community president and other residents for permission to remove the urns since he was concerned that they might suffer further damage. The community approved his request and we spent an afternoon carefully excavating the urns and packaging them for transport back to Borba and then later on to Claide's lab in Manaus. I found the work physically monotonous, but strangely gratifying. When I later shared my enthusiasm over participating in my first "excavation" with Claide, he smirked and told me that the quick and dirty job we had completed was more of a salvage effort than an excavation, but he was pleased with the end result (figure 3.1).

In August Claide returned to conduct a more thorough investigation of Vila Gomes while Anne was working in Manaus. Once again, I accompanied him in his work over the course of several days. After conducting two transects through the community, Claide calculated that *terra preta* covered nearly 40 hectares of the bluff (Moraes and Neves 2012). Residents also pointed out to him that a ditch circumscribed the area. He believed this had been dug by the indigenous population in the late Pre-contact era as a defensive structure.[10] The

FIGURE 3.1.   Archaeologist Claide de Paula Moraes photographs a funerary urn (Vila Gomes, 2010).

ditch was shaped like a half-moon around the bluff, over a kilometer in length, between 10 and 12 meters in width, and up to 3 meters in depth. It demarcates an area of approximately 20 hectares, or half of the total extent of *terra preta*. Claide hypothesized that the increased threat of attack led to a constriction of living space during the late Pre-contact period, when populations had expanded and warring over territory and resources increased in the region.

The soils of the site also contributed to our understanding of the dynamics of the settlement. The *terra preta* beyond the ditch was relatively shallow and tapered off at the edges of the settlement while in the center of the site, it reached a depth of one meter or more. The distribution of potsherds and other artifacts that we collected and recorded during the transects followed the same distribution. Clearly, the spaces that had been occupied for the longest periods of time led to the deepest concentrations of *terra preta*. Furthermore, Claide's excavation of a cross-section of the defensive ditch revealed two primary strata of *terra preta*, showing that as the ditch was dug, Oxisols from below the soil's surface were heaped on top of the initially formed layer of *terra preta*. Following the construction of the ditch, a second layer of *terra preta* formed over the Oxisol fill during the final period of the site's settlement.

The findings of Claide's research support the hypothesis that *terra preta* soils are in fact the product of large, sedentary agricultural villages, as Herbert Smith originally suggested. It is, however, difficult to generalize about the development of these dark earths in an area as broad and heterogeneous as the Amazon basin, especially over a time frame that spans several thousand years. What can be said is that the majority of the sites investigated in central Amazonia appear to have been occupied between 2,500 and 500 years ago (Neves et al. 2003). Yet many of the sites studied in central Amazonia, like Hatahara outside of Manaus, have long, complex histories of multiple occupations and several distinct archaeological phases (Rebellato et al. 2009). It seems that early *terra preta* development resulted from kitchen middens (i.e., sites of organic waste disposal), which later attracted attention for agricultural use (Rebellato et al. 2009; Woods and McCann 2009).

Several archaeologists working in the region have made the case that the development of manioc (*Manihot esculenta*) agriculture over two thousand years ago, coupled with the subsequent increase in both the population and the size of sedentary villages, led to the formation of the largest patches of *terra preta* that are still witnessed today (Arroyo-Kalin 2008, 174–175; Schmidt 2010). Studying daily livelihood activities and patterns of waste deposition in a contemporary Kuikuru village in southern Amazonia, Morgan Schmidt concluded through his extended doctoral research on *terra preta* that manioc by-products are an important source of organic matter and likely one of the key ingredients in the soil's formation (Schmidt 2010, 882). In addition to manioc by-products, the deposition of fish and animal remains, human waste, palm thatch, and other forms of organic waste are believed to have contributed to these environments of heightened soil fertility (Birk et al. 2011; Glaser et al. 2001, 40). Lastly, one of the most important elements, overlooked in early models of *terra preta* formation, is something deceptively simple: charcoal.

Charcoal derived from charred plant material—sometimes referred to as "pyrogenic carbon," "black carbon," or "biochar"—is found throughout the *terra preta* soil matrix, and its presence is considered one of the primary reasons for the soil's fertility. The carbon plays an important role in maintaining nutrients in the soil and preventing nutrient leaching, a common problem in Oxisols and Ultisols of Amazonia (Glaser et al. 2001). Research has shown that the addition of charcoal to soil can significantly increase the pH as well as the availability of phosphorus and total nitrogen concentrations (Glaser et al. 2002; Lehmann, Pereira da Silva, et al. 2003). And in one study, it was shown that *terra preta* could possess up to seventy times more pyrogenic carbon than adjacent soils (Glaser et al. 2001).

In slash-and-burn agriculture, which is common practice for smallholders in Amazonia today, the burning of slashed vegetation produces mostly ash, which doesn't allow for effective retention of nutrients in the soil matrix. Lehmann (2002) posited that indigenous peoples may have implemented a method of "slash-and-char," in which slash was burned in smoldering, oxygen-deprived fires, which allows for more effective production of charcoal. Nigel Smith (1980) had previously offered an alternative hypothesis, suggesting that charcoal from village fires was worked into the soil over time, thus explaining its ubiquity in *terra preta*. Glaser et al. (2003) support Smith's theory claiming that most of the charcoal in the *terra preta* soil matrix is most likely a product of hearths, although some may have resulted from forest fires or slash-and-burn agriculture. Yet regardless of its origins, pyrogenic carbon is chemically and microbially stable and can persist in an environment for centuries. This explains why sites, like Vila Gomes, that were abandoned centuries ago continue to maintain large quantities of carbon despite the time that has elapsed since indigenous occupation.

It is difficult to determine whether pre-Columbian indigenous groups intentionally created such soils, but from the evidence available, it appears as though *terra preta* may simply be an unintended consequence of sedentary living. Through the accumulation of organic waste and charcoal from village fires over decades and even centuries, the dark soils formed in and around habitation sites. With their formation, indigenous groups came to recognize their value for growing specific crops, most likely those that thrived in nutrient-rich soils.

Some researchers hypothesize that transitional soils surrounding *terra preta* sites, which usually lack potsherds and are slightly lighter in color, could also be evidence of managed agricultural fields (Arroyo-Kalin 2010; Fraser et al. 2011; Sombroek 1966; Sombroek et al. 2002). These soils, referred to by some as *terra mulata*, may have been intensive agricultural production sites that received organic inputs and soil amendments, including in-field burning to introduce charcoal into the soil and enhance its fertility over time. Only further archaeological and geochemical research will enable us to assess the likelihood that this form of soil management was used by indigenous populations in the late pre-Columbian era.

AGRICULTURE AND SOIL MANAGEMENT
IN RURAL AMAZONIA

My brief foray into archaeological research with Claide and Anne was a welcome break from the monotony of household surveys, and I found simple satisfaction in counting potsherds and assisting in the archaeological transects at Vila Gomes. But in my moments of free time, I interviewed the residents of the community to discuss the crops they cultivated on *terra preta* and to investigate how such soils could be helpful for understanding both the limits and possibilities of Amazonian agriculture.

Residents proudly pointed out groves of cacao (*Theobroma cacao*), bananas (*Musa* × *paradisiaca*), and papayas (*Carica papaya*) that flourished in the *terra preta*. Community president seu Jorge, puffing away on a stout, hand-rolled cigarette that hung from his mouth, showed me his prized tobacco (*Nicotiana tabacum*), which he cultivated in a small patch of *terra preta* just beyond the soccer field (see Oyuela-Caycedo and Kawa 2015). Yet in spite of such seemingly successful agricultural production, residents didn't necessarily see *terra preta* in the same light as some of the more optimistic descriptions I had first read about the "miracle" soil of the Amazon. My conversations with the residents of Vila Gomes led me to revisit my previous research on *terra preta* and some of the limitations that Borba's farmers had previously pointed out to me.

In 2007, I conducted a brief survey in Borba of twenty-seven different upland farms, of which fourteen were located on Oxisols and thirteen were located at least in part on *terra preta* (Kawa 2008; Kawa et al. 2011). Through informal and semi-structured interviews, I asked the participants of the study about their management practices on *terra preta* and other upland soils. During these interviews, I inquired about general management practices, including use of agrochemicals (e.g., chemical fertilizer, herbicide, insecticide), organic fertilizers, crop rotation, and fallowing. I also collected data on the species of useful plants under cultivation in the home gardens, orchards, and fields of each household. Lastly, I calculated a measure for evaluating the "market orientation" of each household, dividing the total area of crops destined for market by the total area of cultivation at the time of the study, disregarding land left fallow (see Kawa et al. 2011).

The results were surprising. Half of the *terra preta* farmers I interviewed used chemical fertilizers while only a little more than 15 percent of Oxisol farmers made use of them, even though *terra preta* soils were generally considered to be more fertile. Most of the *terra preta* farmers explained that they typically used chemical fertilizers to maximize production of valuable market crops like papayas and watermelon (*Citrullus lanatus*). In fact, all but one of the *terra preta* farmers who used chemical fertilizer produced watermelon. Although the chemical fertilizer appeared to be used very minimally, at least when compared to large-scale mechanized operations, many farmers noted that if *terra preta* soils were cultivated consistently for a decade or more, fertilizers were necessary to sustain production of demanding crops.

The average market orientation of *terra preta* farms (61.0 percent) was also significantly higher than that of Oxisol farms (47.3 percent) (Kawa et al. 2011). This could be attributed to the fact that many farmers who focus on production for larger markets seek out *terra preta* soils to exploit their fertility, as observed earlier by other researchers (German 2003, 196; Major et al. 2005). Many farmers in Borba almost exclusively associated market production of watermelon and papayas with *terra preta*. In the community of Puruzinho specifically, watermelon was said to have been cultivated for decades on the large stretches of *terra preta* soils that looked out on Puruzinho Lake. Residents reported that in decades past as many as 40 or 50 hectares of land were dedicated to watermelon production between the months of April and July. Residents who owned properties with *terra preta* even leased their lands to other farmers who were willing to invest in watermelon production. When the watermelon was harvested, a fraction of the profit was then shared with the landowner. In the community of Caiçara, not far from Puruzinho, a similar form of market production was found on *terra preta*, except the focus was largely on papayas, another valuable market crop that typically requires richer soils.

In addition to watermelon and papayas, cacao was another crop closely associated with *terra preta*. In my study, it was found on 71.4 percent of *terra preta* farms, as compared to only 30.8 percent of Oxisol farms. Unlike many native Amazonian fruit trees, cacao is relatively nutrient-demanding and often requires more fertile soil environments to thrive (Almeida and Valle 2007). Although some farmers had planted cacao in high sections of the floodplains, I also witnessed many people lose large swaths of cacao production in those environments during years of extreme flooding. For this reason, *terra preta* serves as a useful alternative location where farmers can cultivate cacao in an area of relative stability and elevated soil fertility.

Despite *terra preta*'s benefits for the production of unique market crops that fare poorly in other soils of the Amazonian uplands, it presents one major drawback. As noted by other scholars, the proliferation of weeds on *terra preta* is one of the major disadvantages of the soil (German 2001; German 2003; Major et al. 2005). Due to the heightened fertility of *terra preta*, weeds thrive in areas shortly after clearing, rapidly occupying fields and sometimes threatening to choke out crops if not properly managed. Some of the farmers I interviewed managed large fruit orchards in which shade helped to block out the majority of insistent weeds, but this state would only occur after plants had begun to fully mature, which usually takes around three to four years. For those who managed annual crops, the use of herbicide was quite common. "A terra preta cerra muito" ("*terra preta* weeds up a lot") was a refrain I often heard. Due to this tendency of weeds to grow more quickly on *terra preta*, farmers who managed larger areas of land often described a need for either more labor or machinery in order to combat their proliferation. One farmer even inquired if I could use my contacts in the local agricultural extension agency to acquire a weedwacker for him as he was tired of fighting unruly invasive plants.

Like most of the Amazon basin, the region surrounding Borba is subject to two distinct seasons: the dry season (*a época de seca*; *verão*) and the wet season (*a época de chuva*; *inverno*). The rhythm of life in the region is defined by this seasonality, which affects fishing, hunting, and of course, farming. All of the farms I visited in Borba relied upon rain for irrigation. On many occasions, farmers mentioned that the reliance on rain-fed irrigation was another factor that complicated production. One *terra preta* farmer known as "Tiger" shared the following:

> Every year the summer [dry season] arrives at a different time of the year. The year before it had been raining up until June. This year, summer arrived early and we probably would have been better off if we had planted in March instead of April. The problem that we are now facing is that when the dry season really hits its peak, the soil

dries out, but the plantation really needs some rainwater if the watermelons are going to reach good form before the harvest.[11]

Although *terra preta* is recognized for retaining moisture better than upland Oxisols—probably because of *terra preta*'s higher levels of organic matter—farmers still complained that the soil dried out in the summer. As another farmer shared: "When the summer hits, the land dries out and production isn't very good, not even on *terra preta*. Only on the floodplain is [production] good because it's moist."[12] Others suggested that dark earths are generally more fertile than other upland soils and can produce crops like corn (*Zea mays*) and beans (*Vigna unguiculata*) except during the height of the dry season (*no verão forte*), when the drought limits production on the uplands.

Those I interviewed often discussed the fertility of the floodplain (*várzea*), which was seen to be the most fertile soil in the region. However, they pointed out that the floodplain was relatively limited close to Borba and only opened into larger stretches near the upriver town of Manicoré. Despite its fertility, the floodplain poses risks for agriculture, because the floods vary greatly from year to year in their timing and extent (Chibnik 1994; Padoch and de Jong 1992; see also Pinedo-Vasquez et al. 2011). This irregularity can be very problematic for those farmers who depend primarily on floodplain agriculture. And while farmers who cultivate upland soils are not exposed to the same degree of risk, they too are greatly affected by yearly variation in the arrival of the rains and the intensity of the dry season. This is the predicament of Amazonian agriculture: the fertile floodplains are completely unpredictable and the stable uplands are subject to drought and soil infertility. To make matters worse, climate change, which is one of the defining features of the Anthropocene, is likely to increase the irregularities in rainfall, further complicating smallholder agricultural production in Amazonia.

In May 2010 I walked through Puruzinho's watermelon fields with Zé. I weeded some of the field while he sprayed the young plants with insecticide. He told me, "People have slowed down now but Puruzinho was once the champion in watermelon." "How many years ago?" I asked. "Just ten years ago, maybe seven," he replied. As we continued across the field, I asked him why things had changed. "Because the soil went bad. People worked but couldn't get any more out [of the soil] so everyone stopped."[13]

Several months later, when I returned to Puruzinho for the watermelon harvest, the crop had failed. Instead of the two or three thousand watermelons that Zé had hoped to send downriver to Manaus, there were less than several hundred puny fruit littered throughout the field. They eventually ended up as fodder for the neighbors' pigs. Planting watermelon was like gambling, I was told—when you got it right, you made it big. And when you didn't, well, you know the story.

For most contemporary farmers in Borba, the primary benefit of *terra preta* is its ability to produce nutrient-demanding or pH-sensitive crops with relatively little inputs over the short term, usually between two and three years. Watermelon, corn, beans, papayas, West Indian gherkin (*Cucumis anguria*), and cacao were all crops that farmers claimed to produce well on *terra preta* but performed poorly in upland Ultisols and Oxisols. However, as farmers have sought to produce for larger regional markets, the adoption of more demanding crops has limited the long-term productive capacity of *terra preta*, especially when farmers do not invest in considerable agricultural inputs, usually in the form of organic or chemical fertilizers. Although *terra preta* soils are capable of producing more demanding crops with minimal inputs for several years, the soils also present farmers with a number of complications, particularly invasive weeds as well as pests and disease. To maintain long-term production, farmers must either focus on crops that require less intensive management like manioc, or they have to invest greater time, energy, and inputs—all sacrifices that most rural farmers are usually unable or unwilling to make. Despite the many benefits of *terra preta* soils and their unique relationship to prehistoric land use, they are no more likely to yield truly sustainable agricultural systems than the surrounding Oxisols of the region without the use of inputs, crop rotation strategies, and labor-intensive management.

TERRA PRETA NOVA

Even farmers with access to the most fertile soils face significant obstacles. Reducing the myriad challenges of tropical agricultural management to issues of soil fertility alone is clearly myopic and misguided. However, many researchers continue to view *terra preta* as an important model for agricultural production. This is largely because the use of charcoal, or biochar, not only has the potential to enhance the fertility of a soil but also works to sequester carbon. It is hoped that the widespread use of biochar as an agricultural amendment can help to combat global climate change. Questions remain, however, about how this model will be enacted and by whom.

During the first Amazonian Dark Earth Workshop, held in Manaus in 2002, the late Dutch soil scientist Wim Sombroek proposed the idea of the Terra Preta Nova (TPN) project. Sombroek, who conducted some of the most important modern pedological studies of *terra preta*, wanted to direct research toward the replication of dark earths, with the intention of improving the productive capacity of smallholder farmers in the Amazon region and other areas of the developing tropics (Sombroek et al. 2002). The project was also presented as an opportunity for *terra preta* researchers to network and collaborate. Participants in the workshop agreed with the proposal, and institutions from Brazil, the United States, Germany, and the Netherlands were invited to take part. Universities, research institutes, and a museum were integrated into the project in addition to EMBRAPA, the Brazilian Agricultural Research Corporation. It was hoped that a model for a new *terra preta* could be produced through international collaborative research.

At the time that the TPN project was conceived, the corporation Eprida was founded in the United States. The founder of the company, Danny Day, had collaborated with laboratories from the US Department of Energy to develop a process by which plant biomass would yield hydrogen-rich biofuel. Day found that the charcoal by-product resulting from this process could be utilized as an agricultural amendment following the *terra preta* model. By taking advantage of farm waste like peanut shells, Day showed, it was possible to produce biofuel and biochar in a way that was actually "carbon negative."

When plants carry out the process of photosynthesis, they remove carbon dioxide from the atmosphere and turn it into biomass. If plant biomass is harvested and then heated in the absence of oxygen—a process known as pyrolysis—it yields volatile organic molecules that can be used as biofuel, in addition to producing biochar, a recalcitrant form of carbon (Woolf et al. 2010). With biochar, carbon that would normally be released into the atmosphere during a plant's decomposition is locked up in the form of charcoal instead. When introduced into the soil, it can persist for centuries and even millennia. In this way, biochar is a relatively simple technology that removes carbon dioxide from the air and stores it underground, with the added benefit of improving soil fertility.

Since Eprida opened for business, a wide number of other alternative energy companies in over a dozen countries have adopted similar models for the production of biochar and biofuels. With the advent of carbon markets, it is believed that the use of biochar for carbon sequestration can render such models profitable. As the Food and Agriculture Organization of the United Nations has demanded greater investment in research and development for improving the capacity of agricultural lands to sequester carbon (FAO 2004), researchers and private corporations have responded: opportunities exist for the use of biochar not only in agricultural lands under active management but for degraded areas as well (Lal 2004a; Lal 2004b).

International media outlets have also produced enthusiastic articles about the potential that *terra preta* and biochar have for promoting environmentally sound agricultural management and curbing climate change (e.g., Binns 2006; Mann 2002; Marris 2006). However, some scholars worry that the original objectives of the TPN project are being overlooked as more and more focus is placed on the use of biochar in big agribusiness. In response to a *Nature* article on the subject, three researchers spoke specifically about this trend: "One might be left with the impression that the biochar initiative is solely directed toward agribusiness applications. From the start, this has certainly not been the case. Indeed, innovative biochar field trials involving a variety of crops are currently being conducted in Amazonia. . . . These trials are specifically designed for implementation by smallholders, who comprise most of the world's farmers" (Woods et al. 2006, 144). For big farmers, biochar can facilitate a shift toward industrial agriculture that is perceived as "environmentally friendly." What rural smallholders of Amazonia can gain from these developments is still unclear.

One source of optimism, however, is the work of Rubem César Rodrigues Souza, a researcher from the Center for Amazonian Energy Development (Centro de Desenvolvimento Energético Amazônico) at the Federal University of Amazonas (UFAM) in Manaus. Souza and his team have developed a machine for a small community in the state of Amazonas that processes açaí (*Euterpe oleracea*) seeds and creates a form of biodiesel that can be used to power the community's generator. As diesel is rather expensive and often in high demand in the rural communities of the interior of the Amazon, a consistent energy source for individuals in these communities is a major priority. With the generous supplies of biomass that represent potential fuel in place for these communities, all that is missing is the technology that can convert these sources into fuel. Since Eprida and other corporations have shown that technology used to harness fuel from this biomass can also be used to create biochar, this might serve as an added bonus for local farmers and even serve to sequester carbon.

Although it would require considerable investment, pyrolizers modeled after those of biochar corporations could not only contribute to the development of a "new *terra preta*" in the Amazon but also potentially provide rural communities with an excellent solution for energy independence, a hugely important step toward development in rural Amazonia. As state and federal governments actively invest in infrastructure and agricultural finance projects to minimize the migration of rural peoples to urban capitals, technologies modeled after biochar pyrolizers could represent practical alternatives for providing communities with energy, subsequently improving the quality of living in these areas and deterring potential out-migration.

It has been calculated that biochar could potentially offset as much as 12 percent of current anthropogenic carbon dioxide emissions on the planet (Lehmann et al. 2006; Woolf et al. 2010). Still, many big questions remain concerning its global implementation. One of biochar's primary selling points for farmers is increased crop yields, but experimental research in this area has shown mixed results, revealing that the benefits of biochar for crop production depend greatly upon soil properties and conditions, especially soil texture and pH (Jeffrey et al. 2011). For farmers who do want to convert their agricultural residues into biochar, investment must be made in pyrolizers and equipment for tilling biochar into the soil. This is also problematic because tillage and soil disturbance encourage the release of carbon dioxide from the soil into the atmosphere, thus diminishing biochar's benefits for carbon sequestration (McHenry 2009). Industrial agriculture's continued reliance on fossil fuels for chemical fertilizer also runs counter to the benefits of biochar for curbing greenhouse gas emissions. And while much has been written about the potential of biochar for improving agricultural production on smallholder farms, initiatives that have sought to implement this model have been limited mostly to small-scale "trials" (Leach et al. 2012, 299). The investments needed for pyrolizers and the added labor required for processing biochar and distributing it in fields represent major challenges for any small farming operation.

So can industrial farmers and big agribusinesses lead the charge in spreading biochar across the globe? Can this model simultaneously be adapted to the needs of smallholder farmers, who represent the majority of the world's farming population? And a much broader question but one that must be asked is: can the global-scaling of such technologies help us engineer our way out of ecological crisis?

One of the characteristics of the Anthropocene is the increased homogenization of life on the planet. Industrial agriculture has played a large role in this process as more and more of the global landscape is dedicated to the production of a select few crops—largely soy (*Glycine max*), corn (*Zea mays*), rice (*Oryza sativa*), and wheat (*Triticum aestivum*). Although humanity genuinely needs viable technological solutions for addressing climate change, the widespread adoption of biochar could have the unintended consequence of further homogenization of the landscape geared toward biomass production for biofuels and biochar, and could even encourage the release of greenhouse gases if forested areas are cleared for their production (Fargione et al. 2010; Groom et al. 2007; Searchinger et al. 2008). Widespread adoption of biochar could have unforeseen impacts on soil ecology too. Depending on the source of biomass used in pyrolysis, biochar might introduce undesirable contaminants, toxicants, and metals into the soil (Kookana et al. 2011; McHenry 2009). And there is fear that its use could have drastic impacts on vulnerable human populations: demand for biochar production has the potential to induce or exacerbate land grabbing in parts of the developing world (Leach et al. 2012; TNI 2009).

In many ways, "the biochar solution" is consistent with the ethos of the modern industrial era—it is believed that with the "right" technological fix, we can solve the problem of climate change and reengineer the earth to work for our benefit. As Charles Clement reminds us though, soils are not factories but rather dynamic living systems (2011, 832). And the thing about living systems is that they change and evolve and, inevitably, escape our control.

CONCLUSION: THE GROWTH OF THE SOIL (RESISTANCE, ACCOMMODATION, COLLABORATION)

Humans have maintained intimate relationships with Amazonian soils for centuries, altering them in profound ways, as research on *terra preta* attests. In my conversations with rural farmers, however, I found that even when a soil has been enriched by the accumulation of organic refuse over generations and generations, it continues to require attention and maintenance for long-term agricultural productivity.

Farmers do not work in a vacuum but rather constantly encounter resistance from other elements in the environment, including pests, invasive or undesirable plant species, floods, droughts, and others threats posed by an unpredictable climate.

What appears to be an unintended consequence of Amerindian settlement—the accumulation of charcoal that contributed to the development of *terra preta*—is now being reinvented as biochar technology aimed at curbing the climate change that largely defines this new geological epoch. But does biochar technology represent a new path toward a more "sustainable" future? Can the *terra preta* model be scaled globally to meet the needs of both large industrial farmers and smallholders of the developing tropics? And can it been done in a way that is sensitive to the needs of both human and nonhuman populations alike?

The ability of science to isolate the critical components of a phenomenon, essentialize them, and then facilitate their translation to other contexts is what gives it such great power. But the case of *terra preta* should remind us that while humans either knowingly or unknowingly altered Amazonian soils in ways that enriched them, or at the very least altered their characteristics to allow for other forms of agricultural production, it would be wrong to assume that the environment simply opens itself up to facile human manipulation and control. As Andrew Pickering argues in his writings on the sociology of science, humans are engaged in a perpetual "dance of agency" with the material world, always seeking novel ways to accommodate its resistances (2009, 21). To assume that humanity can short-circuit this process of resistance and accommodation and give itself the upper hand without facing any consequences is at best naïve, and at worst dangerous.

The soil is the skin of the earth. It is literally the foundation of biological life. Although *terra preta* doesn't exactly reproduce itself in the way that some researchers had once hoped (Woods and McCann 1999), it is in other ways very much alive. New studies show that *terra preta* soils have unique microbial and bacterial populations when compared to adjacent Oxisols and Ultisols (Grossman et al. 2010; Tsai et al. 2009). One study in western Amazonia found *terra preta* to have 25 percent greater species richness for soil bacterial populations than adjacent forest soils (Kim et al. 2007). Another study by Grossman and colleagues (2010) reported more than a 90 percent difference between the communities of Archaea (single-celled micoorganisms without a cell nucleus) living in *terra preta* and in adjacent soils. These researchers believe that the distinctive microbial communities that thrive in *terra preta* may also partially explain their persistence over time. *Terra preta* teems with life, as most soils do.

The Amazonian farmers whom I've met over the years often refer to their daily work as "a batalha," or the battle. However, I also see their work as a form of collaborative engagement with this diversity of lifeforms. They would probably smirk at this suggestion, but truly, farming involves the co-laboring of many different beings. Humans are just one of these, and arguably a very consequential one, but there are always others. To ignore this fact is to give the false impression that humanity can very well do as it pleases without repercussion, without resistance. Instead, *terra preta* should be a reminder that humanity maintains deep, binding relationships with the environment, and that such relationships require sensitivity to the actions and responses of the other beings that animate the world, even those that live right beneath our feet.

Chapter 4

PLANTS

BOTANIZING IN BORBA

When I grew tired of thinking about Amazonian soils, I turned my attention to plants. It's no secret that Amazonia is a region of stunning botanical diversity, with tens of thousands of endemic species. At least 138 of these were under active cultivation or management by indigenous populations prior to European arrival (Clement 1999), and today Amazonia continues to harbor a great deal of cultivated biodiversity in its agricultural landscapes.

At the time I began collecting data on the diversity of botanical species managed in rural Amazonian communities, I had no intention of studying "magic" plants.[1] But shortly after starting my research, a succession of stories drew me away from my typical routine of household surveys and species tallying. I heard, for example, about poraquê, or the "electric eel plant" (unidentified sp.), which I was told could be tucked into my belt while playing soccer to protect me from the aggressive body checks of the opposing team's defenders. I also learned about castanha-da-índia (*Thevetia peruviana*), which produced a fruit that farmers tied to their belt with a piece of string to shield them from venomous snakes as they weeded their manioc fields. During my surveys of home gardens, I encountered several plants that had the power to ward off the evil eye or deter unwelcome guests from entering a family's home. Others served as active ingredients in healing baths (*banhos*) that treated children afflicted by folk illnesses (i.e., culturally specific maladies) or hunters who had been hexed. Some plants were even said to have the power to attract money and good luck, and even good looks. As I spent more time in rural communities in Borba, I began to appreciate that such plants' symbolic and magical properties had important consequences, whether these were "real" or "imagined." Not only did these plants have powers as social agents imbued with meaning but many of them were weedy species that actively colonized areas inhabited by humans. In other words, more than just being passive recipients of human action, some plants actively responded to the human presence in the landscape.

The conceptual foundations of the Anthropocene and the modern industrial era encourage the view that humans alone have the capacity for "agency." In most scholarly circles, "agency" refers to action with intention (see Pickering 1995, 17–19). However, if this definition is modified to regard agency as simply "purposive behavior," it becomes obvious that humans are not the only ones with agency in the world. Purposive behavior is exhibited by lots of things that are not human and, as Dorion Sagan remarks, such behavior does not even require brains, since "an amoeba swims toward nutrients" and "sunflowers follow the sun" (2013, 129). By placing human agency on a pedestal, we ignore the fact that other organisms also act in the world, and sometimes they can directly challenge the actions of humans and even foil the best of human intentions.

This chapter examines the social lives of plants that Amazonian people cultivate and manage, paying specific attention to those that have distinctive magical and symbolic powers. Although "magic" plants can be seen as simple fetishes, I contend that the powers imbued in them can have important consequences, from healing a loved one to deterring potential thieves from a family home. Not only that, but such plants also open up possibilities for a broader consideration of the agency of nonhuman others. Sometimes they are wielded as weapons or employed practically as remedies, but other times they can arguably be considered actors in their own right. To put it plainly, even in the Anthropocene, humans are not the only ones in on the action.

PIÃO ROXO

Between visits to the rural countryside, I spent time in the town of Borba catching up on laundry, checking my email, and appreciating the simple pleasures of city life that I had previously taken for granted. I savored cold glasses of ice water and the smell of freshly baked bread that wafted through the streets in the early morning. But after a day or two in town, I would get restless, and begin to wander, hoping to stumble upon new observations that might be relevant to my ethnographic research.

On one such day, I started to casually survey the different species of ornamental plants found on the street where I lived. One species ap-

FIGURE 4.1. A fruiting pião roxo plant standing outside Diana's house.

peared consistently in the front yards of houses on the block, including my own. The plant had deeply lobed leaves that were maroon and green in color. When I picked a leaf, a milky-white latex dripped down from the freshly broken stem. I asked Diana the name of the plant and she told me it was known as "pião roxo" (*Jatropha gossypiifolia*). She said that the plant had started growing in the yard voluntarily and she had left it because she "liked the way it looked" (figure 4.1). Since then several *filhos*, literally "children" or offshootings, had appeared as well.

When I inquired about the uses of pião roxo, Diana explained that some people applied its white latex to their skin to heal wounds or scars. But later, my friend Valdo informed me that other people used it to protect the household from the evil eye, which is known in Brazil as *mau olhado* or *olho gordo*. From that day on, I began to notice pião roxo in front of residences in both the city and the rural communities where I conducted my botanical surveys. It seemed to crop up everywhere.

When I began to search for scholarly references to pião roxo, I found it commonly cited in studies of medicinal and healing plants of the Americas (Duke 2008, 389–391; Ortencio 1997, 337; Di Stasi and Hiruma-Lima 2002). The name of the plant's genus, *Jatropha*, is derived from the Greek words *iatros*, meaning "doctor," and *trophe*, meaning "food"—a reflection of its broad medicinal uses (Sabandar et al. 2013). In English, it is referred to as the "bellyache bush," indicating its common use as a purgative and for treating stomachache (ibid.). It has also been reported as a remedy for a wider host of afflictions, including anemia, diabetes, diarrhea, fever, hypertension, hemorrhaging, infection, inflammation, and malaria (Félix-Silva et al. 2014; Sabandar et al. 2013; Di Stasi and Hiruma-Lima 2002). In Brazil, it has even been traditionally used as a pesticide, insecticide, and vermifuge (Agra et al. 2013; Albuquerque et al. 2007).

Beyond its everyday utilitarian employment, pião roxo holds a close relationship to the Afro-Brazilian religion Candomblé (Albuquerque et al. 2007; Voeks 1997). It's considered to belong to the deity Omolu, a survivor of smallpox known for his bellicosity. Since Omolu is said to watch over the plant, followers of Candomblé frequently keep it in their front yards to scare off the evil eye, just as I had seen in Borba (Voeks 1997, 106). Having originated in the Americas (Prentis et al. 2009), pião roxo is one of a whole host of Neotropical plants that had been adopted by African slaves and incorporated into their medicomagical pharmacopeia. In the process of adapting their religious activities to a new environmental context in Brazil, Africans also introduced new sets of practices and beliefs, many of which would find their way into the Amazon region.

Did Africans learn about the magical and medicinal uses of pião roxo from indigenous peoples and adapt it to their own needs? Or did they simply find a fitting use for this weedy plant through a process of experimentation, which later spread to other peoples of Brazil? And did the Portuguese introduce the notion of the evil eye to African and indigenous populations, or did an analogous concept already exist in their different belief systems? It's hard to know where the stories of pião roxo and the evil eye intersect in Brazil, but what can be said is that their marriage was the product of the colonial encounter and that mixture of diverse belief systems, people, and plants. And throughout Brazilian Amazonia, pião roxo can still be found in the front yards of homes. Some might say that they simply like the way it looks. Others will confide that they keep it around to ward off dangers of the evil eye.

THE EVIL EYE, ENVY, AND
THE SOCIAL LIVES OF PLANTS

Reference to the "evil eye" invokes a common folk belief that an individual has the power to cause harm to others or their property simply by looking at them or praising them (Dundes 1992, 256). This might occur either voluntarily or involuntarily, but at its core, the evil eye is rooted in feelings of envy. The concept originated in the Old World, most likely in the eastern Mediterranean or the Middle East, and migrated to the Americas during the colonial period. Regardless of its origins, it is a concept that reflects an arguably universal preoccupation in humanity with envy and its potentially injurious consequences. George Foster pinpoints this preoccupation in his article "The Anatomy of Envy," writing: "In every society people use symbolic and nonsymbolic cultural forms whose function is to neutralize, or reduce, or otherwise control the dangers they see stemming from envy, and especially their fear of envy" (1972, 165).

Like magic plants themselves, envy is often a taboo subject. This is especially true when the topic is mentioned by an outsider. I suspected that my inquiries about the evil eye frequently made my interlocutors uncomfortable. Perhaps this was because they thought that I as a foreigner was interested in studying the evil eye as a "backwards" superstitious belief, antithetical to so-called modern living. However, I believe there were other reasons for the reticence of those whom I interviewed. An acknowledgment of fear of the evil eye requires recognition of social tensions within a community, inviting speculation about personal competition, animosity, and the possibility of violence that can emerge as a consequence. Perhaps even worse, the presence of the evil eye is an admittance of our fear of the envy of others as well as the fear of our own capacity to envy others, whether in regard to their health, wealth, or social standing.

I was always conscious of my own ability to inspire envy. I never brought my laptop computer to the communities where I worked, in part because electricity was only available for a few hours in the evening, if at all, but also because no one else possessed a computer. There were already enough ways to mark my difference, and I wanted to try to minimize the most conspicuous technological ones. However, I did frequently carry around a digital camera and voice recorder. I also brought a small MP3 player that I shared with others. Eventually one man begged me to sell it to him. At the time, however, I still had several long boat rides ahead of me and the idea of enduring them without music was difficult to accept. Somewhat pathetically, I attempted to explain to him that I simply could not part with it.

I did give small gifts to the families that hosted me, but minor controversies always surfaced as a result. Who in the household should maintain possession of the photographs of the family? What about the Maglite? Who would get which fishing lures? Which ones were good for catching peacock bass (tucunaré)? Which ones were too small, and worthless for catching a fish of any decent size? I always contributed food to the households where I stayed, including beans, rice, coffee, sugar, powdered milk, crackers, dried pasta, and some cookies for the kids. Once in a while I indulged everyone's sweet tooth with guava jelly and milk cream for an evening dessert. In a few rare instances, I even brought the fixings for pizza.

To enter into social life is to enter into exchange with others. These systems of interaction are always fraught with complications, and my socialization in rural Amazonia was no different. In an attempt to repay people who spent time answering my questions I frequently provided them with seeds of crops that they had requested on prior visits or ones that I thought might be useful additions to their home gardens. I distributed seeds of tomatoes (*Solanum lycopersicum*) and bell peppers (*Capsicum annuum*), chives (*Allium fistulosum*), squash (*Cucurbita* spp.), and watermelon (*Citrullus lanatus*). In some cases I came back months later to find clutches of bright red tomatoes and received a friendly "thanks" in return. Other times it was pointed out that some of the seed that I had purchased in the city had been outdated or had gone bad, which was frustrating for all parties involved. Who knows if the evil eye had been implicated in the process?[2]

As I became more acquainted with rural Amazonia, I also began to see plants as part of the broader fabric of everyday social life. Not only were they objects exchanged between humans but they themselves engaged humans and imposed different demands. At times, they arguably could be seen as actors in their own way.

When Diana claimed that pião roxo had simply appeared in her yard, I thought she may have used this as a convenient explanation because she was embarrassed to acknowledge the plant's association with the evil eye and what some considered *macumba*,[3] or black magic. But then I heard others describe its unexpected appearance in their yards in the same manner. Gisele, a newcomer in the agricultural settlement outside of the town of Borba, told me that she also had pião roxo in her yard and she knew quite well its ability to ward off the evil eye. But she hadn't planted it there. It had simply appeared, she insisted.

If a plant is completely unwanted in a yard, a weed in the truest sense, then it is almost always removed. Most rural Amazonians keep the area surrounding their house, known as the *terreiro*, cleared to prevent snakes or pests from having a place to hide. Sometimes weedy plants that appear voluntarily in the yard are left to grow, which is considered by scholars a form of "passive cultivation." But the term "passive cultivation" could also be seen as an elaborate designation for acknowledging human inaction while ignoring a plant's active colonization of spaces inhabited by humans. Isn't the plant responding to the human presence in the landscape? Isn't it doing something of its own accord?

While perusing an online forum dedicated to gardening in the United States, I came across a discussion of pião roxo, including the following post by a man living in Houston, Texas: "Beautiful plant, but a weed, nevertheless! It shoots its seeds all over the place. It kind of sounds like caps being struck and the next thing, it is hurling seeds through the air. I have been pulling this plant for 4 years and I still get one occasionally peeking its head through the mulch."[4]

This post flirts with anthropomorphizing the plant as it flings seeds[5] and peeks its "head" out from the oppressive mulch. But upon further reflection I asked myself, doesn't the plant do precisely this? As much as gardens are intentionally designed and cultivated, is it too far-fetched to claim that humans aren't the only ones responsible for the action that occurs within their confines?

Rick Stepp and Dan Moermann (2001) have demonstrated from their research among the highland Maya in Chiapas, Mexico, that weedy species are commonly used as healing plants and medicinals. They argue that short-lived weedy species are more likely to have secondary bioactive compounds that inhibit the growth of other plants or guard against herbivory, and such compounds often have curative properties for humans. These authors also explain quite logically that easy-to-find plants are much more useful to a household when someone falls ill. Although some conservationists have made the argument that primary forests need to be conserved to protect reserves of unknown plants that may offer benefits to modern medicine, in many parts of the world people rely on plants that thrive in disturbed areas or environments where humans are active. This may also explain why

Afro-Brazilians adopted pião roxo. It was not necessarily a plant that they sought out, but rather one that *came to them*.[6]

Pião roxo is an important starting point for understanding magic plants in Amazonia because it embodies a number of their complexities. Such plants can be viewed as medicines used for healing scars or wounds. In other cases, they are wielded as symbolic weapons that fight the power of envy or protect individuals from illnesses caused by it. In some instances they are considered no different than innocuous ornamentals that casually occupy yards. Other times they are viewed as aggressive weeds that actively thwart any attempt at repression. How much of their power is projected upon them? How much is inherent to them? And can we distinguish between the two?

PLANTS WITH POWERS TO REPEL, PROTECT, AND ATTRACT

After I had gathered information on pião roxo, other magic plants started working their way into my studies (Table 4.1). Many were used to ward off the evil eye or repel unwanted guests, including pião branco (*Jatropha curcas*), pião barrigudo (*Jatropha podagrica*), mucura-caá (*Petiveria alliacea*), jiru (unidentified sp.), pimenta malagueta (*Capsicum frutescens*), and cipó alho (*Mansoa alliacea*). Rue (*Ruta graveolens*), known in Portuguese as arruda, also fit into this group. It was among the first plants introduced by Europeans into the New World and its history of religious and medicinal use extends back to the Greek and Roman empires (Pollio et al. 2008). The genus *Ruta* appears frequently in the Corpus Hippocraticum, which is considered the most ancient systematic record of medical practice of the Mediterranean world (Pollio et al. 2008). Rue also receives mention in the Bible and even found its way into the Roman Catholic Church. Due to its abundance of little leaves, it served to sprinkle holy water and bless the faithful, thus becoming known as the "herb of grace" (ibid.).

But the Roman Catholic Church would not have approved of all of the plant's uses. It was employed as an abortifacient in the eastern Mediterranean, and after being introduced to Brazil, it seems that Afro-Brazilians adopted it for this same purpose to avoid bringing children into slavery (Voeks 1997, 24). Afro-Brazilians also adopted the practice of hiding sprigs of rue in their clothing or wearing it behind the ear to protect them from the evil eye. Cattle ranchers and *caubois* in

Amazonia maintained the same practice to protect them while work-ing out in their pastures. And in the community of Auará Grande, a lanky man named Mario once told me that the old-timers (*os antigos*) believed that you had to steal a cutting of rue if you wanted to plant it in your yard, otherwise it would lose its effect if it was knowingly loaned from someone. This presented a fascinating irony: you have to steal a magical plant that protects you from the evils of envy.[7]

It is often assumed that the use of magic plants in Amazonian com-munities is the product of local indigenous tradition, but many reli-gious and medicinal plants found in contemporary rural Amazonian communities, like rue, are in fact of Old World origin. As a result of the Columbian Exchange, several species were adopted because of their cachet as exotic plants, and perhaps also because they were be-lieved to possess heightened powers for healing and magic. Others may have been quick to spread into the region on their own, coloniz-ing areas occupied by humans and eventually forcing their way into the social lives of rural communities.

Some plants kept in Amazonian home gardens are used to ward off not just envy and the evil eye, but also physical aggression. One of these I encountered was poraquê (unidentified sp., Araceae fam-ily), named after the Amazonian electric eel. I heard about the plant while visiting in the community of Vila Gomes with dona Maria Gua-dalupe, one of the few people who talked about magic plants with-out the slightest hint of self-consciousness. Most others that I inter-viewed chuckled awkwardly when I inquired about the subject, either because they were embarrassed to discuss what may be perceived as superstition or because they were simply reluctant to acknowledge the beliefs associated with them. At first, dona Maria's sons laughed ner-vously when she told me about the different magic plants she kept, but shortly thereafter they began helping to point out a few specimens themselves. Her eldest son showed me the plant known as poraquê, which he said could be used when playing soccer. You simply had to tuck a leaf in your belt and if some other player tried to body check you, he informed me, you wouldn't feel a thing. Instead, the poraquê would bounce them right off of you as if they had received a shock from an Amazonian electric eel itself.

Other plants, like castanha-da-índia (*Thevetia peruviana*), are used to repel the physical threats of animals. The fruit of castanha-da-índia is said to have the power to scare off snakes. Farmers pierce a hole through the fruit and tie it to their belt with a piece of string, and it's used to protect them as they work in the fields, either clearing a new piece of land or weeding their manioc plots. Poisonous snakes like the surucucu are perennial threats to farmers, and friends told me of numerous horror stories about snakebites. The surucucu pico-de-jaca (*Lachesis muta*) is considered the most dangerous, and one killed a horse owned by the head of the agricultural extension agency in Borba shortly before I arrived in 2007. Since castanha-da-índia is a toxic plant, which is even responsible for an "epidemic of self-poisoning" in Sri Lanka (Eddleston et al. 1999), its toxicity is perhaps seen as countering that of a venomous snake. Moreover, it serves as a talisman for farmers when they must work in fields. Several others are also used to protect against snakebite, including an unidentified aroid known as tajá-buceta, whose name is curiously derived from a colloquial term for "vagina."

Plants are used not just to keep human envy and snakes away but also to protect the household from the threat of thieves and other dangerous individuals. Comigo-ninguém-pode, which translates directly, albeit somewhat awkwardly, as the "nobody can [fool] with me" plant (*Dieffenbachia seguine*), is one of these. It is a common and somewhat innocuous-looking ornamental that can be purchased at garden stores in North America and Europe, although it is native to South America. The plant is particularly shade tolerant and can be kept indoors, but in Amazonian home gardens it is often kept close to the entrance of the house. When I was on a visit to the community of Floresta, a young woman revealed to me that comigo-ninguém-pode was not just cultivated for aesthetic reasons but was also used to keep unwanted guests or enemies away from the household. Sometimes referred to as "dumb cane" in English, the leaves of the plant contain calcium oxalate, and if chewed, it can leave an individual's capacity for speech severely impaired. Perhaps unsurprisingly, it is reported to have been used as a punishment for insubordinate slaves in South America (Barnes and Fox 1955). A lesser-known fact is that during World War II, a physician proposed to Heinrich Himler that extracts of the plant could serve the Nazi party to sterilize "racially undesirable" prisoners (Kenny 2002).

The symbolic power of comigo-ninguém-pode is most likely linked to its toxicity, similar to that of castanha-da-índia and even rue, which can poison humans if ingested in significant doses. But why might it be kept as a sentinel outside of people's homes? As I spent more time in the small communities in Borba, I saw that far from being idyllic oases of harmony and social order, most communities grappled with problems

TABLE 4.1 LIST OF "MAGIC" PLANTS IDENTIFIED IN BORBA, AMAZONAS, BRAZIL

Family	Scientific Name	Local Common Name	English Name	Native/ Exotic (1/0)	Origin	Magic Use	Other Uses
Amaranthaceae	*Alternathera* sp.	cuia-mansa		1	South America	banho	
Amaranthaceae	*Chenopodium ambrosioides*	mastruz	wormseed	1	Mesoamerica	banho	medicinal
Annonaceae	*Annona montana*	araticum	mountain soursop	1	Amazonia	banho	food
Apiaceae	*Eryngium foetidum*	chicoria	culantro	1		banho	condiment
Apocynaceae	*Thevetia peruviana*	castanha-da-índia		1	Andes	repel (snakes)	ornamental
Araceae	*Caladium* sp.	cachorrinho		1	Neotropics	attract (people)	ornamental
Araceae	*Dieffenbachia seguine*	comigo-ninguém-pode	dumb cane	1	Neotropics	repel	ornamental
Araceae	*Scindapsus aureus*	jibóia	ivy	0	Old World (Asia)	attract (people)	ornamental
Araceae	Unidentified	tajá-buceta				repel (snakes)	ornamental
Araceae	*Caladium bicolor*	vence-tudo	caladium	1	South America	banho	ornamental
Araceae?	Unidentified	poraquê		?	?	repel	ornamental
Aristolochiaceae	*Aristolochia* sp.	uecá		0	Neotropics	attract (luck)	ornamental

Family	Scientific name	Portuguese name	English name		Origin		
Asparagaceae	*Sansevieria trifasciata*	espada de São Jorge	snake plant	0	Old World (Africa)	repel	ornamental
Asteraceae	*Tagetes erecta*	cravo; cravo de defunto	marigold	1	New World	banho	ornamental
Asteraceae	*Acmella oleracea*	jambu		1	Amazonia	banho	food
Asteraceae	*Ayapana tripilinervis*	japana		1	Amazonia	banho	
Asteraceae	*Pluchea sagittalis*	marcela		1	Americas	banho	medicinal
Bignoniaceae	*Mansoa alliacea*	cipó alho	garlic vine	1	Amazonia	banho	medicinal
Bignoniaceae	*Fridericia chica*	crajiru		1		banho	medicinal
Commelinaceae	*Callisia repens*	dinheiro-em-penca		1	Neotropics	attract (money)	ornamental
Costaceae	*Costus spicatus*	pobre velho; cana mansa		1	South America	banho	
Crassulaceae	*Bryophyllum pinnatum*	coirama		0	Africa	banho	medicinal
Euphorbiaceae	*Euphorbia milii*	coroa de cristo	crown of thorns	0	Old World	repel	ornamental
Euphorbiaceae	*Jatropha podagrica*	pião barrigudo	gout plant; Buddha belly plant	1	Mesoamerica	repel	medicinal
Euphorbiaceae	*Jatropha curcas*	pião branco		1	Mesoamerica	repel; banho	medicinal

(continued)

TABLE 4.1 (CONTINUED)

Family	Scientific Name	Local Common Name	English Name	Native/Exotic (1/0)	Origin	Magic Use	Other Uses
Euphorbiaceae	*Jatropha gossypiifolia*	pião roxo	bellyache bush	1	South America	repel; banho	medicinal
Euphorbiaceae	Unidentified sp.	caboclo roxo		?	?	repel	
Lamiaceae	*Ocimum campechianum*	alfavaca	Amazonian basil	0	Neotropics	banho	condiment
Lamiaceae	*Aeollanthus suaveolens*	catinga de mulata		1	Old World (Europe)	banho	medicinal
Lamiaceae	*Mentha* sp.	hortelazinha	mint	0	Old World (Europe)	banho	food; medicinal
Lamiaceae	*Ocimum americanum*	manjericão	basil	0	Old World	banho	food
Lamiaceae	*Pogostemon heyneanus*	oriza; uriza	patchouli	0	Old World (Asia)	banho	
Malvaceae	*Gossypium barbadense*	algodão	cotton	1	South America	banho	utilitarian
Monimiaceae	*Peumus boldus*	boldo		1	South America	banho	tea
Monimiaceae	*Siparuna guianensis*	capitiu	fevertree	1	Neotropics	banho	medicinal
Phytolaccaceae	*Petiveria alliacea*	mucura-caá		1	Neotropics	banho	

Family	Species	Local name	English name		Origin		
Piperaceae	Piper callosum	paregórico; panquilê		1	South America	banho	medicinal
Poaceae	Cymbopogon citratus	capim cheiroso; capim santo	lemon grass; citronella	0	Old World	banho	tea
Poaceae	Vetiveria zizanioides	patichulim	vetiver	0	Asia	banho	
Portulacaceae	Portulaca pilosa	amor-crescido	kiss-me-quick	1	Americas	banho	
Rutaceae	Ruta spp.	arruda	rue	0	Old World	repel	
Solanaceae	Capsicum frutescens	pimenta malagueta	hot pepper	1	South America	repel	food
Unidentified	Unidentified	jiru		?	?	repel	ornamental
Unidentified	Unidentified	Maria bonita		?	?	attract	ornamental
Unidentified	Unidentified	vai-vem		?	?	attract	
Unidentified	Unidentified	mutuquinha		1	Neotropics	banho	
Zingiberaceae	Zingiber officinale	gengibre; mangarataia	ginger	0	Asia	banho	food; medicinal

*Data collected from 138 households in the municipality of Borba between 2009 and 2010.

related to burglary and theft. Boat motors, fattened hogs ready for slaughter, hidden caches of marijuana, and numerous other valuable goods and items were stolen under the cover of night in the communities where I stayed. I reasoned that plants like comigo-ninguém-pode represented ways of coping with threats from undesirable characters in the community, at least in an indirect or deflected manner. However, I also found during a brief visit to the Peruvian Amazon that individuals who commanded a heightened knowledge of plants were considered curers or witches and were much less likely to be crossed by others. In this way, the ability to command or exploit the symbolic power of plants can sometimes translate into other forms of social power. And as I have described here, the symbolic threat of such plants often rests on their ability to yield very painful (and even deadly) biophysical effects.

Sometimes interviewees pointed out plants that were kept close to the home not to fend off threatening individuals or the evil eye, but rather to attract money, good luck, and even other people. Although I encountered far fewer of these plants, it is worth noting that plants are used not simply for protection or defense but also to fortify social relationships and even elevate one's social standing. One example is dinheiro-em-penca (*Callisia repens*), which appeared in two home gardens I visited and is said to attract money to the household. It is typically kept in a small hanging basket, spilling out over the sides with its numerous small leaves, much like an overflowing basket of money. Sir James Frazer (2009 [1922]) described "homeopathic" or "imitative" magic as a form in which one attempts to attain a result through its mimicry, and this plant is employed symbolically following the same rationale. Rather than protecting the household from the envy of others, this plant perhaps serves as inspiration for those who aspire to *be* the envy of others.

Still other plants are used to attract people. Jibóia (*Scindapsus aureus*) is a small creeping vine similar to ivy that's named after the boa constrictor and is believed to attract "good" people to a home. Since snakes are widely hated or feared by Amazonians, it seemed somewhat counterintuitive that a plant named after a boa was said to entice people. I considered that the plant may have been given the name because of its winding, snakelike gestalt, but instead it's attributed to the fact that the boa is known for hypnotizing its prey (Nigel Smith, pers. comm.). On a related note, the owner of a general store in the town of

Borba kept a small dead boa constrictor preserved in a jar because he said it also helped to draw in customers.

One of the last plants that drew my attention due to its ability to attract people was cachorrinho (*Calladium* sp.), or the "puppy plant." A young woman pointed it out to me in her yard and informed me that it was good for a married man to keep around his house. I inquired as to why and she told me: "Because his wife will follow him around like a puppy, responding to his every command." Although we laughed about this, later reflection made me consider a more serious reason for its usage. In rural Amazonian communities, infidelity is a major concern among couples, and for this reason, the cultivation of cachorrinho may represent a way of confronting doubts regarding marital infidelity, or perhaps even serve as a guilty reminder to an unfaithful spouse.

If we approach social life from a relational perspective, following the lead of Bruno Latour,[8] it is possible to see plants as social actors, or in the terms of Latour's actor-network theory, "actants." In reflecting on the bumper sticker "Guns don't kill people; people kill people," Latour argues that action cannot lie simply with the people who use guns or the guns themselves but rather the way they work together. In Latour's words, "responsibility of action must be shared among various actants" (1999, 180). From this vantage point, plants share responsibility with humans for a broad number of actions, from temporarily inhibiting an individual's speech to curbing the infidelities of a cheating spouse to even potentially poisoning an enemy. Clearly, plants— just like guns or books or cameras—require knowledge or skill on the part of their owners for effective manipulation. And to be successfully used as deterrents or incitements, they require that their potential be recognized by others. In other words, their power is both projecting and projected, both material and symbolic, both "real" and "imagined." And therein lies some of their magic.

PLANTS WITH POWERS TO HEAL

When I began asking rural Amazonians about pião roxo and plants used against the evil eye, many respondents also discussed plants they kept in their home gardens that were used in healing baths, or *banhos*. In fact, many of the same species used to ward off the evil eye were used for *banhos*, including pião roxo, pião branco, cipó alho, mucura-caá, and arruda. In addition, japana (*Ayapana tripilinervis*), manjericão (*Ocimum americanum*), cuia-mansa (*Alternathera tenella*), alfavaca (*Ocimum micranthum*), cravo (*Tagetes erecta*), hortelazinha (*Mentha* sp.), jambu (*Acmella oleracea*), and uecá (*Aristolochia* sp.) were also commonly used in healing baths. The use of herbs in cleansing baths is another common characteristic of Afro-Brazilian religious traditions like Candomblé (Albuquerque 2001; Voeks 1997), demonstrating the intimate relationship between religion and healing and the ways in which physical health is directly tied to spiritual belief and practice.

In Brazil, as in much of Latin America, emotions are considered to have the power to cause sickness or become sicknesses in themselves (Rebhun 1994). This holds particularly true in rural Amazonia, where many folk illnesses are attributed to the effects of the evil eye. Children are seen to be particularly vulnerable, and mothers can be wary of individuals who compliment their children, especially if such individuals are childless. *Banhos* are usually used to treat infants and children either when they catch colds or when they are afflicted with folk illnesses such as *quebranto* or *vento caído* (Fraxe 2004, 209; Smith 1996). In an excerpt from Nigel Smith's *Enchanted Amazon Rain Forest*, he discusses how the magical power of such plants overlaps with their use in preventive medicine:

> Many people in the region believe in the evil eye, known in the Brazilian Amazon as "mau olhado" or "quebranto." Young children are especially vulnerable to the evil eye. If a child is the object of a great deal of admiration, for example, he or she may become weak or feverish. A victim of mau olhado is listless and has no or little desire to eat. . . . To ward off its harmful influence, women plant pião roxo, pião branco, vassoura, and rue in their yards, especially by the front entrance of their home. (1996, 126)

Much in the same way that these plants protect the household from their neighbor's envy, baths with the leaves of these plants are used to heal children who may be affected by envious or excessively affectionate neighbors and strangers, which are oftentimes viewed as the sources of these folk illnesses. In other cases, if a father carelessly throws his sweat-drenched shirt on a child after a long morning of work in the sun, then the child can fall ill from direct contact with this item.

When I asked a friend, dona Nanda, how she learned to use plants in healing baths, she told me that she began when she had her first children. In many parts of rural Amazonia, where medical assistance is sorely lacking, learning home remedies for common problems and illnesses is a critical skill for young mothers. In addition to dona Nanda, other women reported similar stories, explaining that they learned about such plants from their mothers when they first had their own children. This explains why female household representatives reported a significantly higher number of magic species on average than male household representatives in my research (Kawa 2012). Some male respondents demonstrated an intimate knowledge of magic plants, but on more than one occasion I was told by a male respondent that it would be best to talk to his wife about such matters. I could not discern, however, whether this was because of his ignorance on the subject or a lack of willingness to entertain a discussion about magic plants.

Even though magic plants are most often used by rural Amazonian women to bathe children, they can also be used to bathe adults. Cuiamansa was reported to be used to bathe men when they become angry and belligerent, as it is said to have a calming effect. Pião roxo can be used similarly, as I learned when a friend began acting aggressively after a long day of drinking in the town of Borba; his mother grabbed some leaves from the yard and quickly bathed him in the hope that he would calm down.

Healing baths are also used to treat *panema*, a lowland South American cultural concept that can be understood as a hex or a form of bad luck. In rural Amazonia, *panema* is most commonly diagnosed when a man has difficulty hunting game or catching fish (Harris 2011; Smith 1996, 101; Wagley 1976, 78). A number of practices and habits are performed both to prevent *panema* and to treat it. For example, I was told not to walk on the scales of either the pirarucu (*Arapaima gigas*) or aruanã (*Osteoglossum* spp.) fish because they could give me *panema*.[9] Men are also supposed to avoid menstruating women when engaging in hunting or fishing activities, and it is said that a man exposed to a menstruating woman can even ruin the luck of others in his party (Harris 2011, 42).

To free an individual of *panema*, several women told me, baths made with the vine known as cipó alho were best. The plant's leaves release a pungent garlic smell when crushed, giving it the name "the garlic vine." A plant with a similar odor is mucura-caá, or the "possum plant," which is used for the same purpose. In western Amazonia, it is also sometimes prepared with the hallucinogenic plant ayahuasca in a ritualistic cleansing practice against witchcraft (McKenna et al. 1995). One common characteristic of many of the plants used in *banhos* is their distinct smells and aromatic qualities when crushed and mixed in water. After I interviewed a woman named Evani, who patiently responded to several questions about such plants, she did her best to sum up the tradition of *banhos*: "We were raised with our parents doing this when we were ill. They bathed us with stinky plants!"

While I was writing notes on an early draft of this chapter, a neighbor came over to pick some leaves of japana from the backyard of Diana's house. Diana had numerous plants that were used for baths and healing, many of which she had inherited from her mother. When I later asked her about using plants to ward off the evil eye, she told me that the plants she had served simply as herbal remedies. However, since Diana was a nurse in town, she had a different relationship to healing and medicine, which perhaps made her feel uncomfortable entertaining the notion that her use of plants could be related to ritualistic and spiritual practice as much as Western biomedicine. Although many of the plants described here have scientifically documented medicinal benefits, I would argue that most are used in rural Amazonia today because of their inherited sociocultural value in the practice of healing. And, on numerous occasions, I found friends, neighbors, and acquaintances stopping by Diana's house to pick a few leaves or sprigs of plants to bathe a sick child or an ailing relative.

It is difficult to create clear-cut categories of plants used strictly for magical reasons and others used for homeopathy (see also Desmarchelier et al. 1996; Macia et al. 2004). These ambiguities relate to the fact that traditional healing and magic are interchangeable in many places in the world. Because of the intimate relationship between magic and healing, Evans-Pritchard referred to magic plants in his study of the Azande as "medicines" and provided a revealing justification for this translation: "The Zande word which I have translated as 'medicine' or 'magic,' according to the context, is *ngua*. *Ngua* means 'tree' or 'wood' or 'plant'; so when we ask a Zande what medicine is used for a certain activity we are asking him what tree or plant is used, though our question may also have a general sense of what magical rite is performed" (1958 [1937], 440). In this way, magical and medicinal plants may be seen as one and the same. And regardless of how these plants are categorized, their powers play an important role in their continued adoption and use in rural communities, allowing them to remain fundamental parts of everyday social life.

CONCLUSION: THE POWERS OF PLANTS

Some magic plants found in Amazonian home gardens are actively cultivated by people and directly depend upon humans for their continued propagation. Others, like pião roxo, are opportunists that take advantage of people's company but also thrive independently of human management. In fact, pião roxo has become so successful at occupying territory and expanding its range outside of South America that it is now considered to be a "globally invasive plant." It has traversed most of the American tropics and subtropics, crept through the Caribbean, and fanned out across Australia, southeastern Asia, western Africa, and the Pacific Islands (Prentis et al. 2008; Prentis et al. 2009). According to Prentis and colleagues, it is currently considered "one of the world's worst tropical weeds," thanks to its ability to spread, displace existing pasture grasses, and even poison livestock that eat its toxic seeds (2008, 150). While humans are changing the global landscape, pião roxo is following in hot pursuit. Its rebellious nature makes it a challenge for any who attempt to control its movement or suppress its expansion.

In some parts of the world, like Australia, people are working to eradicate pião roxo from the landscape because of its threat to livestock animals and their grazing lands. Trials have been undertaken to attempt to control it through the use of fire, albeit with limited success (Bebawi and Campbell 2002). In Central America and the Caribbean, researchers are examining the prospect of using leaf-eating insects, fungi, and other predators to serve as "biological controls" of its populations. Meanwhile, in Brazil and India, other researchers are exploring the possibilities of taking advantage of it as a source of biodiesel (de Oliveira et al. 2009; Mukewar et al. 2006).

Whether social scientists agree that plants can have agency is of little concern to pião roxo. It doesn't appear particularly interested in philosophical debate. Instead it's busy building its numbers, expanding its range, and flinging its seeds across the landscape.

Other magic plants appear more attuned to human insecurity and the human desire for control, finding more subtle ways to work themselves into our lives. Oftentimes they are adopted for use because of the meanings that we have attached to them or the importance that we have given them—whether this is related to the food they produce, the medicines they offer, or the spiritual significance they carry. It would be wrong, I suppose, to project notions of agency onto plants for those reasons. But who wears the pants in the relationship or has the grand plans might be beside the point.

After returning from Brazil to the United States, I found myself in the nursery of a large home improvement store one afternoon. Looking for a houseplant to brighten my home, I came upon a fine *Dieffenbachia* specimen, the same plant rural Amazonian households use to protect themselves from unwanted visitors. I felt compelled to purchase the plant in part to maintain a connection with Amazonia and its people but also because I reasoned it never hurt to have a little added security at home. Evans-Pritchard noted that he had adopted the habit of consulting oracles before traveling to reassure his Azande counterparts that their journey would be a safe one. He concluded, "If one must act as though one believed, one ends in believing, or half-believing, as one acts" (1976, 244).

Leaving the store, I looked down at the plant. A few years prior it would have been completely meaningless to me and probably would have sat on the shelf waiting to catch someone else's eye. At that moment, I began to understand the magic hidden in such plants with their ability to capture our imagination and ensnare us with their stories. It seems they might have something to teach us all.

THE NATURE AND CULTURE
OF AMAZONIAN FORESTS

Amazonia is known for its forests. In fact, it is *the* tropical rainforest—more than any other in the global imaginary. And for much of modern history it has been emblematic of "nature" in its rawest, most pristine, unadulterated state.

Recently, however, anthropologists and archaeologists have begun to paint a more complicated picture of Amazonian forests. They have shown that far from being pristine, the region's forested landscapes have been shaped by human populations since hunter-gatherers first arrived in lowland South America. Pre-Columbian Amazonians encouraged the growth and expansion of Brazil nut trees (*Bertholletia excelsa*) and hosts of fruit-bearing palms in managed agroforestry systems. In some instances, indigenous management practices appear to have even increased botanical diversity and ecological heterogeneity in the region (Balée 1989; Balée 1994; Posey 1985; Shepard and Ramirez 2011). And today, many contemporary rural Amazonians benefit from the useful species found in forests that are in part the product of past human management and subsistence activities.

In recognizing the long-term effects of human populations on forests, new research has provoked some hard-to-answer questions regarding the degree to which Amazonian nature is in fact "natural." Although many anthropologists working in Amazonia recognize the dialogical relationship between human populations and the environment, the increasingly customary distinction made between "anthropogenic" and "natural" forests represents one of many problematic efforts to classify and smooth over complex histories of interaction. In the attempt to dissolve the boundaries of nature and culture, a habit of dichotomizing nature has emerged instead, leading to such distinctions as "natural" and "cultural" forests, or essentially, "natural nature" and "cultural nature."

Whereas the perception of Amazonian forests as idealized "natural" spaces obscures the history of humans in the landscape and their interactions with other species, the identification of forests as "cultural" spaces has the opposite problem of fixating solely on human uses and manipulations of them, overlooking the ways in which forests act or exist independently of humans. Today, as humans are increasingly viewed as the primary drivers of regional environmental change, the capacity of the environment to resist human control is largely ignored and underestimated. Once again, the failure to recognize the actions of nonhuman others is a reflection of the deeply entrenched anthropocentrism that characterizes the current conception of the Anthropocene.

This chapter offers a view of Amazonian forests that seeks to move "beyond nature and culture" (Descola 2013). Here I examine the ways that Amazonian forests reflect human management at varying scales and intensities, while also directing attention to the manner in which forest environments are constituted through the work of other beings and things. Drawing from the "decentered" perspective of posthumanism read alongside Amazonian mythology, I show how the massive snake known as Cobra Grande in Amazonian folklore is an important metaphor for the force of the Amazonian environment. As Cobra Grande is often invoked to explain the appearance of creeks and waterways resulting from seasonal shifts in regional hydrology, it also serves to illustrate the emergent qualities of the Amazonian landscape. And like contemporary posthumanist philosophy, the stories of Cobra Grande underscore the need to situate human lives within broad networks of relations with other beings and forces, offering a much-needed counterpoint to the anthropocentrism of the Anthropocene.

HEAVEN, HELL, AND HISTORICAL ECOLOGY

In the generations following the initial European exploration of Amazonia, the region came to be seen as an earthly Eden. In the final chapter of his book *The Naturalist on the River Amazons*, Henry Walter Bates lays bare his ambivalent feelings regarding his return to England after eleven years collecting insects and other biological specimens in Brazilian Amazonia. On one hand he describes his contentment with returning to "civilization" but on the other he expresses the difficulty in having left behind a tropical "paradise":

> [The desire] of seeing again my parents and enjoying once more the rich pleasures of intellectual society, had succeeded in overcoming the attractions of a region which may be fittingly called a Naturalist's Paradise. . . . I was quitting a country of perpetual summer where my life had been spent like that of three-fourths of the people in gipsy fashion, on the endless streams or in the boundless forests. I was leaving the Equator where the well-balanced forces of Nature maintained a land-surface and climate that seemed to be typical of mundane order and beauty. . . . It was natural to feel dismayed at the prospect of so great a change, but now, after three years of renewed experience of England, I find how incomparably superior is civilized life, where feelings, taste, and intellect find abundant nourishment, to the spiritual sterility of half-savage existence, even if it were passed in the garden of Eden. (1863, 416)

In this closing statement of his account, Bates promotes a prominent perception in the nineteenth century that is carried by many Europeans and North Americans up until the present: Europe and the northern latitudes represent the home of "Civilization," while Amazonia and the equatorial tropics are the home of "Nature." And like many natural historians of the Victorian era, Bates projected his image of a timeless heaven onto the tropical forest (see also Grove 1996).

At the beginning of the twentieth century, Brazilian writers depicted the Amazon region in another light—one that stood in direct opposition to the edenic narrative found in Bates's account. In 1908, Alberto Rangel published the book *Inferno verde*, or "green hell." It appealed to a growing number of Brazilians who were concerned about integration of the Amazon region into the nation, seeing its abundant nature as a formidable obstacle to that task, as exemplified in the following passage: "The jungle makes the worker into an alert watchman. If he abandons his post, it vigorously breaks past the edges of his field, empowering itself again" (63–64).[1]

For different reasons, a similar view was reinforced in Amazonian anthropology of the mid- to late twentieth century, especially through the work of the late North American archaeologist Betty Meggers. In her book *Amazonia: Man and Culture in a Counterfeit Paradise*, she asserted that the Amazonian environment, and specifically the poor soils of the uplands, inhibited cultural development in much of the basin. In a synthesis of her argument in an earlier work she wrote: "The evidence suggests that the environment exerts an unsurmountable limiting effect on the culture it supports as long as it permits only a hunting and gathering subsistence pattern, and that this limitation extends to all areas of culture, even those that seem remotely or not at all related to the subsistence requirements. No amount of inventive genius or receptivity to borrowing that might be theoretically attributable to the people psychologically is sufficient to overcome this barrier" (Meggers 1954, 807). Meggers's model thus argued that the tropical forest severely limited indigenous populations' productive activities and cultural development. As a consequence, Amazonian forests were largely viewed as virginal, pristine, and primeval. They were forests without history.

Over time, however, archaeologists and anthropologists began to question Meggers's interpretations and called for a reexamination of the evidence. Building upon early archaeological studies (Hartt 1874; Hartt 1885; Ferreira Penna 1869; Palmatary 1949; Palmatary 1960), many researchers have argued in recent decades that the Amazonian environment reflects considerable human influence from the pre-Columbian era (Balée 1989; Balée 1994; Erickson 2005; Heckenberger et al. 2003; Roosevelt 1991; Rostain 2008; Rostain 2010; Schaan 2004). The research program of historical ecology has played a critical role in revising this history, emphasizing the recursive nature of human–environmental interaction. Historical ecologists contend that humans do not simply adapt to their surroundings, but rather play an active role in shaping them through time (Balée 2006). From this perspective, human–environmental interaction is conceived of as a dialogical and co-evolutionary process.

One of the key areas of study in historical ecology has been the effect of past human activity on contemporary biodiversity, especially botanical diversity. In Amazonia and neighboring regions, human populations have been shown to have a profound effect on the floristic composition of contemporary forests (Balée 1989; Balée 1994; Junqueira 2010; Levis et al. 2012; Posey 1985; Shepard and Ramirez 2011). In the influential study "The Culture of Amazonian Forests," William Balée (1989) outlined different forms of forests shaped by historical human presence that can be found across the basin, including palm forests, bamboo forests, Brazil nut groves, and liana forests. Balée's research suggested that historical human management and selection of useful plants contributed to the formation of such "anthropogenic" forests in more than 11 percent of the Amazon region. Similarly, studies by the late Darrell Posey demonstrated that the Kayapó of southern Amazonia planted trees that led to the establishment of forest islands (*apêtê*) in what was otherwise largely scrub savanna, known in Brazil as *cerrado* (Posey 1985). Such forest islands not only harbored high concentrations of useful species managed by the Kayapó, but also possibly served as safe havens away from disease during the indigenous demographic collapse of the post-contact era.

Studies by Posey, Balée, and others have provided necessary correctives to what William Denevan (1992b) has described as the "pristine myth," or the notion that the Americas were a sparsely populated wilderness prior to European arrival. Some historical ecologists, however, have also been critiqued for overemphasizing human influence on the environment and making the related assumption of human intentionality in environmental transformation. In the rejection of environmental determinism and simplistic models of human adaptation, historical ecologists have occasionally overextended their arguments in support of human agency by characterizing environmental phenomena that may be by-products of human activity, like *terra preta* soils, as examples of "human engineering" (e.g., Erickson 2008, 171). In the decision to describe environments as "anthropogenic," it is also often overlooked that many indigenous groups do not necessarily view their management as intentional activity (Posey 1992).

The ongoing debate over the extent to which pre-Columbian human populations shaped the Amazonian forest is largely bound by the problems inherent to the nature–culture divide and its conceptual framing. The view led by Betty Meggers, and carried on by several contemporary ecologists and biologists, holds on to the idea that "nature" can (and should) exist in a discrete sphere independent of human influence. Meggers for her part saw Amazonian nature as imposing insurmountable obstacles to the development of large-scale societies. From her viewpoint, Amazonian forests remained largely insusceptible to human intervention and meddling in prehistoric times. A new group of scholars have sought to reassert this position, claiming that *interfluvial* areas of Amazonia—those isolated from the region's major rivers—were largely unoccupied during the pre-Columbian era, experiencing only minimal human influence through the activities of hunter-gatherers (Barlow et al. 2012; Bush and Silman 2009; McMichael et al. 2012; Peres et al. 2010). They also insist that pre-

Columbian indigenous populations were largely concentrated in eastern Amazonia, while the western portions of the basin experienced relatively little to no human impact (Bush and Silman 2009; McMichael et al. 2012).² Although these scholars rightly claim that it is difficult to generalize about human land use patterns in an area as large as Amazonia, they argue that pre-Columbian human influence on the region was patchy and limited in its distribution.

The alternative view, coming from many contemporary anthropologists working within the research program of historical ecology, offers a more complex portrait, in which humans have adapted to forested environments and altered them over time through their subsistence and management practices. But while this group of scholars emphasizes dialogical interaction between humans and their environments, an ongoing tendency within this area of research has been to highlight "anthropogenic" environments, or ones defined by human signatures. These studies have done much work to expose the flawed assumptions of researchers who tend toward environmentally deterministic thinking, yet, at the same time, the idea of the Amazonian environment as a human creation can mislead, or encourage "misreadings" of the landscape (see Fairhead and Leach 1996). Clearly, the characterization of a forest as "anthropogenic" privileges the role of humans in the forest's formation, and ignores the roles of other organisms in the creation and existence of the ecological communities found therein. This denies the work of seed-dispersing birds and rodents, winged pollinators, soil microbes, and decaying bodies that contribute humic matter and release nutrients crucial to the forest's perpetuation.

Although I had initially sought to understand the long-term effects of human management on the Amazonian environment, I also began to see the pitfalls of privileging "cultural" histories over "natural" ones. One cool November morning while visiting an older man named Nilo, I re-confronted this problem.

O SÍTIO DO MANOEL

After borrowing a small canoe with a noisy *rabeta* motor, Nilo took me out to look at the future manioc (*Manihot esculenta*) field he was clearing on the uplands across from the strip of floodplain where he resided. I had met Nilo a few weeks earlier while distributing agricultural implements and seeds with the extension agents from town. We had stopped in Nilo's community to drop off a few small motors that the government was distributing to aid in the processing of manioc or, in case of emergency, to take a sick individual into town for medical attention.

From the beginning, I could tell that Nilo was a curious type. After I introduced myself as a visiting American researcher, Nilo quickly struck up a conversation, telling me that a group of evangelical Christians from the United States had paid him a visit a year or two prior. They had donated reading glasses, medicines, toys, and clothing, including the T-shirt he was wearing that day. "Very kind and generous people. Real children of God," he said. "For you Americans to come to the Amazon, it's a real dream, isn't it? To see all these forests and animals and the river. You don't have anything really like this, do you?"

I pondered the question as Nilo and I motored across the floodplain lake, before arriving at a stretch of land that was occupied by tall old-growth forest. Climbing up a steep, gravelly bank, we entered the dark forest. Surrounding us were a number of towering rubber trees (*Hevea brasiliensis*) mixed in with old mangos (*Mangifera indica*) and a host of palms clumped together. Further in the background was a small clearing, where Nilo intended to plant manioc. The land we stood on had been owned by his grandfather, who had passed it down to his father and then on to him (figure 5.1). He said he wanted to post a small sign in front that read "Sítio do Manoel" (Manoel's farm) in honor of his grandfather, who had tapped rubber and planted many of the trees that we gazed up at that day.

Next to the future manioc plantation, Nilo pointed out the clumps of bacaba palms (*Oenocarpus bacaba*) that were found throughout the land, which he described as an old *bacabal*, or bacaba palm stand. Alongside the bacaba palms, we found Brazil nut trees, bacuri (*Platonia insignis*), andiroba (*Carapa guianensis*), and hogplums (*Spondias mombin*) as well as caiauê (*Elaeis oleifera*) and urucuri palms (*Attalea phalerata*), all possible indications of past human presence. Impressed by the diversity of useful plants on Nilo's land, I asked him which species, to his knowledge, had been planted by his father and grandfather. He explained that they had planted the andiroba and some of the rubber trees we had examined, which were scarred from years of tapping. Other trees may have also been planted by them, but he wasn't entirely sure which had been cultivated and which had not. In reference to the bacaba palms, he said that they were "native," or naturally occurring, but because of their dense concentration, I questioned whether they were potentially living relics of an old Indian site (see Le-

FIGURE 5.1. Nilo stands in the dense cluster of useful tree species planted by his father and grandfather (2009).

vis et al. 2012). He didn't seem to discount the idea, and together we briefly contemplated the possibility in silence. How was one to know for sure?

Considering what Nilo knew of the biography of that swath of particular forest, it was fair to say that many of the trees that he utilized and managed were a direct inheritance from his father and grand-father. Deeper into the history of the land, it was also likely that the area had once been occupied by early indigenous inhabitants of the region. The fact that several stretches of *terra preta* existed nearby, including a site known as Maloca (longhouse), made this possibility all the more likely.

Looking at the trees before me and thinking about their origins, I began to reconsider what it meant for a forest to be deemed "anthropogenic," as such a designation can create simplifications of intertwining and complex histories. Was Nilo's plot of land the result of human management from only the past one hundred or one thousand years? Could we (or should we?) distinguish clumps of bacaba palms that were the result of indigenous management or subsistence activities from those that had resulted from the work of other animals or beings?

In North America, trees bent in peculiar forms with severely angled trunks and deformed branches can be found in many old tracts of forest. These are Indian trail marker trees, once serving as blazes on paths traveled by native North Americans (Barr 2011; Jannsen 1941). Sometimes these trees were used to indicate nearby bodies of water, important landmarks, or burial sites. Some say they were even used to conceal objects in their nooks (Jordan 1997). Still, many of the trees that carry signs of the human past outlive the very people who shaped them as they continue to evolve and grow, extending their presence in their surroundings. To underestimate their vitality would be a mistake.

In examining the biography of nearly any tract of forest, it becomes incredibly difficult to excise the "natural" from the "cultural," as the processes by which the forest came into being are inextricable and entwined. For the study of contemporary biodiversity, it is important to demonstrate that individuals like Nilo have inherited a number of useful plants from the past and that such diversity can be passed over generations like any form of inherited wealth. Attempting to distinguish the accreted diversity due to human history from that which results from natural history is a much more difficult task, and should compel us to develop more precise questions about the specificities and particularities of a forest's past. Rather than attempt to distinguish cultural and natural forests, or "anthropogenic" and "non-anthropogenic" forests, perhaps it's better to discuss the information available about such forests, whether this be *archaeological* (known material evidence or archaeological soils), *ecological* (distinctive patterns of species richness and abundance or species oligarchy), or *historical* (oral histories associated with the forest, and its use and management over time). These lines of investigation reveal more about the dynamic histories of a forest's past, and can help to eliminate the tendency toward a dichotomous view of forests, other than perhaps "forests with known histories" and "forests without history."

Social theory tends to rely on dualisms and binaries. It is important, however, to recognize the simplifications that they impose, the perspectives that they privilege, and the biases that they perpetuate. Might our view of Amazonian forests change if we blur the distinction between "natural" and "cultural" forests? What other types of forests might be discerned if we shift our perspective or look just a little bit closer?

A FOREST BEYOND NATURE AND CULTURE

"So how should we think with forests?" asks Eduardo Kohn (2013, 21). "How should we allow the thoughts in and of the nonhuman world to liberate our thinking?"

Kohn and other ethnographers have been working to develop an anthropology that "extends beyond the human" (see also Candea 2010; Candea 2013; Haraway 2003; Haraway 2008), building upon a philosophical position sometimes referred to as "posthumanism."[3] In contrast to the humanistic approach, which centers strictly on the actions of humans, posthumanist scholarship seeks to adopt a *decentered* perspective that accommodates and accounts for the actions of other beings and things.

A useful illustration of the posthumanist perspective is offered by Andrew Pickering, a sociologist of science, in the edited volume *The Mangle in Practice* (2008). In the introduction of the book, Pickering describes how the city of New Orleans finds itself in an ongoing struggle against the shifting course of the Mississippi River. As the river pushes away from the city, the city's inhabitants must respond by fortifying its levees, building them higher and higher until the boats passing on the river now float high above their heads. Pickering describes this give-and-take between the people of New Orleans and the Mississippi River to demonstrate that human action in this context can only be understood in relation to the actions of the river. Despite the commonly held belief that techno-scientific knowledge enables human control of "nature" and the environment, Pickering's brief examination of New Orleans convincingly illustrates the point that humanity is engaged in a continual process of negotiation with the material world in which it is embedded.

Kohn's ethnographic work, in contrast, has focused specifically on the lives of Quichua-speaking Runa of the Ecuadorian Amazon and the many kinds of beings that inhabit the forests surrounding them. Not only does his provocatively titled book, *How Forests Think* (2013), argue for a recognition of the diversity of actors (including humans) involved in the forest's constitution, but he extends his analysis even further, through the semiotic work of Charles S. Peirce, to claim that the interactions and relations within the forest require the interpretation of signs by all living beings (not just humans), thus substantiating the idea that the forest itself *thinks*.

Kohn's work builds upon scholarship by Philippe Descola (1996; 2013), Eduardo Viveiros de Castro (1998), and other Amazonianists who have developed ethnographic insights from working with indigenous societies to point out the deep problematics of the modernist division of the world into two halves—a world of objective nature and a world of subjective culture. These scholars note that in animistic societies, a number of which can be found in Amazonia, humans are not the only beings that have subjectivity or an "interiority" (Descola 2013, 129). Instead, spirits and plants and animals have their own agency, and they can openly challenge the workings and doings of people.

In an interview with Descola, Kohn lays out what he sees as the implications of this basic ethnographic observation: "Animism forces us to come to grips with the fact that we humans are not the only ones who know the world. Therefore, our human-centered analytics—those that underpin all of the human sciences as well as the basis for its division from the natural ones—have to be rethought to show how the human is open to these other ways of knowing, and being, in the world" (2009, 1).

A simple lesson from Amazonian indigenous ethnography and posthumanist scholarship is that humans are not the only actors of consequence in the world, nor are humans the only ones who can "see" or "think" or "know." Furthermore, the placing of humans in one category ("culture") and the rest of the world in another ("nature") severely inhibits any understanding of the dynamic interplay between the wide diversity of beings and things on the planet,[4] including those found in a small patch of Amazonian forest. Dividing the world along lines of "nature" and "culture"—the "naturalist ontology," following

Descola (2013)—is what encourages anthropocentrism since it privileges humans while slighting those considered less-than-human. To fight against this, Kohn implores us (ethnographers, scientists, scholars, humans) "to free our thinking of that excess conceptual baggage that has accumulated as a result of our exclusive attention—to the neglect of everything else—to that which makes us humans exceptional" (2009, 22). He explains further that "as we learn to attend ethnographically to that which lies beyond the human, certain strange phenomena suddenly come to the fore, and these strange phenomena amplify, and in the process come to exemplify, some of the general properties of the world in which we live."

And when I turned my attention away from the human presence in the forest, strange phenomena appeared indeed. But it was not posthumanist philosophy or contemporary Amazonian ethnography that first helped me to see this. Rather it was rural Amazonian people and their stories of Cobra Grande, the "Big Snake."

THE BIG SNAKE

On a Saturday morning in late October, I accompanied Zé, Cândida, and some of Cândida's brothers on a fishing trip to Lago Comprido, a seasonal lake found on an island in the middle of the Madeira River. After we arrived, we crossed swamps on fallen logs and then made a short canoe trip through a shallow flooded section of forest before arriving at a temporary camp that was situated on relatively stable ground. Cândida's stepfather and brothers frequently camped out on the island during the dry season to fish pirarucu, the largest scaled fish in Amazonia, and arguably its most lucrative.

After getting settled in camp and starting a small fire, some of us went to search for a seasonal *poço* (small pond) that was said to be full of the armor-plated catfish known locally as bodó that we hoped to prepare for our afternoon meal (figure 5.2). As we set off toward the *poço*, we entered a gnarly *bamburral*, or swamp forest, full of fallen palm fronds with needle-like spines that stuck in the feet of those of us who had carelessly, or foolishly, made the trip without rubber boots.

Farther along, as we hiked through the muddy, flooded forest, we came upon a deep, dried creek bed that looked like a canal. We descended into the creek bed and followed its course. While walking, Cândida's brother Sapo[5] casually mentioned that the canal we were passing through was a trail created by Cobra Grande, the mythical

FIGURE 5.2. Bodó (*Pterygoplichthys pardalis*) fish held in a pan of water after being caught on a fishing trip (2010).

snake of Amazonian folklore and indigenous oral tradition. As I continued to walk, spines deep in the soles of my feet, I pondered this revelation.

Minutes after learning this, Cândida's oldest brother, who followed from behind, called out to us. "Hey guys," he shouted, "you just stepped on a *sucuriju*!" He was informing us, in other words, that we had walked over an anaconda (*Eunectes murinus*). I emitted a laugh, in partial disbelief, but I turned around nonetheless. I walked back slowly, suspecting that Cândida's brothers were playing a practical joke on me. Instead, her oldest brother stuck his hand down in the mud and unearthed a snake, about 5 feet long. It was, after all, a small *sucuriju*, or a young anaconda. Sapo grabbed the snake from his brother and held it up: "There you go," he exclaimed, "this is one of the little ones left behind by their mother, Cobra Grande" (figure 5.3).

Cobra Grande is a massive snake, much larger than the largest anaconda, and in many Amazonian folktales it is implicated in the region's ever-shifting topography and hydrology (see, for example,

FIGURE 5.3.   Sapo holds up a small anaconda (*Eunectes murinus*) left
behind by its mother, Cobra Grande (2009).

Chernela and Pinho 2004; Smith 1981). Seasonal fluctuations in pre-
cipitation result in constant changes in the size and form of regional
waterways, and the accumulation of silt on an odd sandbar can sometimes lead to the formation of an island overnight. In other cases, a
shallow spot on the edge of the floodplain may sometimes form an en-
closed pond, trapping fish, like the bodó that we were after, which
hang out in muddy bottoms. As Hugh Raffles (2002) documented in
his thought-provoking book *In Amazonia*, a number of Amazonian
waterways are also carved out by rural Amazonians, some being simply cleaned or widened while others are laboriously excavated by community work parties. Amazonian waterways are thus defined by processes that are arguably both natural and cultural.

When the origin of a channel or *furo* is ambiguous, or no history
is associated with its formation, then it is sometimes acknowledged as
the work of Cobra Grande, a supernatural(-cum-cultural) force. When
I talked with one affable farmer about his youth in the floodplain community where he had been born and where I had spent time visiting,
he told me without prompting that the "old-timers" said that the chan-

nel (*furo*) that connected the floodplain lake to the Madeira River was created by a big snake. I had heard similar stories from other interlocutors when discussing the origins of channels and cuts that simply "appeared" along the river overnight. More specifically, a story about Cobra Grande's appearance in the community of Cantagalo (Cock's crow), upriver from the town of Borba, was related to me on several occasions. Many variations of the account exist, but most versions give the following details. During a large party in honor of a saint, a reveler commits an offensive act that provokes the ire of Cobra Grande. With a whip of its tail it beats the earth, causing a major crack to form across the riverbank in front of the community. The crack rapidly widens until a massive slab of land breaks off into the Madeira River, hurling the unfortunate partygoers perched near the floodplain's edge, who are subsequently swallowed up by the muddy river water below (see also Smith 1981, 117; Smith 1996, 91–93; Guerreiro and Guerreiro 2003, 73–76).

In this story, Cobra Grande is seen not only as the embodiment of the force of nature, but also as a moral agent that has the capacity to punish humans. In this way, the figure of Cobra Grande parallels another popular folkloric character, known as Curupira, considered a protector of game and the forest. In fact, Curupira is known literally as a "mother of the forest" (*mãe do mato*) who threatens to enchant or disorient hunters who harvest more than their fair share of wild game. Although Curupira more clearly enforces moral guidelines for human activity in the forest world, both figures serve as important metaphors of the force, and even agency, of the Amazonian environment, which openly challenge humans and their desires. Even while these can be interpreted as myths designed to reinforce a strict moral order among humans, they also reflect Amazonian peoples' notions about the power of their environment as well as the ways other beings that inhabit the world respond to human action.

If our concern is to understand the Amazonian environment, and the relationships between all the things and beings that exist within it (i.e., Amazonian ecology in the broadest sense), then there is good reason to believe that mythologies that speak to the agency of nonhuman others within the shifting Amazonian landscape are important for understanding the regional environment, how its people relate to it, and how see they see themselves positioned within it. Cobra Grande does not necessarily exist in the biological way that anacondas do, but it inhabits the Amazonian imaginary and continues to shape how many

Amazonian peoples understand their surroundings. Jimison, a history student from the town of Borba, offered this insight while we were sharing stories during a long boat ride from Manaus. He pointed out that the myth of Cobra Grande is important for explaining the ongoing transformation of the topography and hydrology of the region as it lifts islands, pulls banks into the river, cuts *furos*, and weaves new watercourses for the river to travel. As a student of history, Jimison argued that folklore and oral history provide much-needed complements to science and natural history. Even while he himself didn't believe that Cobra Grande was a biological creature that created islands or cuts in the river, he recognized that it remained a powerful metaphor of the evolving Amazonian landscape. Like most stories, it's a "lie" that tells a truth.

Just as oral histories and patterns of botanical species are important sources of information for dissecting the history of swaths of Amazonian forest, mythologies that explain the seasonal creeks that run through them, the rhizomic[6] waterways that intersect and overlap, should also be considered pertinent details for the study of the Amazonian environment. The story of Cobra Grande is a compelling narrative, much like that of Curupira and other mythical beings of Amazonian folklore, but it is more than a quaint folktale. Cobra Grande is a central Amazonian metaphor that reminds us that our surroundings are in constant flux, and that humans are not the only creatures responsible for this ongoing transformation. Although we cannot always identify the other forces responsible for shaping our evolving world, an imaginary snake can be a useful reminder that they are always present.

REENCOUNTERING THE AMAZONIAN FOREST

On some mornings during my stays in the community of Puruzinho, I would leave Zé and Cândida's house and walk out the back door, past the chickens pecking around the yard in search of the remaining corn from their morning meal. I'd continue past the banana trees and the little garden protected by chicken wire where Cândida kept her pepper and tomato plants, and I'd follow the narrow path that went down to the lake. I would walk past the *canarana* and other tall grasses at the edge of the clearing around their property and then enter the narrow strip of seasonally flooded forest that surrounded the lake (figure 5.4). I'd admire the tall palms, protected by long sharp spines encircling their trunks, paying careful attention to avoid stepping on the

FIGURE 5.4. Looking up from a clearing in the secondary forest behind Zé and Cândida's house.

fallen fronds, which were full of the same severe spines. I'd try my best to remain silent, immersing myself in the buzz of insects as I carefully plodded along the increasingly mucky path, mud squirting through the gaps between my toes. For brief moments, I would stand utterly still, eavesdropping on the forest.

I wasn't entirely sure what I wanted to see or hear on such walks. But I suspect that I was hoping to experience some of the "wild" Amazon that I had grown up with on television and in books—an Amazon that grew increasingly distant as I became familiar with Borba's rural communities while visiting with people, playing soccer, drinking orange soda, sitting patiently in a canoe while checking gill nets, watching the evening *novelas*, reading in my hammock, dreaming of friends at home, taking nips from bottles of warm cachaça, bathing in the river with a gourd and a slippery bar of soap, waiting to see *something happen*, but settling for a few thoughtful words and a good afternoon meal of grilled fish and manioc flour.

One Sunday, Cândida's brothers came to visit, as they frequently did to either play soccer or see if Zé had any work for them. But on that day, they wanted to have an afternoon lunch on the edge of the lake in the shade of the forest where I liked to walk. They caught several fish with a gill net and started a fire. A bottle of wine materialized. Cândida's brothers gutted and de-scaled the fish, and then fashioned thin branches they'd collected from nearby trees into sharpened skewers that they shoved into the fishes' mouths. They then dug the opposite ends of the skewers into the ground at 45 degree angles and the fish began to cook over the fire, their skin slowly blackening, their eyes turning white in the heat. When the fish were done cooking, we laid them out on banana leaves, swatting the flies that quickly began to congregate. Cândida brought a big calabash gourd full of *farinha* and then laid out the essential condiments of salt, hot pepper, and lime. And there we feasted in the shade of the forest at the edge of the lake, sitting on logs, relishing the smoky fish, and the wine, and the shared company.

This wasn't the Amazonian forest I had dreamt of as a child. *That forest* was almost exclusively the realm of wild animals, not a place to hold picnics and imbibe overly sweet wine. Of course, while living in Amazonia I heard plenty of stories about dangerous encounters in the forest with jaguars and snakes. Crazy Pedro, who lived across from Puruzinho, had been carrying big sacks of fresh limes down to his canoe one evening and stepped on a *surucucu* (*Lachesis muta*), which bit him right in the calf. Zé had to rush him to the emergency room in the town of Borba that night. They say when the *surucucu* doesn't kill, it cripples.[7] And my friend Valdo, who lived in town, told me that a friend of his came face-to-face with a spotted jaguar while hunting in the forest. He was able to scare off the large feline with a quick gunshot before he tracked it down and killed it. Valdo then told me the story of another man, who had gone hunting with two friends but had trekked off alone to relieve himself in the woods. A jaguar attacked him from behind when he was most vulnerable. Valdo morbidly joked that when the man's friends finally found the animal and killed it, its mouth was still full of the victim's shit.

But the forest is much more than a place of violent encounters between people and animals—it can also be a place of respite and relief. Many of the stretches of forest surrounding homes and clearings are places where people seek shade from the sun's powerful rays at midday. The forest is also a place to which men abscond to defecate in private, or in other cases, to covertly cultivate small crops of marijuana. It is even a space for romantic liaisons, or so I heard. In other words, the forest is a place of overlapping uses and benefits: a place to hunt and to hide, but also a space for intermittent social happenings. A place where humans escape from the sun, eat, seek solitude, and encounter others. And in considering the diverse uses of the forest by humans, it is also apparent that forests are not shaped by human activity alone. In fact, the forest is a place where the presence of humans is often ephemeral, fleeting, and inconstant. Just like any Sunday picnic.

CONCLUSION: TOWARD A DECENTERED ANTHROPOLOGY IN THE ANTHROPOCENE

Some areas of Amazonian forest have been intensively shaped by human activity and management, and these continue to be passed down among generations like any other form of inherited wealth. Others, however, reflect only vague and subtle clues of past human presence, worn away by the work of time and the overlapping histories of others. As I have argued above, Amazonian forests are emergent spaces that are just as likely to be molded by humans as by nonhuman beings and forces, from trees and seasonal creeks to the massive snakes of Amazonian mythology. Although it is possible to distinguish between forests that proffer deep human histories (i.e., "anthropogenic" forests) and those that do not, I have come to view such dichotomization as problematic, because it obscures the interactions between humans and the vast diversity of other beings that inhabit such spaces. As an alternative, perhaps it is better to examine the clues available to understand the patterns of human–environmental interaction as well as to gauge the intensities of those interactions.

Oral histories and patterns of botanical species are important references for understanding the dynamic pasts of Amazonian forests as well as their present constitution, but so too are the myths of Cobra Grande and other folkloric figures that consider the agency of the Amazonian environment. Currently, as more and more anthropologists and other social scientists draw from the "decentered" perspective of posthumanism, an important shift is occurring and greater attention is being paid to the lives and activities of those that are "other-than-human." To be sure, this perspective is nothing entirely new. In fact, it has long been established and popularized in Amazonian thought, thus revealing the hidden imbrication of contemporary social theory with Amazonian folklore.

The anthropologist David Graeber recently wrote:

Contemporary anthropology often seems a discipline determined to commit suicide. Where once we drew our theoretical terms—"totem," "taboo," "mana," "potlatch"—from ethnography, causing Continental thinkers from Ludwig Wittgenstein to Sigmund Freud and Jean-Paul Sartre to feel the need to weigh in on the resulting debates, we have now reduced ourselves to the scholastic dissection of terms drawn from Continental philosophy (deterritorialization, governmentality, bare life . . .)—and nobody else cares what we have to say about them. And honestly, why should they—if they can just as easily read Deleuze, Agamben, or Foucault in the original? (2010, n.p.)

To end this "bizarre process of self-strangulation," as Graeber puts it, it is necessary to recognize the ways that folkloric stories, like that of Cobra Grande, resonate with contemporary (academic) social theory. Perhaps privileging one over the other isn't necessarily as productive as discovering the ways in which they may buttress one another, potentially forging new directions in the study of our evolving world. Considering the anthropocentrism that underlies the Anthropocene and much of modern thought, Cobra Grande and posthumanism offer useful alternative perspectives for thinking more broadly about ecology and the lives of others at a time when it is very much needed.

FROM THE ANTHROPOCENE
TO THE ECOZOIC?

Chapter 6

CERTAINTY AND DOUBT

"What's worse: certainty or doubt?"[1] I saw this question spray-painted on a canal wall in downtown Recife in April 2010 (figure 6.1). I was taking a break from my research in Amazonia to visit friends and grapple with the end of a long-distance relationship. I have to admit that the piece of graffiti struck me, and I later scrawled the question it posed in one of my notebooks. Was it worse to know that it was all ending or to wonder if it was really over? In writing this book, I have come to see the onset of "Anthropocene" as presenting a similar dilemma: is it worse to believe that we have irrevocably altered the planet and that we shall all suffer as a consequence? Or is it more exasperating to face a completely uncertain future and wonder if we will survive?

Some scholars (e.g., Clark 2011) have pointed out quite rightly that an apocalyptic view betrays our anthropocentrism, which lies at the very root of the problem. To assume that we alone can destroy the earth and all life on it is a reflection of our sheer hubris as a species. While the question of how to face our future is not the only one we should be asking, I find it a useful issue to keep in mind as we move forward and attempt to avoid being paralyzed by fear, or worse yet, arrested by apathy. And it seems that accepting uncertainty may be an important step forward (see Prigogine and Stengers 1984; Prigogine and Stengers 1997; also Skrimshire 2010).

In this final chapter, I examine some of the uncertainties that loom in Amazonia's future in the Anthropocene. Returning to Puruzinho, I discuss the effects of extreme flooding experienced by residents in 2009 and the future challenges rural families are facing with the onset of global climate change (figure 6.2). I also highlight the problem of biodiversity loss that is being witnessed across the planet.[2] In this discussion, I offer a critical examination of how research and conservation efforts can also encourage problematic forms of outside intervention, and I reflect upon the responses of some rural Amazonians to my presence as a foreign researcher in the region. To conclude, I examine what I refer to as "the predicament of nature." Nature is an idea that many of us cannot easily abandon, but if we refuse to let it go, then it must be thoroughly reconceptualized. My contention is that nature cannot be something "over there" that needs to be either protected or feared or admired. Instead, it should be seen as something we are all part of and have never been separated from. Only when this conceptual reconfiguration takes hold may we begin to address the current ecological crisis or, at the very least, the current crisis in our ecological thinking.

FIGURE 6.1. Graffiti on a canal wall in downtown Recife (2010): "What's worse: certainty or doubt?"

FIGURE 6.2.　A house on the Madeira River in Borba stands underwater after the 2014 flood.

AFTER THE FLOOD

In 2009 the central Amazon suffered one of the largest floods in the region's history. I returned to Borba in October of that year after the floodwaters had already receded. People said they hadn't seen anything like it since 1953.

It was raining lightly on the morning that I took the boat to Puruzinho. After getting let off on the riverbank, I started up the slick clay slope to Zé's house. I wasn't entirely sure that I could make it to the top without crawling. Two children appeared above, and I recognized one of them as Zé's son, Zezinho. "Hey, Zezinho, remember me?" I shouted up the embankment. He perked up and came down to help me with my bags: "Jeez, Nickson,[3] we thought you weren't coming back."

When I got to Zé's house, I gave some awkward hugs and handshakes and then dropped my bags off inside. I noticed that the house had changed considerably since my visit two years prior. The old house had been knocked down and the new house they had finished building during my last visit was painted and decorated inside. A picture of Christ hung next to a sign that read "Don't envy me. I'm not rich, I just work."[4] The front room contained a little sofa, a TV, a DVD player, and a speaker for music. When I walked into the kitchen I found a spacious room with a wall full of hanging pots and pans, a new oven, and a freezer. Zé told me that they had also purchased a small generator to provide energy for the appliances.

Zé and Cândida's house served as a type of general store, and from it they sold gasoline, diesel, cachaça, beer, cigarettes, and soda as well as other sundry items, from soap to disposable razors. It appeared that they were making a successful go of it as entrepreneurs. Still, Zé continued to fish and traded fish for diesel on the barges that passed by daily. The family had also cleared an area behind the house, where Cândida had planted bananas (*Musa × paradisiaca*), beans (*Vigna unguiculata*), peppers (*Capsicum* spp.), tomatoes (*Solanum lycopersicum*), and West Indian gherkins (*Cucumis anguria*).

Despite the notable material gains in Zé and Cândida's life, the flood had taken a toll on many households in their community and the region. In an attempt to convey the magnitude of the flood, Zé explained that the governor of Amazonas state had even visited to show his solidarity. A tattered welcoming banner for the governor hung in the community center as lingering proof.

At the height of the flood, the elevated river waters forced the family to leave their home. In fact, all but one of the fourteen houses on the floodplain in Puruzinho had been abandoned, and it is estimated that over three hundred thousand people were left temporarily homeless in the region (Clendenning 2009; see also Chen et al. 2010). Zé, Cândida, and their four children ended up living in the church of a neighboring community while they waited for the waters to recede. Although they were able to return home after a few months, the floodwaters had left a dark line running along the walls of their stilted house, nearly a foot above the floorboards. The line served as a fading yet persistent reminder of the threat of the unpredictable annual flooding.

In addition to damaging homes, the flood wiped out large cacao (*Theobroma cacao*) orchards that had been planted on high floodplain areas that usually remained untouched during a "normal" year. Residents who had gambled by planting manioc (*Manihot esculenta*) in the floodplains also lost their crop and had to scramble to find cuttings to replant fields in the uplands while relying on governmental emergency loans, family support, and alternative sources of income to purchase food. Nearly everyone I encountered complained about the exaggerated costs of manioc flour, or *farinha*, the region's primary staple. The price of a liter of manioc flour had tripled, and at times even quadrupled, since the previous year. No one with whom I spoke, however, would consider going without it. For most people I knew, to eat a meal without manioc flour was like not eating at all. "Hunger for manioc flour is the worst thing in the world," Puruzinho resident dona Célia once told me emphatically.

With the flood behind them, however, the rhythm of life in the community had largely returned to normal. Back at Zé and Cândida's house on that first night of my return, we played soccer until dark. Cândida's sister Leila and Zé's sister Jucila joined us and didn't hold back. The game was all the more spirited because their children were playing on the team opposite them. By the time night began to fall, I was dripping with sweat and ready for a bath. I went down to the river with the kids and jumped in, hoping the stingrays would spare me.[5]

When I got back to the house, the electricity was already running and Zé had music on the DVD player. It was playing the latest hit from the group known as the Forró Boys. His four children had been singing the chorus of the song for most of the day—"Sou moleque doido, eu sou moleque doido"[6]—and I translated it into English: "I'm a crazy boy, I'm a crazy boy," which they tried to repeat, giggling in unison. The children begged me to teach them more English and asked about the translations of various words, which I repeated back to them. They learned the words *plane, water, river, fish, mud, hot chocolate, coffee, spoon, fork, plate, boy, girl, hair, head, eye, ear,* and *tooth* (which was the most repeated and mispronounced due to the difficult "th" sound). When their interest in English waned, they tried to play the live show of the Forró Boys, but the disc refused to cooperate. The latest album of the musical group Banda Calypso was selected as an alternative, which we listened to in its entirety until it (thankfully) ended; by that point everyone was in their hammocks ready for sleep.

It pleased me to see Zé and Cândida's house animated with electricity and musical sounds pumping from speakers—"modern" pleasures that had been lacking just a few years prior. I knew their successes had been hard-won, requiring that many days be spent selling fish and diesel and booze. But I also wondered if it was already too late to live the good life that the modern industrial world had promised. Although they had sidestepped the most devastating effects of this flood, I wondered, how many more floods and droughts loomed in the future? How many more could they withstand?

CLIMATE CHANGE, CROP DIVERSITY, AND BIODIVERSITY LOSS

While climate scientists warn against attributing any one extreme weather event to the effects of global climate change, they assert that large-scale warming on the planet will likely increase the frequency and/or intensity of such extreme weather events (Mitchell et al. 2006). After the flood of 2009, other floods of similar magnitude struck in 2012 and 2014. In addition to extreme flooding, drought has become another major threat, including a record drought that hit the region between 2005 and 2006. Climate scientists working in the region are particularly concerned about the coupled effects of climate shifts and ongoing deforestation and forest fragmentation that could push the region to a "tipping point" of large-scale forest dieback (Nepstad et al. 2008).

Rural Amazonians like Zé and Cândida are accustomed to unpredictability, and their diffuse social networks of friends and kin help them contend with extreme events when they occur. However, climate change may impose new kinds of threats, potentially leaving rural inhabitants more vulnerable than ever. While Zé and Cândida have positioned themselves as entrepreneurs, their livelihoods and those of most other rural families still depend largely on farming and fishing, economic activities that are particularly susceptible to dramatic shifts in climate. This raises a troubling question: can their existing productive strategies adapt to increasingly unpredictable conditions?

In 2010 I conducted research on the diversity of manioc varieties managed by the forty-five households in Puruzinho (Kawa et al. 2013), looking at the number of varieties managed in the community and how varietal diversity was distributed among households. Since most rural communities of Brazilian Amazonia rely heavily on manioc, they often cultivate dozens of unique varieties that have distinct characteristics and advantages. Varieties can be selected for different rates of maturation (Elias et al. 2000), resistance to rot and disease (Heckler and Zent 2008), and performance in relation to climatic and soil conditions (Fraser 2010; Fraser et al. 2012). Many manioc varieties are also selected because of socioeconomic considerations, including aesthetic appeal (Heckler 2004), market demand, and consumptive purpose (Dufour 1993).[7] Among some Amazonian indigenous groups, the high number of varieties cultivated by an individual or household can also reflect social prestige (Emperaire and Peroni 2007; Heckler 2004; Heckler and Zent 2008). Not all Amazonian peoples attribute the same value to manioc varietal diversity, however, and in most communities the distribution of such varieties is rarely uniform (Emperaire and Peroni 2007).

My survey showed that households in Puruzinho actively cultivated between one and eight varieties of manioc, with an average of three and a half varieties per household. The community cultivated a total of twenty-eight varieties, but seventeen of these were managed by only one or two households, reflecting a poor distribution of varietal diversity overall.

I asked farmers to list the most important characteristics they looked for in manioc varieties, and I told them to mention as many as they felt appropriate. The most common response that I received (from twenty-four households) was that farmers selected varieties that produced the greatest root biomass ("dá bem batata"), and thus produced the highest yields of manioc flour. However, the second-most common response (twenty-two households) was related to selection of varieties of bitter manioc that had deep yellow roots ("bem amarelinha"). While yellow varieties typically contain higher concentrations of beta carotene, it appears that their selection is also related to regional aesthetic preference and a broader regional market demand for yellow manioc flour. It is difficult to say whether yellow manioc flour has a distinctive taste, but it is nearly always favored over lighter-colored varieties. Extension agents informed me that some producers in Borba even dyed their *farinha* yellow to make it more attractive to consumers and boost sales (Kawa 2011, 101).

My study also revealed that households that were perceived as having the most knowledgeable producers played a central role in the distribution of planting materials in the community. In other words, when community members were in need of manioc cuttings to plant new fields or wanted new varieties to plant, they often sought out the households that they believed had the most knowledgeable and successful producers (Kawa et al. 2013). These producers not only planted larger areas of manioc, but also seemed to have a stronger orientation to the market. And unlike previous studies with indigenous groups, these experts maintained a very limited number of varieties. This is

due in part to the fact that having a small number of highly productive varieties can be seen as an advantage for market-oriented farmers.
Even when these experts lose their most favored varieties in the event
of an extreme flood or drought, they usually have access to a broader
network of contacts outside the community that can introduce new varieties in times of need (Lima et al. 2012). In other words, there appears to be a trend in which farmers that are perceived as knowledgeable and economically successful select just a few varieties that provide
the greatest short-term economic benefit. This, however, can open
those individuals to possible vulnerability as they put all of their pro-
verbial eggs into one basket. Furthermore, the adoption of a limited
number of varieties by these experts can have broader consequences
for communities since they are often relied upon by others for planting materials.

In the wake of the flood, nearly everyone in Puruzinho complained
about the shortage of manioc cuttings for planting new fields. Even
though most households planted their fields in the uplands, they com-
mented that previous droughts in the uplands had compromised their
ability to take cuttings to replant new fields. The flood also wiped out
fields in the floodplains, thus leading to a general shortage of manioc and manioc planting materials across the region. Most households
were eventually able to acquire cuttings from friends and family members living nearby, but some had to travel to distant communities to
acquire new planting materials. Some individuals, like Zé, ended up
paying for cuttings, which I was told was extremely uncommon.

More research needs to be conducted in communities like Puruzinho to discern how extreme weather events linked to climate change
are affecting rural producers. While it is important not to underestimate the ingenuity and adaptive capacity of rural Amazonians, it is
necessary to investigate how communities respond to these events, and
whether certain management strategies may compromise their resilience. If varietal diversity and its distribution become constrained over
time, this could leave communities especially susceptible to the extreme effects of global climate change.

Unfortunately, loss of crop diversity and biodiversity in general is a
disturbing trend that can be seen worldwide (FAO 1999; Green et al.
2005; Tscharntke et al. 2005). In some cases these losses are the direct
result of conscious human selection. Currently, a very limited number of high-yielding varieties of staple crops—such as wheat (*Triticum aestivum*), barley (*Hordeum vulgare*), soybeans (*Glycine max*),

rice (*Oryza sativa*), and maize (*Zea mays*)—are being planted in most parts of the world (Tilman 1999). These high-yielding crop varieties have been favored over genetically diverse traditional crop varieties in large part because of their productivity. However, such "improved" varieties come with a number of trade-offs. They typically require the use of chemical fertilizers, pesticides, and herbicides to guarantee their high yields while also encouraging production of such crops in massive plantations of individual species, otherwise known as "monocultures" (see Green et al. 2005; Tscharntke et al. 2005).

This trend toward monoculture in industrial agriculture has had many broader homogenizing effects. Today, it is estimated that only twelve species of plants and five species of animals represent 75 percent of global food consumption, and have thus come to dominate the rural landscape (FAO 1999). One afternoon in the Indianapolis airport I overheard a traveling businessman on the phone trying to convey to his colleague the eerie feeling he got during his travels in the American Midwest. He said, "Do you ever see on TV when the guy is at the middle of the intersection in the road and he looks left and looks right and it's cornfields as far as the eye can see? That's where I'm at." Monocultures make for an uncomfortable, oppressive nature indeed.

Today, a square foot of a park outside of South Africa's third-largest city holds a greater diversity of flora and fauna than a Midwestern cornfield. Robert Krulwich (2012) made this observation when comparing two compelling, although not technically "scientific," projects on biodiversity—one by the photographer David Liittschwager and the other by the science writer Craig Childs. Liittschwager spent several years traveling the world with a small metal frame, which he plopped down in the places that he visited. He then documented all the life that entered the cubed frame over a twenty-four-hour period, capturing the diversity of plants, animals, and insects with his camera (Liittschwager 2012). At Table Mountain National Park on the edge of Cape Town, South Africa, he found thirty different species of plants and seventy different insects in one arbitrarily selected patch of grass. In Costa Rica, he left the cube in the branch of a strangler fig in the cloud forest. There he encountered 150 different species of plants and animals that either lived in or passed through that little space of one foot by one foot by one foot. He saw birds, beetles, butterflies, bromeliads, and much more. And yet when writer Craig Childs ventured to Grundy County, Iowa, to spend a few days in the middle of a six-hundred-acre cornfield in a search of its biodiversity, what he found was perhaps more shocking than anything Liittschwager documented. There was corn and corn and very little more. Childs found a single red mite and a spider eating a crane fly. He came upon one tiny mushroom and a few grasshoppers and an ant. And after three days and two nights in the middle of the Iowan cornfield, that was the extent of what he found (Childs 2012).

Humans have developed remarkable ways to keep insects, pests, and fungi at bay, thereby preventing attacks on the agricultural lands that are so crucial to human subsistence and industry. But much new evidence has shown that agro-chemicals can also have major side effects on populations of organisms that are important to agriculture in other ways. Many industrialized countries in the world are currently experiencing what is referred to as "Colony Collapse Disorder" (CCD), which affects bee populations (vanEnglesdorp et al. 2009). Bees, which are vital pollinators for the production of so many different foods—from apples to oranges to almonds—seem to have gone missing. In China, the loss of the bee population has required orchardists to painstakingly hand pollinate the individual flowers of apple and pear trees to enable their fruiting (Partap et al. 2001). As CCD begins to impact other countries across the globe, the loss of bees may have huge economic impacts since it will require humans to do the labor that is carried out by these little pollinators.

Broader trends of biodiversity loss are becoming apparent on the planet as well. Biologists Rodolfo Dirzo and Peter Raven present a startling picture regarding the rate of species loss: "For the past 300 years, recorded extinctions for a few groups of organisms reveal rates of extinction at least several hundred times the rate expected on the basis of the geological record." To which they add, soberly: "The loss of biodiversity is the only truly irreversible global environmental change the Earth faces today" (2003, 137).

Biodiversity loss is alarming not simply because of the important work that other species do for us or even because of our sentimentality over their existence. It is deeply concerning because the endangerment and extinction of other species reminds us of our own inherently precarious situation in the world. What is more, we have begun to realize that we may need other species more than we once knew, including species that offer no obvious or direct material benefit to our own. Only now are we starting to confront the reality that our fate is tied, either directly or indirectly, to a whole host of other beings that inhabit this planet, some of which we are only vaguely aware. And as more and more of these species slip into oblivion, we are reminded that our fate could be the same.

Since Amazonia is recognized as a region of extraordinary biological diversity, it is not surprising that it has attracted so much attention in the past few decades as biodiversity loss weighs more and more on people's minds. However, exactly who should be "saving the Amazon," or whether the Amazon needs someone's saving, is very much up for debate. The push to salvage the earth's biodiversity is directly tied up in politics that cannot be overlooked or swept aside. In fact, the conflicts that have arisen over Amazonian conservation reveal deeply problematic relationships on this planet that are also at the root of the perceived crisis.

"SAVING THE AMAZON"

When I was growing up in the United States, it was not uncommon to hear lectures at an early age on the importance of environmental conservation and the value of biodiversity. The Amazon, of all the world's regions, was always, and inevitably, named as my classmates and I were told about the rapid rates at which forests were being leveled. "They're clearing parcels of land the size of Connecticut every year," we would hear in between recess and lunch. Some researchers and teachers told us that the Amazonian forests would be largely clear-cut by the end of the twentieth century (see Fearnside 1982). Those who were slightly more optimistic, or perhaps of an activist bent, warned that the Amazon would be largely denuded if action was not taken, suggesting that it was our responsibility to fight for the preservation of Amazonian forests. The lives of all the world's inhabitants were said to be hanging in the balance.

One of the purported justifications for "saving the Amazon" was the notion that Amazonian forests represented "the lungs of the world." Following this line of reasoning, it was suggested that destruction of Amazonian forests could disrupt the cycling of carbon dioxide and oxygen on the planet, leading to a dearth of oxygen in the earth's atmosphere.[8] This seemingly logical argument, however, is fundamentally flawed. In fact, rainforests add relatively little net oxygen to the atmosphere through photosynthesis (Moran 1993b, 10). Despite this, the idea circulated widely and was often accepted unquestioningly as a valid reason to support conservation efforts in the region.

A second argument suggests that cures for cancer and AIDS could very well be hiding somewhere beneath the dense forest canopy of the Amazonian jungle. This call for Amazonian conservation was perhaps best illustrated in the Hollywood film *The Medicine Man*, starring Sean Connery, who played a biochemist who finds a cure for cancer in a species of ant that lives in epiphytic plants perched high on trees in old-growth Amazonian forest. The moral of the film was clearly spelled out for the viewing public: if ongoing destruction of the Amazon is permitted, then humanity will suffer great losses, including, potentially, the sources of its own salvation.

However, these myths that have fixated foreign imaginations on the region are more than just harmless projections of widely held hopes and fears; they also have important consequences for the ways in which foreign nations engage Amazonian countries and their people. Candace Slater speaks directly to this point in the introduction to her book *Enchanted Edens*:

> How US lawmakers vote on a foreign aid bill that will affect Amazonian countries depends much on whether they think of the region as a Green Hell or a Green Cathedral. A region billed as "the world's lungs"—and, increasingly, its "toxin-removing kidneys"— is bound to trigger different reactions than a place that appears as its ear, its brain, or its solar plexus. Is the Amazon a primeval garden from which we should help exclude all or certain people in order to preserve it? Is it a source of cancer cures on which we must get patents? A jungle to be developed, or plundered for its natural resources, or cleared for agriculture? If we can identify the true source of our own desire for an unspoiled natural paradise, we may find ourselves more able to see the rich variety not just of life forms, but also of human experience that exists in the Amazon. (Slater 2002, 8)

As Slater argues, the myths of the Amazon must be confronted and dissected before we can reach any real understanding of the region and the place it holds in the world today. Of course, it is equally critical to understand how the people living in its midst see it as well.

I suppose it is not surprising that much of the research I have conducted as an anthropologist in Amazonia has focused on questions of an environmental nature. Considering my exposure to Amazonia as an adolescent, it would have seemed almost counterintuitive for me to have done otherwise. And although much of this book is dedicated to the study of Amazonian human–environmental relationships, over the years I have reflected considerably on the politics of research in

Amazonia, the construction of Amazonia in the imaginary of non-Amazonians, and my own personal and oftentimes conflicted feelings about studying Amazonian environmental management.

When I was teaching English in Manaus, several different students asked me if I had been taught that the Amazon was an "international patrimony," belonging not to Brazil and other Amazonian countries, but rather to all of the world's inhabitants. I informed them that my teachers had emphasized Amazonia's great importance for the world, but never once did they suggest that it belonged to any other countries than those of northern South America. The students, not afraid to contradict me, told me (sometimes politely, other times less so) that in the United States, it was taught in geography classes that the Amazon was an international reserve. Despite my protests, and my adamancy that I had never heard such a claim, they refused to believe it was anything but true.

I decided to investigate the issue further, and what I found was revelatory. In May 2000 one of Brazil's primary newspapers, *O Estado de São Paulo*, published an article claiming that geography textbooks given to children in the United States displayed maps that described Amazonia and the Pantanal (wetlands of southwestern Brazil) as "international reserves" rather than property of the Brazilian state (Giobbi 2000). For many, this simply confirmed the existing fear that North Americans were teaching their children that the Amazon belonged to them as much as it did to Brazilians, Bolivians, Peruvians, Ecuadorians, and Colombians. Understandably, the Brazilian public reacted to the article with considerable indignation and outcry.

After the article was published, however, it was discovered that the claim was completely erroneous. An ultra-nationalist Brazilian organization appeared to have infiltrated the email account of a researcher at the University of Texas at Austin, from which the forged map was sent to the journalist at *O Estado*. Despite the fact that no such geography book ever existed, and that the map's text relied on poorly translated English, the rumor refused to die (see Guzmán 2010 and Mitchell 2010 for further discussion).[9]

AMAZONIA AND INTERNATIONAL COVETOUSNESS

In 1960 Arthur Cézar Ferreira Reis, scholar and former governor of Amazonas state, published the first edition of his book *A Amazônia e a cobiça internacional*. The title can be translated awkwardly but accurately as "Amazonia and international covetousness." The book was designed as a call to protect Amazonia from outside interests in the region.[10] Ferreira Reis, a historian, was well aware of the extended legacy of foreign exploitation in the Amazon region, which began in the colonial period and which continued on through the rubber boom and beyond. The fascination with Amazonia as one of the last bastions of nature in its most pristine state can be seen as a simple extension of this history of foreign desire to control the region, its people, its land, and its forests.

Even though the geography textbook map that described Amazonia as an "international reserve" was a complete forgery, it reignited and reaffirmed Brazilian fears of the "international covetousness" that was earlier described by Ferreira Reis. At the same time, other international developments provided more credible reasons for concern. Fiction, as the old cliché goes, never strays far from the truth. In October 2006 the British secretary of state for environment, food, and rural affairs, David Miliband, planned to propose an initiative that would call for the privatization of parts of Amazonia (Hennessey 2006). When the news was released by the British newspaper the *Daily Telegraph*, Miliband's office denied the story, in attempt to avoid mounting political backlash. Responding to the notion of such a plan, Brazil's foreign minister and environment minister simply stated: "Amazonia is not for sale" (Geraque and Canônico 2006).

In the 1970s, it was declared that Brazilians had to "integrar para não entregar"—integrate Amazonia so as not to hand it over to scheming neo-imperialist powers or let it fall prey to neighbors that passed through its porous borders. More recently, however, the concern over foreign meddling in Amazonia has become less about the land itself and more about the wealth of biological specimens that attract foreign interest. Ever since Henry Wickham left the lower Amazon with a ship full of rubber seeds that led to the bust of the rubber boom, Brazilians have been uncomfortable with the activities of foreigners in the region, especially those involved in biological prospecting. Although Wickham's act could be interpreted as one of sheer opportunism, today he is reviled in Brazil, referred to by tourist guides as "the prince of thieves" and, perhaps worst, a pioneer of "biopiracy" (Mann 2011, 339).

Biopiracy is a concept that describes foreign extraction activities that lead to the development of products derived from endemic biota "without fair compensation to the peoples or nations in whose territory the materials were originally discovered" (Pickett 2000). In 2003, while attending a festival dedicated to the cupuaçu fruit (*Theobroma grandiflorum*) in the town of Presidente Figueirdo north of Manaus, I heard about a more current example of biopiracy in the region. It appears that researchers at the National Institute for Amazonian Research, where I was later affiliated, had developed an alternative form of chocolate from the seeds of the native cupuaçu fruit. The production of this alternative chocolate, known as cupulate, began in the early 1980s in Brazil. Decades later, however, Japanese researchers worked to improve the techniques to extract fat from cupuaçu seeds and applied for international patents, which they were granted. To add insult to injury, the Japanese corporation Asahi Foods placed a trademark on the name "cupuaçu" for the sale of its products derived from the fruit, further aggravating Amazonians (see Vale et al. 2008; Tang 2008). At the festival dedicated to the fruit, hundreds of visitors signed a large banner proclaiming "Cupuaçu is ours!"[11]

Of course, Brazilians have capitalized on the adoption of plants from other parts of the world, including coffee (*Coffea arabica*) and soy, for which the country is the world's largest exporter. In fact, Warren Dean points out that coffee seeds had been smuggled into Brazil from French Guiana in the early 1700s (1987, 23), an event that is often overlooked in contemporary discussions about biopiracy in Brazil. The reality is that the vast majority of humans on this planet rely on plants that originate from outside their home regions; humans have always engaged in the trade and transfer of useful plants. Nonetheless, I could not help but sympathize with Amazonians and their fight for cupuaçu. Perhaps their campaign was a slightly misdirected one, especially given Brazil's own problematic history of imperialism (especially with regards to its indigenous populations; see Guzmán 2010), but it highlighted an important issue concerning the deep inequalities in access to and use of resources in the world and the role researchers may play in perpetuating such inequalities.

When conducting surveys and interviews with rural farmers in Borba, I usually attempted to sidestep discussion about the asymmetrical nature of our relationship. On many occasions, however, rural Amazonians required that I acknowledge the very differences that I conveniently sought to overlook. On a small creek, outside the town of Borba, I interviewed a man named Leo about the stretch of *terra preta* he farmed. He had been living on the land for twenty years, working it directly. As we walked through his fields, inspecting watermelons and rows of tomato plants, I inquired about the depth of the organic horizon of the dark *terra preta* soils. He dug down for a bit to show me their extent and then inquired if I was going to take some samples. I was quick to explain that as a foreign researcher I didn't have any plans of taking any biological materials, hoping that I would dismiss any possible suspicions of me as an heir of Wickham, or a biopirate. I explained further that I had simply wanted to ask some general questions about his agricultural management strategies on the soil.

Leo paused, looked at me, and then responded with a long, indirect monologue. He told me how farmers worked the land over their lifetime, developing their own understanding of agriculture with their *mãos na massa* (hands in the dough), getting their hands dirty, while professors, researchers, and other *estudiosos* occasionally stopped in to see what knowledge they could extract from them without doing any work at all. Leo was not being outwardly hostile, but he clearly wanted me to understand the problem from his perspective. And although it made me feel uncomfortable, I valued his critique. He had worked his whole life in agriculture and I had simply stopped in just to learn a thing or two without putting in the necessary time or work or sweat.

For a moment, I thought I could formulate a coherent response to his critique. I did not want to present a defense so much as an explanation for my presence. Yet somehow it seemed all wrong, and I knew something about what he had said was right. I have had several years to ruminate on what Leo said to me that day. And yet I still struggle to find an appropriate response—one that I think both he and I would find satisfactory. What I have concluded is that anthropological inquiry offers an important opportunity for people like Leo to directly question the motives of conservationists and international researchers like myself. It opens up possibilities for the creation and the circulation of counternarratives like that of the "international covetousness" that Amazonians use in response to foreign demands on their land and resources. The open and reflexive nature of ethnography also allows for the concerns of Amazonians, like the threat of biopiracy, to emerge as topics that merit as much attention as "anthropogenic" soils and agricultural sustainability. Lastly, ethnographic research encourages personalized, grounded views of Amazonia that challenge and call into question abstracted notions of the region, including that of the monolithic rainforest in need of saving.

I believe that all of these are important justifications for anthropological research in Amazonia. However, I suspect they might ring strangely in Leo's ears. So to put things more clearly, I can say this: I was in Amazonia to see it with my own eyes. I was there to hear what people with deep, historical ties to the land had to say about it, how they saw it, and what they felt about it. And I hoped in reporting on that, a different Amazonia might begin to emerge. Not the lungs of the earth. Not the source of botanical wonders that could save us from cancer and AIDS. Not an "Earthly Eden." Not a "Green Hell." Rather, a place where people like Leo live and work, growing tomatoes and watermelons, with their hands covered in dark, ancient dirt.

THE PREDICAMENT OF NATURE

The problem with the idea of "nature" (or "Nature" if you prefer) is that it turns lived-in places like Amazonia into a distant object "over there," separate from us and easily vulnerable to distortion. Timothy Morton vividly illustrates this concern in his book *Ecology without Nature*, in which he writes: "Putting something called Nature on a pedestal and admiring it from afar does for the environment what patriarchy does for the figure of Woman" (2007, 5). Not only does the idea of "nature" allow for the objectification and exploitation of the environment and nonhuman others, but it also compromises the position of the people who live in those environments. Peasants and indigenous groups are sometimes forcibly removed from the landscapes they inhabit in the name of conservation and the protection of nature while in other cases they are required to justify their presence as one that is a "natural" state of affairs (see Conklin and Graham 1995).

Despite these problematic consequences, "nature" is an idea that many people cannot easily shake. Herein lies what I see as "the predicament of nature." Echoing James Clifford's sentiments about culture, nature is a "deeply compromised idea" that many of us cannot yet do without (1988, 10). Even if we were to try to abandon the idea of it, its hold is far too strong in Western thought to be completely abandoned or abolished. This does not mean, however, that the idea of nature cannot change or evolve, or that the relationships between humans and other beings that inhabit this world cannot be reconfigured or reconceptualized.

If we embrace the view of nature as an active and evolving creation for which we are in part responsible, then it cannot be seen as a passive object to be admired or feared; rather, we must view it as something that we are part of and something that we've never really been separate from. In this way, we may begin to see ourselves as part of a living collectivity that pulls us in unanticipated directions. Large snakes, pineapple mealy bugs, creeping lianas, pesky weeds, pet pacas, massive caimans, armor-plated catfish—they all have bearing on our existence, even as much as we may have on theirs. Ironically, the greatest lesson of the Anthropocene is that rather than encourage deeper anthropocentrism, it should urge broader eco-centric thinking and a greater attunement to the lives of others on this earth, those living in forests, subsisting on soil, growing up out of sidewalks, crawling into our homes.

FINAL CONCLUSIONS: ON TO THE ECOZOIC?

So what's worse, certainty or doubt? It is my hope that the many doubts about humanity's future can motivate a radical rethinking of the human place on the planet. As I have attempted to convey in this book, this requires a rethinking of not only human relationships to the environment but also relationships among humans. Ethnography can serve an undoubtedly valuable role in this process as Peter Redfield articulates in *Space in the Tropics*: "The practice of ethnography retains a vital allure, the promise that if well done, it will offer rich rewards: moments of experience, an echo of different voices, and the crucial reminder that things could be otherwise" (2000, 12). And perhaps this will be ethnography's greatest contribution to the future: the continued reminder of how things can and should be different.

The success or survival of many species and life-forms on this planet has recently hinged on their ability to adapt to human needs and the human presence. But mounting evidence, from Colony Collapse Disorder to global climate change, suggests that humanity will face greater problems if we continue to neglect our relationship to others on this planet and resist the idea of ceding them room. It is time that we come to recognize that humanity maintains deep, binding relationships with the environment and that such relationships require sensitivity to the actions and responses of other beings that animate the world. Even more than that, we must accept our obligations of reciprocation toward them.

As I have discussed here, the practices of rural Amazonians offer a number of ways for thinking differently about humans' relationships to others, from the plants that they cultivate to ward off envy to the snakes that remind them of their constantly evolving landscape. Their continuous negotiation with worms and weeds, massive floods and unforgiving droughts often weighs heavily on their minds, and I believe encourages a greater awareness of the lives of other beings and forces in the landscape. In this way, rural Amazonians come to view nonhuman others as agents and active members of society—sometimes they are seen as enemies, other times allies, and even at times kin. The ways in which Amazonians socialize "nature" may seem bizarre to some non-Amazonians, but then again, this is while people in other parts of the world take their dogs out to restaurants in sweaters and feed their cats filet mignon.

Currently much of the world is suffering from a crisis in ecological thinking. With the many technological marvels and profound insights produced through the work of science, we have fallen victim to the illusion that we can exert ultimate control over our surroundings. Instead, the Anthropocene should teach us that science and technology have increased only our potential to alter life on the planet, not necessarily our dominion over it.

The entire debate over the very idea of the "Anthropocene" is in many ways rooted in a growing realization that we are in a state of ecological crisis over which we may have very little control. This has become clearer as floods, drought, tsunamis, and carbon dioxide threaten to displace or destroy human populations in various points across the globe. In our attempts to isolate ourselves from the "natural" environment, building up boundary walls—both physical and social—with our technologies, we are only now starting to appreciate how vitally important our connections to the rest of the world's beings really are.

If we embrace the uncertainty of the Anthropocene, this might push us toward a deeper appreciation of our tenuous ties to others and help us to cultivate a more inclusive ecology—an "ecology" in the broadest sense of the term. When such a project takes hold, we can begin to usher in a new era, one that Thomas Berry has referred to as the "Ecozoic." Only then will we finally begin to experience the universe as it should be known, as "a communion of subjects, not a collection of objects" (2009, 86).

And perhaps even a "more inclusive ecology" is much too little—what we seek does not yet have a name.[12]

USEFUL BOTANICAL SPECIES SURVEYED IN BORBA, AMAZONAS, BRAZIL

Appendix

Scientific Name	Family	Local Common Name	English Name	Native/Exotic[†]	Origin
Acmella oleracea	Asteraceae	jambu		native	Amazonia
Aeollanthus suaveolens	Lamiaceae	catinga de mulata		exotic	Africa
Alibertia edulis	Rubiaceae	puruí		native	Amazonia
Allium fistulosum	Amaryllidaceae	cebolinha	chives	exotic	Old World
Aloe vera	Xanthorrhoeaceae	babosa	aloe vera	exotic	Old World
Alpinia nutans	Zingiberaceae	vendicaá; vindicá	dwarf cardamom	exotic	Asia
Alternanthera sp.	Amaranthaceae	cuia-mansa		native	South America
Anacardium occidentale	Anacardiaceae	caju	cashew	native	South America
Ananas comosus	Bromeliaceae	abacaxi	pineapple	native	South America
Annona montana	Annonaceae	araticum	mountain soursop	native	Amazonia
Annona muricata	Annonaceae	graviola	soursop	native	South America
Annona squamosa	Annonaceae	ata	sweetsop	native	Mesoamerica
Aristolochia sp.	Aristolochiaceae	uecá		native	Neotropics
Artocarpus altilis	Moraceae	fruta-pão	breadfruit	exotic	Southeast Asia
Artocarpus heterophyllus	Moraceae	jaca	jackfruit	exotic	India
Astrocaryum aculeatum	Arecaceae	tucumã	star nut palm	native	Amazonia
Attalea attaleoides	Arecaceae	palha branca		native	Amazonia
Attalea maripa	Arecaceae	inajá		native	Amazonia

Attalea phalerata	urucuri		native	Amazonia
Attalea speciosa	babaçu		native	South America
Averrhoa bilimbi	limão caiano	bilimbi	exotic	Southeast Asia
Averrhoa carambola	carambola	starfruit	exotic	Southeast Asia
Ayapana tripilinervis	japana		native	
Bactris gasipaes	pupunha	peach palm	native	Amazonia
Bertholletia excelsa	castanha	Brazil nut	native	Amazonia
Bixa orellana	urucum	annato	native	Amazonia
Brassica oleracea var. viridis	couve	cabbage; collard greens	exotic	Mediterranean
Bryophyllum pinnatum	coirama; escama de pirarucu		exotic	Africa
Byrsonima chrysophylla	murici	nance	native	Neotropics
Caesalpinia ferrea (Caesalpinoideae)	jucá		native	
Caladium bicolor	vence-tudo	caladium	native	Neotropics
Caladium sp.	cachorrinho	caladium	native	Neotropics
Calathea allouia	ariá	sweet cornroot	native	South America
Callisia repens	dinheiro-em-penca		native	Neotropics
Capsicum annuum	pimentão	bell pepper	native	Mesoamerica
Capsicum chinense	pimenta (various)	pepper	native	Amazonia

(continued)

Scientific Name	Family	Local Common Name	English Name	Native/Exotic[†]	Origin
Capsicum frutescens	Solanaceae	pimenta malagueta	hot pepper	native	South America
Carapa guianensis	Meliaceae	andiroba		native	Amazonia
Carica papaya	Caricaceae	mamão	papaya	native	Mesoamerica
Cassia leiandra	Fabaceae (Mimosoideae)	marimari		native	Amazonia
Cedrela odorata	Meliaceae	cedrinho	Spanish cedar	native	Amazonia
Chenopodium ambrosioides	Amaranthaceae	mastruz	wormseed	native	Mesoamerica
Citrullus lanatus	Cucurbitaceae	melancia	watermelon	exotic	Africa
Citrus × *limon*	Rutaceae	limão tangerina		exotic	Asia
Citrus aurantiifolia	Rutaceae	lima		exotic	Asia
Citrus cf. *limon*	Rutaceae	limão	sour lemon	exotic	Asia
Citrus reticulata	Rutaceae	tangerina	tangerine	exotic	Asia
Citrus sinensis	Rutaceae	laranja	orange	exotic	Asia
Cocos nucifera	Arecaceae	côco	coconut	exotic	Southeast Asia
Coffea arabica	Rubiaceae	café	coffee	exotic	Africa
Coriandrum sativum	Apiaceae	cheiro verde; coentro	cilantro	exotic	Old World
Costus spicatus	Costaceae	pobre velho; cana mansa		native	Americas
Couepia cf. *subcordata*	Chrysobalanaceae	mari		native	Amazonia

Species	Family	Local name	Common name	Status	Region
Crescentia cujete	Bignoniaceae	cuia	calabash gourd	native	Amazonia
Croton sacaquinha	Euphorbiaceae	sacaquinha		native	South America
Cucumis anguria	Cucurbitaceae	maxixe	West Indian gherkin	exotic	Africa
Cucumis melo	Cucurbitaceae	melão	melon	exotic	Africa
Cucumis sativus	Cucurbitaceae	pepino	cucumber	exotic	Old World
Cucurbita spp.	Cucurbitaceae	jerimum	squash	native	Neotropics
Cymbopogon citratus	Poaceae	capim cheiroso; capim santo	lemon grass; citronella	exotic	Neotropics
Dieffenbachia seguine	Araceae	comigo-ninguém-pode	dumbcane	native	Neotropics
Dioscorea trifida	Dioscoreaceae	cará	cocoyam	native	South America
Dipteryx odorata	Fabaceae (Papilionoideae)	cumaru	Tonka bean	native	Amazonia
Duguetia spixiana	Annonaceae	biribarana		native	Amazonia
Elaeis oleifera	Arecaceae	caiauê	American oil palm	native	South America
Eleutherine bulbosa	Iridaceae	marupaí		native	South America
Eryngium foetidum	Apiaceae	chicoria	culantro	native	Amazonia
Eugenia stipitata	Myrtaceae	araça-boi		native	Amazonia
Euphorbia milii	Euphorbiaceae	coroa de cristo	crown of thorns	exotic	Africa (Madagascar)
Euphorbia tirucalli	Euphorbiaceae	dedo de Deus	Indian tree spurge	exotic	Africa

(*continued*)

Scientific Name	Family	Local Common Name	English Name	Native/Exotic[†]	Origin
Euterpe oleracea	Arecaceae	açaí	acai	native	Amazonia
Euterpe precatoria	Arecaceae	açaí do mato; jussara	acai	native	Amazonia
Fridericia chica	Bignoniaceae	crajiru		native	South America
Genipa americana	Rubiaceae	jenipapo	genipap	native	South America
Gossypium barbadense	Malvaceae	algodão	cotton	native	South America
Hevea brasiliensis	Euphorbiaceae	seringueira	rubber tree	native	Amazonia
Hibiscus rosa-sinensis	Malvaceae	pampola; papola	hibiscus	exotic	Asia
Hibiscus sabdariffa	Malvaceae	vinagreira	roselle	exotic	Old World
Himatanthus sucuuba	Apocynaceae	sucuba		native	South America
Inga edulis	Fabaceae (Mimosoideae)	ingá	ice cream bean	native	Amazonia
Inga longiflora	Fabaceae (Mimosoideae)	ingá chato		native	Amazonia
Inga spp.	Fabaceae (Mimosoideae)	ingazinho		native	Amazonia
Ipomoea batatas	Convolvulaceae	batata doce	sweet potato	native	South America
Jatropha curcas	Euphorbiaceae	pião branco		native	Americas
Jatropha gossypiifolia	Euphorbiaceae	pião roxo	bellyache bush	native	South America
Jatropha podagrica	Euphorbiaceae	pião barrigudo	bout plant	native	Americas

Lactuca sativa	Asteraceae	alface	lettuce	exotic	Old World
Leonurus sibiricus	Lamiaceae	cibalena		exotic	Asia
Licaria puchury-major	Lauraceae	puxuri		native	South America
Lippia alba	Verbenaceae	erva-cidreira		native	
Lippia origanoides	Verbenaceae	salva de Marajó		native	
Luffa operculata	Cucurbitaceae	buchinha	luffa	exotic	Old World Tropics
Malpighia emarginata	Malpighiaceae	acerola	Barbados cherry	native	Neotropics
Mangifera indica	Anacardiaceae	manga	mango	exotic	Southeast Asia
Manihot esculenta	Euphorbiaceae	mandioca; macaxeira	manioc; cassava	native	Amazonia
Mansoa alliacea	Bignoniaceae	cipó alho	garlic vine	native	Amazonia
Mauritia flexuosa	Arecaceae	buriti		native	South America
Mentha sp.	Lamiaceae	hortelazinha	mint	exotic	Europe
Mentha sp.	Lamiaceae	hortelã grande	mint	exotic	Europe
Mimosa spp.	Fabaceae (Mimosoideae)	jiquiri; jequiri		native	
Morinda citrifolia	Rubiaceae	noni		exotic	Oceania
Musa × *paradisaca*	Musaceae	banana	banana	exotic	Southeast Asia
Nephelium lappaceum	Sapindaceae	rambutan	rambutan	exotic	Southeast Asia
Nicotiana tabacum	Solanaceae	tobaco	tobacco	native	South America

(*continued*)

Scientific Name	Family	Local Common Name	English Name	Native/ Exotic†	Origin
Ocimum americanum	Lamiaceae	manjericão	basil	exotic	Old World
Ocimum campechianum	Lamiaceae	alfavaca		native	Neotropics
Oenocarpus bacaba	Arecaceae	bacaba		native	Amazonia
Oenocarpus bataua	Arecaceae	patauá		native	Amazonia
Oenocarpus minor	Arecaceae	bacabinha		native	Amazonia
Opuntia ficus-indica	Cactaceae	palmeira	prickly pear cactus	native	Mesoamerica
Oryza sativa	Poaceae	arroz	rice	exotic	South Asia
Passifloria edulis	Passifloraceae	maracujá	passion fruit	native	South America
Pectis elongata	Asteraceae	cuminho	cumin	exotic	South America
Persea americana	Lauraceae	abacate	avocado	native	Mesoamerica
Petiveria alliacea	Phytolaccaceae	mucura-caá		native	Neotropics
Peumus boldus	Monimiaceae	boldo		native	South America
Pfaffia glomerata	Amaranthaceae	emenda-osso		native	South America
Piper callosum	Piperaceae	paregorico; panquilê		native	South America
Piper marginatum	Piperaceae	caapeba		native	Neotropics
Piper nigrum	Piperaceae	pimenta do reino	black pepper	exotic	South Asia
Platonia insignis	Clusiaceae	bacuri		native	Amazonia
Plectranthus amboinicus	Lamiaceae	malvarisco	Cuban oregano	exotic	Africa

Pluchea sagittalis	Asteraceae	marcela		native	Americas
Pogostemon heyneanus	Lamiaceae	oriza; uriza	patchouli	exotic	Asia
Portulaca pilosa	Portulacaceae	amor-crescido	kiss-me-quick	native	Americas
Pouteria caimito	Sapotaceae	abiu	abiu	native	Amazonia
Psidium guajava	Myrtaceae	goiaba	guava	native	South America
Psidium guineense	Myrtaceae	goiaba-araçá		native	Amazonia
Ricinus communis	Euphorbiaceae	mamona	castor bean	exotic	Africa
Rollinia mucosa	Annonaceae	biribá		native	Amazonia
Ruta spp.	Rutaceae	arruda	rue	exotic	Old World
Saccharum officinarum	Poaceae	cana de açucar	sugarcane	exotic	Oceania
Sambucus sp.	Adoxaceae	sabogueiro	elderberry	native	Neotropics
Sansevieria trifasciata	Asparagaceae	espada de São Jorge	snake plant	exotic	Africa
Scindapsus aureus	Araceae	jibóia	ivy	exotic	Asia
Scutellaria agrestis	Lamiaceae	trevo roxo		native	South America
Sesamum indicum	Pedaliaceae	gergelim	sesame	exotic	Old World
Siparuna guianensis	Monimiaceae	capitiu	fever tree	native	Neotropics
Solanum lycopersicum	Solanaceae	tomate	tomato	native	Mesoamerica
Solanum melongena	Solanaceae	berinjela	eggplant	exotic	Africa
Solanum sessiliflorum	Solanaceae	cubiu	Orinoco apple	native	Amazonia
Spondias dulcis	Anacardiaceae	cajarana	Polynesian plum	exotic	Southeast Asia

(*continued*)

Scientific Name	Family	Local Common Name	English Name	Native/Exotic[†]	Origin
Spondias mombin	Anacardiaceae	taperebá; cajá	hog plum	native	South America
Swietenia macrophylla	Meliaceae	cedrinho mogno	big-leaf mahogany	native	Amazonia
Syzygium cumini	Myrtaceae	azeitona	Java plum	exotic	Southeast Asia
Syzygium malaccense	Myrtaceae	jambo	Malay apple	exotic	Southeast Asia
Tagetes erecta	Asteraceae	cravo; cravo de defunto	marigold	native	Central America (Mexico)
Talinum fruticosum	Talinaceae	cariru		native	Americas
Talisia esculenta	Sapindaceae	pitomba		native	South America
Theobroma cacao	Malvaceae	cacau	cacao; cocoa	native	Amazonia
Theobroma grandiflorum	Malvaceae	cupuaçu		native	Amazonia
Theobroma mariae	Malvaceae	cacau jacare		native	Amazonia
Theobroma speciosum	Malvaceae	cacau-rana		native	Amazonia
Thevetia peruviana	Apocynaceae	castanha-da-índia	yellow oleander	native	Andes
Urtica dioica	Urticaceae	urtiga	stinging nettles	exotic	Europe; North America
Vernonia condensata	Asteraceae	boldo japonês		exotic	Old World
Vetiveria zizanioides	Poaceae	patichulim	vetiver	exotic	Asia

Vigna unguiculata	Fabaceae (Faboideae)	feijão de praia	cowpea	exotic	Africa
Vigna unguiculata	Fabaceae (Faboideae)	feijão de corda	Surinamese long bean	exotic	Africa
Vitex agnus-castus	Lamiaceae	pau de Angola		exotic	Europe
Zea mays	Poaceae	milho	corn, maize	native	Mesoamerica
Zingiber officinale	Zingiberaceae	gengibre; mangarataia	ginger	exotic	Southeast Asia
Unidentified	Araceae	tajá-buceta		native	South America
Unidentified	Araceae?	poraquê	electric eel plant		
Unidentified	Euphorbiaceae	caboclo roxo			
Unidentified	Unidentified	maria bonita		?	?
Unidentified	Unidentified	mutuquinha		?	?
Unidentified	Unidentified	miru		?	?
Unidentified	Unidentified	iraporanga		?	?
Unidentified	Unidentified	vai-vem		?	?
Unidentified	Unidentified	curuminzeiro		native	?

Note: Plants were identified from botanical surveys at 138 households in the municipality of Borba between 2009 and 2010. Surveys relied on traditional local classifications of botanical species, to which Latin binomials were later associated. Correspondence between local and scientific names was made by referring to Cavalcante 1991 and Clement 1999.
†Native to the Americas prior to European arrival.

NOTES

PREFACE

1. I use the terms "indigenous peoples," "indigenous populations," and "Amerindians" interchangeably when describing Amazonian peoples who inhabited the region prior to European colonization. In reference to specific ethnic groups, present or past, I try to use appropriate ethnonyms whenever possible.

2. From *Incidentals* (1900). The original reads: "I'm an idealist. I don't know where I'm going but I'm on my way."

3. My initial research was undertaken while I was an intern at INPA in 2003. I returned during my graduate studies to conduct three months of fieldwork, between June and August 2007, and then an additional twelve months of research, from September 2009 to September 2010.

CHAPTER 1: AMAZONIA IN THE ANTHROPOCENE

1. Candace Slater (1996; 2002) has written at length about the "Edenic narrative" attributed to the Amazon. The region is often portrayed as a majestic, paradise-like space of primeval tropical nature (see also Hecht and Cockburn 1989, 8–9).

2. In the book *Amazonia: Um paraíso perdido*, da Cunha wrote, "Mas como todos nós desde mui cedo gizamos um Amazonas ideal, mercê das páginas singularmente líricas dos não sei quantos viajantes . . . sucede um caso vulgar de psicologia: ao defrontarmos o Amazonas real, vemo-lo inferior à imagem subjetiva há longo tempo prefigurada" (2003, 33) (But since, from early on in life, each of us has drawn an ideal Amazonia in our minds thanks to the remarkable lyrical pages left us by countless travelers . . . we experience a common psychological reaction when we come face to face with the real Amazon: we see it as somehow lacking with respect to the subjective image we have long held of it).

3. The date of Borba's establishment is uncertain. Francisco Jorge dos Santos (1999) cites the year 1724 while other authors provide later estimates (e.g., Keller 1875, 44).

4. Amazonas state has a population density of 2.4 people per kilometer squared (IBGE 2010), which is close to that of the US state of Wyoming (US Census Bureau 2013). Although the Amazon is often seen by North Americans as a vast wilderness, Amazonas has a much higher population density than the US state of Alaska (0.5/km²).

5. In Amazonas it is common to hear the phrase "Quem come jaraqui não sai daqui," which translates loosely as "If you eat jaraqui, you won't ever leave."

6. The stream was given this name due to the concentration of puxuri (*Licaria puchury-major*, Lauraceae family), a tree endemic to the Madeira River region whose leaves and nuts are used in perfumes and medicinal teas.

7. These are soil orders from the USDA soil taxonomy. In the World Reference Base for Soil Resources, they are classified as Ferralsols and Acrisols, respectively (FAO 1998).

8. Much has been written about the problematics of ethnographic arrival stories, especially following the publication of *Writing Culture* (Clifford and Marcus 1986), and clearly this one is not exempt from criticism. However, as Shane Greene argues, "the 'writing culture' critique of the canonical ethnographic entrée is itself so canonical by now that it has reached the point of cliché" (2009, 9). As this book is meant to be accessible to a wide audience, this arrival story is used to provide an introduction to the town of Borba and the Amazon region more generally. For thoughtful discussion of anthropological writing and its relation to epistemology, see Clifford Geertz's *Works and Lives: The Anthropologist as Author* (1988, 1–24).

9. I never directly referred to anyone as a *caboclo* since I was aware of the pejorative nature of the term. However, when living in Manaus, I heard friends and acquaintances refer to local men and women (particularly those of lower classes) as *caboquinhos* and occasionally I would reproduce this usage in conversation. As time wore on, though, I became more and more uncomfortable with such usage.

10. Richard Pace (1997), Mark Harris (1998), and Deborah de Magalhães Lima (1999) all look at precisely this question.

11. In Portuguese: "Sou caboclo mesmo!"

12. This view was labeled by Eduardo Viveiros de Castro (1996) as the "Standard Model."

13. This reevaluation within anthropology is currently referred to as "the ontological turn." This movement has been influenced in part by Philippe Descola's schematic of what he identifies as the four primary "ontologies"—animism, totemism, analogism, and naturalism—that order the world of humans and nonhumans in terms of their physical makeup and subjective capacities (2013, xiii). Others who have made important contributions to this area of scholarship include Matei Candea (2010; 2013), Donna Haraway (2008), Eduardo Kohn (2007; 2013), Bruno Latour (2014), and Eduardo Viveiros de

Castro (1998). For further discussion of "the ontological turn," see Viveiros de Castro et al. 2014 and Kelly 2014.

14. The commencement of the Anthropocene is currently a source of much debate. The climate scientists Paul Crutzen, Will Steffen, and their colleagues trace its origins to the industrial revolution, a period in which natural resource extraction and the burning of coal expanded significantly, leading to alteration of the earth's climate (Crutzen and Stoermer 2000; Crutzen 2002; Steffen et al. 2007). In their critique of the term, geologists Whitney Autin and John Holbrook (2012) argue that the Anthropocene "provides eye-catching jargon" but is not necessarily a useful stratigraphic concept. They claim that it is too soon to identify a stratigraphic boundary that would distinguish the Anthropocene from the Holocene, writing: "Because the strata anticipated by the Anthropocene has [*sic*] not yet fully developed and it is only currently possible that a recognizable basal boundary separates it from the Holocene epoch, researchers should find difficulty in using this concept in stratigraphic practice" (60). To counter these arguments, some have proposed the atomic era as an alternative starting point since radioisotopes can be found across the planet after the 1950s (Dean et al. 2014). William Ruddiman (2013) has also added to the debate, arguing for an earlier Anthropocene onset since anthropogenic greenhouse effects can be detected from the period when humans made the transition to food production and agriculture. Contributing to Ruddiman's position, Certini and Scalenghe (2011) have suggested that anthropogenic soils, like *terra preta do índio*, which developed in various parts of the world with the advent of agriculture and large-scale sedentary societies, should be considered the "golden spikes" (i.e., the agreed upon geological reference points) of the Anthropocene.

CHAPTER 2: PEOPLE

1. Most of the fish in Brazilian Amazonia have common names derived from the Tupi language. In Tupi, *pira* is used to designate a fish or something pertaining to fish while *arara* is the common name for the scarlet macaw. The pirarara is thus the "scarlet macaw fish."

2. Eduardo Viveiros de Castro's (1998) "Amerindian Perspectivism" is worthy of reflection here. His insight, drawn from his ethnographic work with Amazonian peoples, is that the way that "humans perceive animals and other subjectivities that inhabit the world . . . differs profoundly from the way in which these beings see humans and see themselves" (470). In a revealing passage, Viveiros de Castro explains further: "Typically, in normal conditions, humans see humans as humans, animals as animals and spirits (if they see them) as spirits; however animals (predators) and spirits see humans as animals (as prey) to the same extent that animals (as prey) see humans as spirits or as animals (predators). By the same token, animals and spirits see them-

selves as humans: they perceive themselves as (or become) anthropomorphic beings when they are in their own houses or villages and they experience their own habits and characteristics in the form of culture—they see their food as human food (jaguars see blood as manioc beer, vultures see the maggots in rotting meat as grilled fish, etc.)" (ibid.). Viveiros de Castro points out, however, that not all animals are involved in this perspectivism and neither do all Amazonian peoples maintain this perspectivism. My curiosity relates to how Zico might think from the fish's point of view, and whether or not his thinking carries any traces of the phenomenon Viveiros de Castro describes.

3. The term, introduced to the social sciences by Marcel Mauss (1979 [1935]) and later expanded by Pierre Bourdieu (1977), generally refers to the totality of learned habits, bodily skills, styles, and "tastes" that "go without saying" for a particular group. Here I playfully suggest that its usage in the social sciences may be expanded beyond human groups.

4. "Bad luck" in fishing is usually described using the Amazonian cultural concept of *panema*, which is examined further in chapter 4 in the discussion of plants used to treat this affliction.

5. Many of these migrants left the Northeast following the extreme drought of 1877 (Weinstein 1985, 94).

6. Although the composition of the migrant population is not well documented, Weinstein (1985) argues that the majority of the migrants were single men or men with families who remained in the Northeast while they worked in the Amazon.

7. Rubber-tappers typically worked in the dry season when rainwater did not interfere with the latex collection (Pace 1998, 75; Weinstein 1985).

8. Wickham's feat was somewhat remarkable considering the narrow window of time he had to collect seeds and transport them to London while they were still viable for propagation. His collections largely took place around the city of Santarém and he enlisted some of the Confederate families (described in chapter 3) that resided in the area to assist him (Dean 1987; Mann 2011, 337–341).

9. "A gente sofreu muito."

10. "Trabalhar na goma elástica era o jeito [nessa época]. . . . Só tinha essas coisas."

11. When I asked seu Hernando, an elderly resident of Puruzinho, if he ever encountered Juma or any other such creatures in the woods while collecting latex, he told me that he hadn't seen anything except the occasional jaguar. However, he added that he worked with a man from Pará state named Fernando (who they called Nicolau) who had had a run-in with Curupira, "the mother of game" (*mãe do mato*). While tapping latex from a sapupema tree, Fernando had heard a deep "peiii peiii peiii" echoing from the forest. He thought it was seu Hernando or one of his brothers nearby. Then the sound repeated itself, and he became scared because he knew it wasn't something good

(*não era coisa boa*). He loaded his pathetic shotgun and waited. He heard the sound approaching even closer, near a large tree. He collected his latex and threw it in a sack. Luckily, Fernando was an experienced woodsman, seu Hernando told me. He explained that when Curupira comes after you, you have to collect a vine (*cipó*), either tiririca or taracuá, and wind it up, hiding the ends of the vine in the bundle, and then leave it on a tree at a fork in the path. Curupira then grabs the vine as (s)he passes by, and since (s)he can't find the ends of the vine to unravel it, (s)he eventually forgets about you. And that's exactly what Fernando did.

12. Original: "O irmão do meu avô que morava na Trocanã me contou essa estória antes dele morrer. Ele trabalhava com balata em Borba e chegou até um ponto que tava bem de vida. Mas ele tava preocupado que os outros homens que trabalhava na balata estavam com ciúmes dele. Uma noite ele sonhou que um urubu estava limpando os ossos dele e ele acordou o dia seguinte com medo que os outros iam matar ele. Ele resolveu ir embora pro Mapiá mas como ele desconfiava, um grupo de homems estava atrás dele e pegaram ele. Ele pensava que ia morrer, mas os homens falavam que iam deixar ele escapar com a vida porque eram amigos. Mas falavam que ele tinha que ir embora e deixar todas as suas coisas. Aí ele foi pro mato lá no Mapiá e passou seis meses só comendo frutras e outras coisas da mata. Todo dia ele rezava o Pai Nosso e Creio em Deus Pai. Depois de varios meses na mata, ele viu que tava sendo acompanhando por um homenzinho todo de branco que falou que ele tava entrando no inferno. Lá ele viu as almas de varias pessoas que ele conhecia em Borba que ainda eram vivos. Ele encountrou a sua irmã, Zuza, que estava de quartro com um cachorrinho na boca dela. O homenzinho de branco disse que ela tinha pecado porque abortou os filhos. Aí, o homenzinho de branco levou ele fora do inferno e falou que ele não ia morrer porque não era a hora dele, mas ele tinha que se arrepender por ter ficado com a mulher do enteado dele. Daí o homezinho falou que ele ia voltar pro seu corpo e aí apareceu na frente dele como um bicho e ele ficou com nojo. Depois disso, encontraram ele na beira de um igarapé e levaram pra cidade e deram roupa para ele. Só nesse momento que ele se deu conta que estava completamente nu."

13. "Agora as pessoas só trabalham por dinheiro, mas na época tinha poucas famílias [em Puruzinho] e a gente se ajudava."

14. This image of rural Amazonians parallels in some ways Claude Lévi-Strauss's discussion of the bricoleur, which he introduces in his book *The Savage Mind* (1966). In essence, the bricoleur does the best (s)he can with the materials and resources available. This attitude is also captured in the common Brazilian idiom "If you don't have a dog, hunt with a cat."

15. Amazonia was the major focus for the collection of cacao and spices known as the *drogas do sertão*, which included sarsaparilla and wild clove. Collecting expeditions, sponsored by missionaries or private parties, began operating at least in the mid-seventeenth century (see Roller 2010).

16. *Riberinho* is a more accurate term for Amazonians who live on the region's waterways. It also lacks the pejorative overtone that *caboclo* carries.

17. This is commonly heard in Manaus in the augmentative form *cabocão*.

18. For an argument against its usage by anthropologists, see the important critique by Richard Pace: "Amazon Caboclo: What's in a Name?" (1997).

19. Lima describes anthropological usage of the social category *caboclo* as an abstract theoretical term or Weberian "ideal type." She is right to argue that the ongoing usage of the term by anthropologists overlooks the fact that no rural Amazonians actively self-identify in this way. From her view, the theoretical employment of the term reflects a lack of understanding or sensitivity to the ways in which rural Amazonians present and represent themselves (Lima 1999, 29). Elsewhere, Brondizio (2004) has argued that redefining the *caboclo* identity as that of a rural producer could be an "important step towards overcoming the prejudices embodied in the term" (19).

20. The idea that rural Amazonians are of "mixed" descent presupposes unassailable categories of "pure" biological race. The supposed "mixed" nature of their racial and ethnic background also stands in strong contrast to the assumed monolithic nature of the Amazonian environment. It is precisely this mode of thinking that Eduardo Viveiros de Castro challenges and inverts with Amerindian perspectivism and the notion of "multinaturalism" (for extended discussion, see Viveiros de Castro 2014). Also worthy of mention is that a social category very similar to *caboclo* exists in the Andes, where it is known as the *cholo*. Mary Weismantel explains that "cholos are neither white (mestizo) nor Indian, a position more often defined in cultural or geographical than explicitly racial terms. Whiteness is Western civilization, modernity, upward mobility, acculturation, even Methodism or the cash market. . . . Cholos are [seen as] moving forward: they had been Indian but are becoming white. . . . [However], the cholo is an Indian who approaches—but never achieves—whiteness" (2001, 89–90).

21. This is a riff on "turtles all the way down"—a story of cosmological infinite regress, known best in anthropological circles in its retelling by Clifford Geertz (1973).

22. See Greg Grandin's book *Fordlandia* (2009).

CHAPTER 3: SOILS

1. When the Spanish and Portuguese traveled to the New World, they brought with them a host of myths that animated and haunted their imaginations. Among these was the story of the Amazons. As Hardwick explains, the Amazons were seen as a "war-like society of women, living on the borders of the known world, renowned for archery and riding skills" (1990, 14). When Francisco de Orellana descended the Andes and began his long journey down the Amazon, he and his crew suffered numerous attacks by the indigenous

tribes along the river's banks (Carvajal 1894). After one such encounter, the Spaniards claimed that the Indian warriors shared a likeness to the Amazons of Greek myth. In relocating the myth of the Amazons, the Spaniards were able to render the exoticism of the Amazon somewhat familiar. The transposition of the Greek myth to northern South America also led to the naming of the world's largest river: the Amazon.

2. There exists an abundance of terms used to describe this pedological phenomenon. Early North American researchers referred to areas of the soil as "black lands" while the soil itself was described as "black earth," "dark earth," "terra preta do índio," or simply "terra preta" (Brown and Lidstone 1878; Hartt 1874; Smith 1879a). Later references included "archaeological black earth" and "archaeological dark earth," reflections of the abundance of potsherds and cultural material often found at such sites (da Costa and Kern 1999). Studies originating from Spanish-speaking countries of Amazonia used the terms *tierras negras* (black earths) and *suelos negros* (black soils) (Andrade 1986; Herrera 1980; Mora 2002). In addition to these referents, a host of other names describing the soil and its variations have been introduced as research has changed and expanded over time. In 1966, Wim Sombroek published his doctoral dissertation entitled "Amazon Soils: A Reconnaissance of the Soils of the Brazilian Amazon Region," which made reference not only to *terra preta* but also to an associated soil he called *terra mulata* (Sombroek 1966). Woods and McCann (1999) later provided their own insights regarding *terra mulata*, and claimed that it could be distinguished from *terra preta* by its grayish-brown color, lower concentration of nutrients, lack of cultural material, and surprisingly higher content of soil organic matter. In their writings, Woods and McCann employ the term "Amazonian dark earth" in consideration of both *terra preta* and *terra mulata*. The first two books dedicated to the study of these soils also opted for the use of the term "Amazonian dark earth" (Lehmann, Kern, et al. 2003; Glaser and Woods 2004).

3. The fazenda at Taperinha was owned by the Barão de Santarém, the same individual who had granted the tract of land to Hastings for the Confederate colony to be established.

4. The Rhome family and plantation is described in a short article Herbert Smith wrote for *Scribner's Monthly* (Smith 1879b).

5. Penna had surveyed numerous *terra preta* sites, including those in Santarém and Marajó Island. Summaries of Penna's contributions to archaeology are included in Helen Palmatary's excellent manuscript discussing pottery of Marajó Island (Palmatary 1949:270–273) as well as Hartt's "Contribuições para a ethnologia do valle do Amazonas" (Hartt 1885). As noted by both Hartt and Palmatary, Penna was the first scholar to investigate the burial mounds at Marajó, including the sites of Pacoval and Camuntins (Hartt 1885, 17; Palmatary 1949, 270). Beyond his work on Marajó, Penna discovered archaeological sites in the Maracá River region in southern Amapá, which were

later surveyed by Guedes (1896), Farabee (1921), and Nimuendajú (1927). His work also inspired recent investigations on the unique anthropomorphic funerary urns of the area (Guapindaia 2008). In addition to these accomplishments, Penna was arguably the first scholar to describe *terra preta* and its relationship to indigenous habitation (Penna 1869, 65–66). He later went on to found the Museu Paraense Emílio Goeldi, the leading institution for social science research in Amazonia.

6. Whether these men were slaves or not is unclear. The relationship between the Amazonian Confederates and Brazilian slaves is poorly documented, although it is certain that some (if not many) Confederates in Santarém owned slaves. After 1865, Brazil was one of the few nations in the world that maintained the institution of slavery. However, many historians downplay slavery's role in attracting Confederates to Brazil (see Dawsey and Dawsey 1995, 17; Harter 1985, 22; Gussi 1997, 101–104).

7. Not surprisingly, Hartt's collections proved to be valuable to later archaeological inquiry. In the early 1980s, Anna Roosevelt examined Hartt's collections at the museums at Cornell and Harvard and took a radiocarbon date of a shell from the Taperinha site, which dated to 5705 BP (Roosevelt 1995). In 1987, Roosevelt and colleagues conducted an archaeological investigation of the Taperinha shell midden and found the oldest pottery to date in the Amazon, with radiocarbon dates suggesting that it was crafted around 8000–7000 years BP (Roosevelt et al. 1991).

8. Pedro Texeira's voyage up and down the Amazon occurred between 1637 and 1639, but by that time there was already evidence of massive die-off of the indigenous population in the region (Myers et al. 2003). The first European voyage down the length of the Amazon had occurred almost one hundred years prior (1541–1542), led by Francisco de Orellana. The chronicler of Orellana's voyage, Gaspar de Carvajal (1894), described very large indigenous populations on the banks of the Amazon, although the reliability of the account has been called into question.

9. Many archaeologists and geologists use "Before Present," or B.P., as a preferred time scale. January 1, 1950, is used as the beginning date from which measurements are made.

10. We later found a similar defensive ditch in a neighborhood of Borba known as La Colonia, which had also been noted by Nimuendaju (2004, 159).

11. "Todo ano o verão chega numa época diferente. O ano passado, tava chovendo até junho. Esse ano o verão chegou cedo e a gente ia se dar melhor se plantou em março em vez de abril. O problema agora é que quando o verão bate forte, o solo seca muito, mas o plantio precisa de chuva para a melancia ficar boa antes da safra."

12. "Quando o verão bate, a terra fica seca e a produçao nao é muito boa, nem na terra preta. Só na várzea é bom porque a terra é húmeda."

13. "O pessoal trabalhava e não tirava mais. Aí parou."

CHAPTER 4: PLANTS

Portions of this chapter appeared, in an altered form, in Nicholas C. Kawa (2012), "Magic Plants of Amazonia and Their Contribution to Agrobiodiversity," *Human Organization* 71(3): 225–233. Reprinted by permission.

1. The word "magic" is a loaded term. To be clear, many of the individuals with whom I spoke would not describe the plants I discuss in this chapter as "magic plants." In fact, I found there to be no cover term applied to them in Borba. Many of the plants are used in spiritual and healing practices and are often identified as medicinals. However, since the forms of healing in which they are employed contrast greatly with Western biomedicine and many plants are used because of their power to ward off the evil eye and other malevolent forces, I describe them here as "magic plants." This is not meant to demean them—quite the contrary. I use this term with the utmost respect for their powers, which sometimes defy scientific or material explanation.

2. I never considered the possibility that my blue eyes might have also led some to believe that I had the evil eye, but this is a phenomenon noted in studies of the eastern Mediterranean (Lykiardopoulos 1981).

3. Macumba is in fact an Afro-Brazilian religion similar to Candomblé, but more commonly practiced in Rio de Janeiro and southeastern Brazil. In Brazilian Amazonia, I usually heard the term "macumba" used in a derogatory manner, in much the same way people in North America use the terms "voodoo" or "black magic."

4. Comment by Z4golfer regarding *Jatropha gossypifolia* or the "Bellyache bush" on the website "Dave's Garden." Accessed 14 March 2013. http://davesgarden.com/guides/pf/go/32205/#ixzz2QG53dnI1.

5. This seed dispersal mechanism is common for many plants in the Euphorbiaceae family, including two of Amazonia's most famous: the rubber tree (*Hevea brasiliensis*) and manioc (*Manihot esculenta*).

6. In the book *Sacred Leaves of Candomblé*, Robert Voeks describes a whole host of cosmopolitan weedy plants used in Afro-Brazilian religion and healing practice (1997, 27–32). These include castor bean (*Ricinus communis*), English plantain (*Plantago major*), dandá-da-costa (*Cyperus rotundus*), folha-da-costa (*Kallachoe integra*), and folha-da-fortuna (*Kallanchoe pinnata*), among many others.

7. Claude Lévi-Strauss had a penchant for recognizing such seeming contradictions in myth through his use of structuralist analysis. Similar examples can be found in his famous work *The Savage Mind* (1962).

8. Latour provides a comprehensive overview of his approach to actor-network theory in the book *Reassembling the Social* (2010). Graham Harman's book *Prince of Networks* (2009) also provides lucid insight into Latour's theoretical work. Of particular value here is the first part of the book, which is dedicated to Latour's metaphysics.

9. Mark Harris (2011) outlines seven different ways in which *panema* can be contracted, including among other things stepping on the entrails of fish or wild game. Fish bones and entrails, he notes, should also be disposed of in a manner that prevents domestic animals from eating them or people from urinating or defecating on them. In his account, however, *panema* is contracted by the person who caught the fish and not the individual stepping on the scales or entrails.

CHAPTER 5: FORESTS

1. Original quote: "A mata faz do lavrador uma sentinela alerta. Abandone o homem seu posto e ela vigorosamente irrompe pelas linhas do roçado, impoderando-se de novo" (63–64).

2. Most contemporary researchers recognize that any analysis of pre-Columbian impacts on the environment is complicated by sampling bias, because the overwhelming majority of ecological and archaeological research has been conducted in sites near the Amazon River and its major tributaries. However, there is also debate about the types of evidence that are suggestive of past human management or influence. While some researchers have looked for charcoal and phytoliths (e.g., McMichael et al. 2012), others have conducted botanical surveys to assess the dominance of useful species (e.g., Levis et al. 2012; Balée et al. 2014) in interfluvial areas of the region. The geoglyphs discovered in western Amazonia are also located largely in interfluvial areas (Balée et al. 2014; Schaan et al. 2007), although other archaeological evidence indicative of large populations is mysteriously lacking. Only more ecological and archaeological research in areas far removed from the Amazon River and its major tributaries will help to create a more complete picture of Amazonian settlement patterns across the basin during the pre-Columbian era.

3. Posthumanism is not to be confused with "transhumanism," which relates to the idea of humans merging with technology and transcending the limitations of the physical body (e.g., Kurzweil 2005). Posthumanism is not an apocalyptic view of life after humans either. Instead, it is an attempt to move past anthropocentrism and the prioritization of human lives over those of other beings and things. Although Kohn (2013) and Haraway (2011) do not identify themselves as posthumanist scholars per se, their work is part of a broader body of anthropological scholarship that seeks to move anthropology and ethnographic research beyond humans and human representations.

4. In the book *Consulting the Genius of the Place*, Wes Jackson shares a letter from his friend Wendell Berry, the renowned agrarian writer and poet, who identifies this problem: "The job we have now is to oppose the proposition that natural diversity and integrity of the natural world can be preserved (1) by making a strict division between the natural world and the human world and (2) by radically reducing cultural, economic, and domestic-genetic

diversity of the human world. . . . (I'm adapting my language only by courtesy to *the absurd notion that nature can be whole in half the world*)" (Jackson 2010, 40; emphasis added).

5. Sapo's name means "toad" in Portuguese. Many rural Amazonians whom I met (especially men) were known by nicknames that were taken from animals and other Amazonian biota. I knew several people named after fish (*traíra, bodó, pacu*), cats and dogs (*gato, cachorrinho*), and domesticated livestock (*boi, pinto*). Two young brothers were also known as "seed" (*caroço*) and "sweet manioc" (*macaxeira*). Others were ant (*formiga*), caiman (*jacaré*), macaw (*arara*), and monkey (*macaco*). One man in town was even known by everyone as "Batman" (using the word from English).

6. This is a nod to Gilles Deleuze and Felix Guattari's notion of the rhizome, which has experienced recent popularity in anthropological theory (e.g., Muehlmann 2012; Ogden 2010; Runk 2009). In their use of this botanical metaphor, Deleuze and Guattari emphasize that unlike roots or branches, which bifurcate and are thus dichotomous, rhizomes have the potential to move in a multitude of ways and directions. They claim that a rhizome has no center, no beginning, and no end, but rather exists in a continual process of "becoming." This openness and sense of possibility are designed to challenge dualisms and given categories, including the distinction between "nature" and "culture," which Deleuze and Guattari consider inherited necessary evils.

7. In Portuguese: "Quando não mata, aleija."

CHAPTER 6: FROM THE ANTHROPOCENE TO THE ECOZOIC?

Portions of this chapter appeared, in a slightly different form, in the following sources: Nicholas C. Kawa (2014), "'Saving the Amazon': Conservation, International Covetousness, and the Politics of Research," *Anthropology Today* 30(2): 21–24; and Nicholas C. Kawa (2014), "Managing Uncertainty in Rural Amazonia: Climate Change, Crop Diversity, and Social Networks," *Anthropology News* 55 (4). Both are used by permission.

1. The original text in Portuguese read: "O que é pior: a dúvida ou a verdade?" This can be translated literally as "What's worse: doubt or truth?" but I believe "certainty or doubt" captures the sentiment more accurately in English.

2. For an anthropological analysis of global biodiversity loss and the broader environmental crisis, John Bodley's *Anthropology and Contemporary Human Problems* (2012) provides a thorough discussion, especially in chapter 2.

3. Many people in the rural countryside referred to me as "Nickson." In Brazil, the suffix "-son" is very common for masculine first names, most likely due to influence and adoption of European surnames. Since it is com-

monplace to hear men named Jackson, Edilson, Emerson, Kleberson, or Wilson, some individuals began referring to me as "Nickson" (or "Nixon") and the name stuck.

4. "Não sinta inveja de mim. Não sou rico apenas trabalho."

5. One afternoon while fishing, I saw one of Cândida's youngest brothers get stung by a ray right at the edge of the river where we bathed. He laid down in his father's canoe and rolled around, grimacing in pain. When his brothers and father came down to the river's edge, they applied some toothpaste and tobacco to the wound and then took off to the town of Borba to get him treated for it. A few months later, Zé's mother was stung on the foot. Nearly everyone told me it was "24 hours of pain" (24 *horas de dor*).

6. I learned that the title was in fact "Só moleque doido" (Just [a] crazy boy).

7. In Brazilian Amazonia, manioc is popularly classified in two general categories: *macaxeira*, or "sweet manioc," and *mandioca*, or "bitter manioc." Sweet varieties of manioc contain few cyanogenic compounds and can be eaten after being peeled and boiled. Bitter varieties, on the other hand, contain higher concentrations of such compounds, and must be processed to extract the poison (McKey et al. 2011). Bitter varieties are used to make manioc flour, the primary source of calories in rural Amazonia. Sweet varieties are less widely consumed and are more frequently eaten as a snack.

8. This claim has been attributed to the Amazonian limnologist Harald Sioli (see Junk 2001; Mittermeier et al. 2005). Due to heavy use of fire for clearing, ecologist Dan Nepstad is reported as saying: "It's not the lungs of the world. It's probably burning up more oxygen now than it's producing" (Chu 2005).

9. To dispel this "urban myth," the US State Department published an online response that examined the original map forgery and text. Unfortunately, the original link to the page online (http://usinfo.state.gov/media /Archive/2005/Jul/07–397081.html) is no longer active. The text is reproduced here: "Since 2000, a forgery has circulated, falsely claiming that the United States and the United Nations have assumed control of the Amazon rainforest in order to safeguard its treasures for all mankind. The forgery, pictured below, purports to be page 76 of a US sixth-grade textbook titled *An Introduction to Geography* by David Norman. There is no indication that such a book exists. The US Library of Congress, with more than 29 million books and other printed materials, has no record of it. The Online Computer Learning Center's WorldCat database, the world's largest database of bibliographic information with more than 47 million books, has no record of the book. Nor can such a book be found in Internet searches on amazon.com or Google." The text also outlined the many spelling and grammatical errors found in the forgery, which "would not necessarily be obvious to non-native English

speakers," including "explorate" instead of "exploit" and "vegetals" instead of "vegetables."

10. In 1962, Luiz Osiris da Silva published *A luta pela Amazônia* (The fight for the Amazon) and two years after that Genival Rabelo published *Ocupação da Amazonia* (Occupation of the Amazon), both of which took up this same theme.

11. On March 20, 2003, the NGOs Amazonlink and Grupo de Trabalhos Amazônicos (Amazonian Working Group), along with several others, filed an administrative procedure order with the Japan Patent Office (JPO) to cancel the trademark registration on cupuaçu. On February 18, 2004, the JPO agreed to cancel the trademark, acknowledging that there was no alternative term to cupuaçu for competitors to use since the word indicates the name of the raw materials themselves. The JPO also denied Asahi Food Co. Ltd.'s application for a patent on the processing of cupuaçu seeds into cupulate because the Brazilian Agricultural Corporation (EMBRAPA) had already disclosed the process in an earlier patent application (Matthews 2011, 149–153).

12. This is a variation on a line from the Brazilian writer Clarice Lispector: "Liberade é muito pouco, o que eu desejo ainda não tem nome" (Freedom is much too little, what I want doesn't have a name yet).

REFERENCES

Adams, Cristina, Rui S. S. Murrieta, and Walter A. Neves, eds. 2006. *Sociedades caboclas amazônicas: Modernidade e invisibilidade*. São Paulo: Annablume.

Adams, Cristina, Rui S. S. Murrieta, Andrea D. Siqueira, Walter A. Neves, and Rosely A. Sanches. 2006. "O pão da terra: Da invisibilidade da mandioca na Amazônia." In *Sociedades caboclas amazônicas: Modernidade e invisibilidade*, ed. Cristina Adams, Rui S. S. Murrieta, and Walter A. Neves, 295–321. São Paulo: Annablume.

Agassiz, Louis, and Elizabeth C. C. Agassiz. 1868. *A Journey in Brazil*. Boston: Ticknor and Fields.

Agra, Maria de Fátima, Kiriaki Nurit Silva, Ionaldo José Lima Diniz Basílio, Patrícia França de Freitas, and José Maria Barbosa-Filho. 2008. "Survey of Medicinal Plants Used in the Region Northeast of Brazil." *Revista Brasileira de Farmacognosia* 18.3:472–508.

Albuquerque, Ulysses Paulino. 2001. "The Use of Medicinal Plants by the Cultural Descendants of African People in Brazil." *Acta Farmacéutica Bonaerense* 20.2:139–144.

Albuquerque, Ulysses Paulino, Júlio Marcelino Monteiro, Marcelo Alves Ramos, and Elba Lúcia Cavalcanti de Amorim. 2007. "Medicinal and Magic Plants from a Public Market in Northeastern Brazil." *Journal of Ethnopharmacology* 110.1:76–91.

Almeida, Alex-Alan F., and Raúl R. Valle. 2007. "Ecophysiology of the Cacao Tree." *Brazilian Journal of Plant Physiology* 19.4:425–448.

Andrade, Angela. 1986. *Investigación arqueológica de los antrosoles de Araracuara*. Fundación de Investigaciones Arqueológicas Nacionales 31. Bogota: Banco de la República.

Aramburu, Mikel. 1994. "Aviamento, modernidade e pos-modernidade no Interior Amazônico." *Revista Brasileira de Ciências Sociais* 9.25:82–99.

Arroyo-Kalin, Manuel. 2008. "Steps Towards an Ecology of Landscape: A Geoarchaeological Approach to the Study of Anthropogenic Dark Earths in the Central Amazon Region." PhD thesis, University of Cambridge.

———. 2010. "The Amazonian Formative: Crop Domestication and Anthropogenic Soils." *Diversity* 2.4:473–504.

Autin, Whitney J., and John M. Holbrook. 2012. "Is the Anthropocene an Issue of Stratigraphy or Pop Culture?" *GSA Today* 22.7:60–61.

Balée, William L. 1989. "The Culture of Amazonian Forests." In *Resource Management in Amazonia: Indigenous and Folk Strategies*, ed. William L. Balée and Darrell A. Posey, 1–21. Bronx: New York Botanical Garden.

———. 1994. *Footprints of the Forest: Ka'apor Ethnobotany—the Historical Ecology of Plant Utilization by an Amazonian People*. New York: Columbia University Press.

———. 1998. "Historical Ecology: Premises and Postulates." In *Advances in Historical Ecology*, ed. William L. Balée. New York: Columbia University Press.

———. 2006. "The Research Program of Historical Ecology." *Annual Review of Anthropology* 35:75–98.

Balée, William L., and Clark L. Erickson, eds. 2006. *Time and Complexity in Historical Ecology: Studies in the Neotropical Lowlands*. New York: Columbia University Press.

Balée, William, Denise P. Schaan, James Andrew Whitaker, and Rosângela Holanda. 2014. "Florestas antrópicas no Acre: Inventário florestal no geoglifo três vertentes, Acrelândia." *Amazônica: Revista de Antropologia* 6.1:140–169.

Barlow, Jos, Toby A. Gardner, Alexander C. Lees, Luke Parry, and Carlos A. Peres. 2012. "How Pristine Are Tropical Forests? An Ecological Perspective on the Pre-Columbian Human Footprint in Amazonia and Implications for Contemporary Conservation." *Biological Conservation* 151.1:45–49.

Barnes, Byron A., and Lauretta E. Fox. 1955. "Poisoning with Dieffenbachia." *Journal of the History of Medicine and Allied Sciences* 10.2:173–181.

Barr, Juliana. 2011. "Geographies of Power: Mapping Indian Borders in the 'Borderlands' of the Early Southwest." *William and Mary Quarterly* 68.1:5–46.

Barreto, Cristiana, and Juliana Machado. 2001. "Exploring the Amazon, Explaining the Unknown: Views from the Past." In *Unknown Amazon: Culture in Nature in Ancient Brazil*, ed. Colin McEwan, Cristiana Barreto, and Eduardo Neves, 232–251. London: British Museum Press.

Bates, Henry Walter. 1863. *The Naturalist on the River Amazons*. London: John Murray.

Bebawi, Faiz F., and Shane D. Campbell. 2002. "Impact of Fire on Bellyache Bush (*Jatropha gossypifolia*): Plant Mortality and Seedling Recruitment." *Tropical Grasslands* 36.3:129–137.

Berlin, Brent. 1992. *Ethnobiological Classification: Principles of Categorization of Plants and Animals in Traditional Societies*. Princeton, NJ: Princeton University Press.

Berry, Thomas. 2009. *The Sacred Universe: Earth, Spirituality, and Religion in the Twenty-first Century*. New York: Columbia University Press.

Binns, Corey. 2006. "Scientists Promote Benefits of 'Black Magic' Soil." Foxnews.com. Accessed Feb. 22, 2007.

Birk, Jago Jonathan, Wenceslau Geraldes Teixeira, Eduardo Góes Neves, and Bruno Glaser. 2011. "Faeces Deposition on Amazonian Anthrosols as Assessed from 5β-stanols." *Journal of Archaeological Science* 38.6: 1209–1220.

Blank, Les, dir. 1982. *Burden of Dreams*. 94 min. Flower Films. El Cerrito, CA.

Bodley, John H. 2012. *Anthropology and Contemporary Human Problems*. 6th ed. Lanham, MD: Altamira.

Bourdieu, Pierre. 1977. *Outline of a Theory of Practice*. Cambridge: Cambridge University Press.

Boyer, Véronique. 1999. "O pajé e o caboclo: De homem a entidade." *Mana* 5.1:29–56.

Brice, William M., and Silvia F. de M. Figueiroa. 2003. "Rock Stars: Charles Frederick Hartt—Pioneer of Brazilian Geology." *GSA Today* 13.3:18–19.

Brondizio, Eduardo S. 2004. "Agriculture Intensification, Economic Identity, and Shared Invisibility in Amazonian Peasantry: Caboclos and Colonists in Comparative Perspective." *Culture and Agriculture* 26.1–2:1–24.

Brown, Charles Barrington, and William Lidstone. 1878. *Fifteen Thousand Miles on the Amazon and Its Tributaries*. London: Edward Stafford.

Buarque de Holanda Ferreira, Aurélio, ed. 1971. *Novo dicionário da língua portuguesa*. Rio de Janeiro: Nova Fronteira.

Bush, Mark R., and Miles R. Silman. 2009. "Amazonian Exploitation Revisited: Ecological Asymmetry and the Policy Pendulum." *Frontiers in Ecology and the Environment* 5.9:457–465.

Camargo, Felisberto. 1941. *Estudo de alguns perfis do solos coletados em diversas regiões da Hiléia*. Belém: Instituto Agronômico do Norte.

Candea, Matei. 2010. "'I Fell in Love with Carlos the Meerkat': Engagement and Detachment in Human–Animal Relations." *American Ethnologist* 37.2:241–258.

———. 2013. "Suspending Belief: Epoché in Animal Behavior Science." *American Anthropologist* 115.3:423–436.

Carvajal, Gaspar de. 1894. *Descubrimiento del Río de las Amazonas*. Sevilla: E. Rasco.

Cavalcante, Paulo B. 1991. *Frutas comestíveis da Amazônia*. 5th ed. Belém: CEJUP.

Certini, Giacomo, and Riccardo Scalenghe. 2011. "Anthropogenic Soils Are the Golden Spikes of the Anthropocene." *The Holocene* 21.8:1269–1274.

Chakrabarty, Dipesh. 2009. "The Climate of History: Four Theses." *Critical Inquiry* 35:197–222.

Chernela, Janet, and Patrícia Pinho. 2004. "Constructing a Supernatural Landscape through Talk: Creation and Recreation in Central Amazon of Brazil." *Journal of Latin American Lore* 22.1:83–106.

Chibnik, Michael. 1991. "Quasi-Ethnic Groups in Amazonia." *Ethnology* 30.2:167–182.

———. 1994. *Risky Rivers: The Economics and Politics of Floodplain Farming in Amazonia.* Tucson: University of Arizona Press.

Childs, Craig. 2012. *Apocalyptic Planet: Field Guide to the Everending Earth.* New York: Pantheon.

Clark, Nigel. 2011. *Inhuman Nature: Sociable Life on a Dynamic Planet.* London: Sage.

Clement, Charles R. 1988. "Domestication of the Pejibaye Palm (*Bactris gasipaes*): Past and Present." In *The Palm-Tree of Life: Biology, Utilization, and Conservation,* ed. Michael J. Balick, 155–174. Advances in Economic Botany 6. Bronx: New York Botanical Garden.

———. 1999. "1492 and the Loss of Amazonian Crop Diversity, I: The Relation between Domestication and Human Population Decline." *Economic Botany* 53:12–25.

———. 2011. Review of "The Biochar Solution: Carbon Farming and Climate Change." *BioScience* 61.10:831–833.

Clendenning, Alan. 2009. "Amazon Hit by Climate Chaos of Floods, Drought." *USA Today.* Accessed Nov. 16, 2013. http://usatoday30.usa today.com/weather/2009-05-25-amazon-drought-and-floods_N.htm.

Clifford, James. 1988. *The Predicament of Culture: Twentieth-Century Ethnography, Literature, and Art.* Cambridge, MA: Harvard University Press.

Clifford, James, and George E. Marcus, eds. 1986. *Writing Culture: The Poetics and Politics of Ethnography.* Berkeley: University of California Press.

Comissão de Estudos da Estrada de Ferro do Madeira e Mamoré. 1885. *Do Rio de Janeiro ao Amazonas e alto Madeira.* Rio de Janeiro: Soares e Niemeyer.

Conklin, Beth A., and Laura R. Graham. 1995. "The Shifting Middle Ground: Amazonian Indians and Eco-Politics." *American Anthropologist* 97.4:695–710.

Costa Pereira, José V. 1975. "Caboclo amazonico." In *Tipos and aspectos do Brasil,* 12–15. Rio de Janeiro: IBGE.

Crist, Eileen. 2013. "On the Poverty of Our Nomenclature." *Environmental Humanities* 3:129–147.

Crosby, Alfred W. 1986. *Ecological Imperialism: The Biological Expansion of Europe, 900–1900.* Cambridge: Cambridge University Press.

———. 2003 [1972]. *The Columbian Exchange: Biological and Cultural Consequences of 1492.* Westport, CT: Greenwood.

Crutzen, Paul J. 2002. "The Geology of Mankind." *Nature* 415:23.

Crutzen, Paul J., and Will Steffen. 2003. "How Long Have We Been in the Anthropocene Era?" *Climatic Change* 61.3:251–257.

Crutzen, Paul J., and Eugene F. Stoermer. 2000. "The 'Anthropocene.'" *Global Change Newsletter* 41:12–13.

Cunha Franco, E. 1962. "As 'terras pretas' do planalto de Santarém." *Revista da Sociedade dos Agrônomos e Veterinários do Pará* 8:17–21.

da Costa, Marcondes Lima, and Dirse Clara Kern. 1999. "Geochemical Signatures of Tropical Soils with Archaeological Black Earth in the Amazon." *Journal of Geochemical Exploration* 66:369–385.

da Cunha, Euclides. 2003. *Amazônia: Um paraíso perdido*. Manaus: Valer.

da Silva, Luiz Osiris. 1962. *A luta pela Amazônia*. São Paulo: Fulgor.

Davidson, David M. 1970. "Rivers and Empire: The Madeira Route and the Incorporation of the Brazilian Far West, 1737–1808." PhD diss., Yale University.

Dawsey, Cyrus B., and James M. Dawsey. 1995. "Leaving: The Context of Southern Emigration to Brazil." In *The Confederados: Old South Immigrants in Brazil*, ed. Cyrus B. Dawsey and James M. Dawsey, 11–23. Tuscaloosa: University of Alabama Press.

Dean, Jonathan R., Melanie J. Leng, and Anson W. Mackay. 2014. "Is There an Isotopic Signature of the Anthropocene?" *Anthropocene Review* 1–12. doi:10.1177/2053019614541631.

Dean, Warren. 1984. *Brazil and the Struggle for Rubber: A Study in Environmental History*. Cambridge: Cambridge University Press.

de Faria, João Barbosa. 1944. "A cerâmica da tribo Uaboí dos rios Trombetas e Jamundá: Contribuição para o estudo da arqueologia pré-historica do Baixo Amazonas." In *Anais III, 9º Congresso Brasileiro de Geografía, Rio de Janeiro*, 3:141–165. Rio de Janeiro: Conselho Nacional Brasileiro de Geografia.

Deleuze, Gilles, and Felix Guattari. 1987. *A Thousand Plateaus: Capitalism and Schizophrenia*. Trans. Brian Massumi. Minneapolis: University of Minnesota Press.

de Melo, Maria Mitouso. 1983. *Um pouco da minha vida*. Rio de Janeiro: Civilização Brasileira.

Denevan, William M. 1992a. "The Aboriginal Population of Amazonia." In *The Native Population of the Americas in 1492*, ed. William M. Denevan, 205–231. Madison: University of Wisconsin Press.

———. 1992b. "The Pristine Myth: The Landscape of the Americas in 1492." *Annals of the Association of American Geographers* 82.3:369–385.

de Oliveira, Jefferson S., Polyanna M. Leite, Lincoln B. de Souza, Vinícius M. Mello, Eid C. Silva, Joel C. Rubim, Simoni M. P. Meneghetti, and Paulo A. Z. Suarez. 2009. "Characteristics and Composition of *Jatropha gossypifolia* and *Jatropha curcas* L. Oils and Application for Biodiesel Production." *Biomass and Bioenergy* 33.3:449–453.

Descola, Philippe. 1996. *In the Society of Nature: A Native Ecology in Amazonia*. Cambridge: Cambridge University Press.

———. 2013. *Beyond Nature and Culture*. Chicago: University of Chicago Press.

Desmarchelier, Cristian, Alberto Gurni, Graciela Ciccia, and Ana M. Giuletti. 1996. "Ritual and Medicinal Plants of the Ese'ejas of the Amazonian Rainforest (Madre de Dios, Peru)." *Journal of Ethnopharmacology* 52.1:45–51.

Dirzo, Rodolfo, and Peter H. Raven. 2003. "Global State of Biodiversity and Loss." *Annual Review of Environment and Resources* 28.1:137–167.

Di Stasi, Luiz Claudio, and Clélia Akiko Hiruma-Lima. 2002. *Plantas medicinais na Amazônia e na Mata Atlântica.* São Paulo: UNESP.

Dufour, Darna. 1993. "The Bitter Is Sweet: A Case Study of Bitter Cassava (*Manihot esculenta*) Use in Amazonia." In *Tropical Forests, People, and Food: Biocultural Interactions and Applications to Development,* ed. Claude Marcel Hladik, Annette Hladik, Olga F. Linares, Hélène Pagezy, Alison Semple, and Malcolm Hadley, 575–588. Man and the Biosphere Series 13. Paris: UNESCO.

Duke, James A. 2008. *Duke's Handbook of Medicinal Plants of Latin America.* Boca Raton, FL: CRC.

Dundes, Alan. 1992. "Wet and Dry, the Evil Eye: An Essay in Indo-European and Semitic Worldview." In *The Evil Eye: A Folklore Casebook,* ed. Alan Dundes, 257–312. Madison: University of Wisconsin Press.

Dunn, Rob. 2011. *The Wild Life of Our Bodies: Predators, Parasites, and Partners That Shape Who We Are Today.* New York: Harper.

Eddleston, Michael, Christeine A. Ariaratnam, W. P. Meyer, G. Perera, Sithara A. M. Kularatne, S. Attapattu, M. H. Rezvi Sheriff, and David A. Warrell. 1999. "Epidemic of Self-Poisoning with Seeds of the Yellow Oleander Tree (*Thevetia peruviana*) in Northern Sri Lanka." *Tropical Medicine and International Health* 4.4:266–273.

Elias, Marianne, Laura Rival, and Doyle McKey. 2000. "Perception and Management of Cassava (*Manihot esculenta*) Diversity among Makushi Amerindians of Guyana (South America)." *Journal of Ethnobiology* 20.2: 239–265.

Ellis, Erle. 2010. "Anthropogenic Transformation of the Terrestrial Biosphere." *Philosophical Transactions of the Royal Society A: Mathematical, Physical, and Engineering Sciences* 369.1938:1010–1035.

Emperaire, Laure, and Nivaldo Peroni. 2007. "Traditional Management of Agrobiodiversity in Brazil: A Case Study of Manioc." *Human Ecology* 35.6:761–768.

Erickson, Clark L. 2005. "The Domesticated Landscapes of the Bolivian Amazon." In *Time and Complexity in Historical Ecology: Studies in the Neotropical Lowlands,* ed. William L. Balee and Clark L. Erickson, 235–278. New York: Columbia University Press.

Evans-Pritchard, E. E. 1958 [1937]. *Witchcraft, Oracles, and Magic among the Azande.* London: Oxford University Press.

Fairhead, James, and Melissa Leach. 1996. *Misreading the African Landscape: Society and Ecology in a Forest Savanna Mosaic.* Cambridge: Cambridge University Press.

Falesi, Ítalo C. 1974. "Soils of the Brazilian Amazon." In *Man in the Amazon*, ed. Charles Wagley, 201–229. Gainesville: University of Florida Press.

FAO (Food and Agriculture Organization of the United Nations). 1998. *World Reference Base for Soil Resources.* Rome: Food and Agriculture Organization of the United Nations.

———. 1999. "Women: Users, Preservers, and Managers of Agrobiodiversity." Accessed Nov. 7, 2008. http://www.fao.org/sd/nrm/Women%20-%20Users.pdf.

———. 2004. *Carbon Sequestration in Dryland Soils.* Rome: FAO Publishing Management Service.

Farabee, William C. 1921. "Exploration at the Mouth of the Amazon." *Museum Journal* 12.3:142.

Fargione, Joseph E., Richard J. Plevin, and Jason D. Hill. 2010. "The Ecological Impact of Biofuels." *Annual Review of Ecology, Evolution, and Systematics* 41:351–377.

Fearnside, Philip M. 1982. "Deforestation in the Brazilian Amazon: How Fast Is It Occurring?" *Interciência* 7.2:82–85.

Félix-Silva, Juliana, Raquel Brandt Giordani, Arnóbio Antonio da Silva Jr., Silvana Maria Zucolotto, and Matheus de Freitas Fernandes-Pedrosa. 2014. "*Jatropha gossypiifolia* L. (Euphorbiaceae): A Review of Traditional Uses, Phytochemistry, Pharmacology, and Toxicology of This Medicinal Plant." *Evidence-Based Complementary and Alternative Medicine*, article ID 369204. http://dx.doi.org/10.1155/2014/369204.

Ferreira Reis, Arthur Cézar. 1960. *A Amazônia e a cobiça internacional.* Rio de Janeiro: Edinova.

Foster, George M. 1972. "The Anatomy of Envy: A Study in Symbolic Behavior." *Current Anthropology* 13.2:165–202.

Franklin, Adrian. 2008. "A Choreography of Fire: Posthumanist Account of Australians and Eucalypts." In *The Mangle in Practice: Science, Society, and Becoming*, ed. Andrew Pickering and Keith Guzik, 17–27. Durham, NC: Duke University Press.

Fraser, James A. 2010. "Caboclo Horticulture and Amazonian Dark Earths along the Middle Madeira River, Brazil." *Human Ecology* 38.5:651–662.

Fraser, James A., Alessandro Alves-Pereira, André B. Junqueira, Nivaldo Peroni, and Charles R. Clement. 2012. "Convergent Adaptations: Bitter Manioc Cultivation Systems in Fertile Anthropogenic Dark Earths and Floodplain Soils in Central Amazonia." *PLoS One* 7.8:e43636. doi:10.1371/journal.pone.0043636.

Fraser, James A., Thiago Cardoso, André B. Junqueira, Newton P. S. Falcao, and Charles R. Clement. 2009. "Historical Ecology and Dark Earths in Whitewater and Blackwater Landscapes: Comparing the Middle Madeira and Lower Negro Rivers." In Woods et al. 2009, 229–261.

Fraser, James A., André B. Junqueira, Nicholas C. Kawa, Claide P. Moraes, and Charles R. Clement. 2011. "Crop Diversity on Anthropogenic Dark Earths in Central Amazonia." *Human Ecology* 39.4:395–406.

Fraxe, Therezinha J. P. 2004. *Cultura cabocla-ribeirinha: Mitos, lendas e transculturalidade*. São Paulo: Annablume.

Frazer, James G. 2009 [1922]. *The Golden Bough: A Study of Magic and Religion*. New York: Cosimo.

Garfield, Seth. 2013. *In Search of the Amazon: Brazil, the United States, and the Nature of a Region*. Durham, NC: Duke University Press.

Geertz, Clifford. 1973. *The Interpretation of Cultures: Selected Essays*. New York: Basic Books.

———. 1988. *Works and Lives: The Anthropologist as Author*. Stanford, CA: Stanford University Press.

Geraque, Eduardo, and Marco Aurelio Canônico. 2006. "Governo do Reino Unido nega 'privatização' da Amazônia." *Folha de São Paulo Online*, Oct. 4. http://www1.folha.uol.com.br/folha/ciencia/ult306u15292.shtml.

German, Laura A. 2001. "The Dynamics of Terra Preta: An Integrated Study of Human–Environmental Interactions in a Nutrient-Poor Amazonian Ecosystem." PhD diss., University of Georgia.

———. 2003. "Ethnoscientific Understandings of Amazonian Dark Earths." In *Amazonian Dark Earths: Origin, Properties, Management*, ed. Johannes Lehman, Dirse C. Kern, Bruno Glaser, and William I. Woods, 179–201. Dordrecht, Netherlands: Kluwer.

Ghosh, Amitav. 2000. *The Hungry Tide*. New York: Houghton Mifflin.

Giobbi, César. 2000. "Equanto é tempo." *O Estado de São Paulo*. www.estadao.com.br. Accessed May 24, 2006.

Glaser, Bruno, Georg Guggenberger, Wolfgang Zech, and Maria de Lourdes Ruivo. 2003. "Soil Organic Matter Stability in Amazonian Dark Earths." In *Amazonian Dark Earths: Origin, Properties, Management*, ed. Johannes Lehmann, Dirse C. Kern, Bruno Glaser, and William I. Woods, 141–158. Dordrecht, Netherlands: Kluwer.

Glaser, Bruno, Ludwig Haumaier, Georg Guggenberger, and Wolfgang Zech. 2001. "The 'Terra Preta' Phenomenon: A Model for Sustainable Agriculture in the Humid Tropics." *Naturwissenschaften* 88.1:37–41.

Glaser, Bruno, Johannes Lehmann, and Wolfgang Zech. 2002. "Ameliorating Physical and Chemical Properties of Highly Weathered Soils in the Tropics with Charcoal." *Biology and Fertility of Soils* 35.4:219–230.

Glaser, Bruno, and William I. Woods, eds. 2004. *Amazonian Dark Earths: Explorations in Space and Time*. Berlin: Springer.

Goodland, Robert J. A., and Howard S. Irwin. 1975. *Amazon Jungle: Green*

Hell to Red Desert? An Ecological Discussion of the Environmental Impact of the Highway Construction Program in the Amazon Basin. New York: Elselvier Scientific.

Graeber, David. 2010. "Endorsements for HAU: The Journal of Ethnographic Theory." Accessed Feb. 29, 2010. http://www.haujournal.org/index.php /hau/pages/view/endorsements.

Grandin, Greg. 2009. *Fordlandia: The Rise and Fall of Henry Ford's Forgotten Jungle City.* New York: Macmillan.

Grandtner, Miroslav M., and Julien Chevrette. 2013. *Dictionary of Trees,* vol. 2: *South America: Nomenclature, Taxonomy, and Ecology.* London: Academic Press.

Green, Rhys E., Stephen J. Cornell, Jörn P. W. Scharlemann, and Andrew Balmford. 2005. "Farming and the Fate of Wild Nature." *Science* 307 (5709): 550–555.

Greene, L. Shane. 2009. *Customizing Indigeneity: Paths to Visionary Politics in Peru.* Palo Alto, CA: Stanford University Press.

Griggs, William Clark. 1987. *The Elusive Eden: Frank McMullan's Confederate Colony in Brazil.* Austin: University of Texas Press.

Groom, Martha J., Elizabeth M. Gray, and Patricia A. Townsend. 2008. "Biofuels and Biodiversity: Principles for Creating Better Policies for Biofuel Production." *Conservation Biology* 22.3:602–609.

Grossman, Julie M., Brendan E. O'Neill, Siu Mui Tsai, Biqing Liang, Eduardo Neves, Johannes Lehmann, and Janice E. Thies. 2010. "Amazonian Anthrosols Support Similar Microbial Communities That Differ Distinctly from Those Extant in Adjacent, Unmodified Soils of the Same Mineralogy." *Microbial Ecology* 60.1:192–205.

Grove, Richard H. 1996. *Green Imperialism: Colonial Expansion, Tropical Island Edens, and the Origins of Environmentalism, 1600–1860.* Cambridge: Cambridge University Press.

Guapindaia, Vera. 2008. "Prehistoric Funeral Practices in the Brazilian Amazon: The Maracá Urns." In Silverman and Isbell 2008, 1005–1026.

Guedes, Aureliano Pinto de Lima. 1897. "Relatório sobre uma Missão Ethnographica e Archeologica aos Rios Maracá e Anauerá-Pucú (Guyana Brazileira)." *Boletim do Museu Paraense de História Natural e Etnografia, Belém* 2.1:42–64.

Guerreiro, Ana Felisa Hurtado, and José Camil Hurtado Guerreiro. 2003. *Tradições orais de Nova Olinda do Norte.* Manaus: Valer.

Gussi, Alcides Fernando. 1997. *Os norte-americanos (confederados) do Brasil: Identidades no contexto transnacional.* Campinas: Centro de Memória–Unicamp.

Guzmán, Tracy Devine. 2010. "Our Indians in Our America: Anti-Imperialist Imperialism and the Construction of Brazilian Modernity." *Latin American Research Review* 45.3:35–62.

Haraway, Donna J. 2003. *The Companion Species Manifesto: Dogs, People, and Significant Otherness*. Chicago: Prickly Paradigm.

———. 2008. *When Species Meet*. Minneapolis: University of Minnesota Press.

Hardwick, Lorna. 1990. "Ancient Amazons: Heroes, Outsiders, or Women?" *Greece and Rome* 37.1:14–36.

Harman, Graham. 2009. *Prince of Networks: Bruno Latour and Metaphysics*. Melbourne: Re.press.

Harris, Mark. 1998. "'What It Means to Be a Caboclo': Some Critical Notes on the Construction of Amazonian Caboclo as an Anthropological Object." *Critique of Anthropology* 18.1:83–95.

———. 2000. *Life on the Amazon: Anthropology of a Brazilian Peasant Village*. London: British Academy.

———. 2010. *Rebellion on the Amazon: The Cabanagem, Race, and Popular Culture in the North of Brazil, 1798–1840*. Cambridge: Cambridge University Press.

———. 2011. "The Enchantments of Food in the Lower Amazon, Brazil." In *Food: Ethnographic Encounters*, ed. Leo Coleman, 39–48. London: Berg.

Harter, Eugene C. 1985. *The Lost Colony of the Confederacy*. Jackson: University Press of Mississippi.

Hartt, Charles F. 1873. *Notes on the Manufacture of Pottery among Savage Races*. Rio de Janeiro: Offices of the South American Mail.

———. 1874. "Preliminary Report of the Morgan Exhibitions, 1870–71—Report of a Reconnaissance of the Lower Tapajós." *Bulletin of the Cornell University (Science)*, 1:1–37.

———. 1885. "Contribuições para a ethnologia do valle do Amazonas." *Archivos do Museu Nacional do Rio de Janeiro* 6:1–174.

Hecht, Susanna B. 2013. *The Scramble for the Amazon and the "Lost Paradise" of Euclides da Cunha*. Chicago: University of Chicago Press.

Hecht, Susanna, and Alexander Cockburn. 1989. *The Fate of the Forest: Developers, Destroyers, and Defenders of the Amazon*. New York: Verso.

Heckenberger, Michael J., James B. Petersen, and Eduardo G. Neves. 1999. "Village Size and Permanence in Amazonia: Two Archaeological Examples from Brazil." *Latin American Antiquity* 10.4:353–376.

Heckenberger, Michael J., J. Christian Russell, Carlos Fausto, Joshua R. Toney, Morgan J. Schmidt, Edithe Pereira, Bruna Franchetto, and Afukaka Kuikuro. 2008. "Pre-Columbian Urbanism, Anthropogenic Landscapes, and the Future of the Amazon." *Science* 321 (5893): 1214–1217.

Heckenberger, Michael J., J. Christian Russell, Joshua R. Toney, and Morgan J. Schmidt. 2007. "The Legacy of Cultural Landscapes in the Brazilian Amazon." *Philosophical Transactions of the Royal Society B* 362 (1478): 197–208.

Heckler, Serena. 2004. "Tedium and Creativity: The Valorization of Manioc Cultivation and Piaroa Women." *Journal of the Royal Anthropological Institute* 10.2:243–259.

Heckler, Serena, and Stanford Zent. 2008. "Piaroa Manioc Varietals: Hyperdiversity or Social Currency?" *Human Ecology* 36.6:679–697.

Hemming, John. 2008. *Tree of Rivers: The Story of the Amazon*. New York: Thames and Hudson.

Hennessey, Patrick. 2006. "Miliband Promotes Plan to Buy Rainforests." *Daily Telegraph*. Accessed Oct. 1, 2008. http://www.telegraph.co.uk/news /uknews/1530220/Miliband-promotes-plan-to-buy-rainforests.html.

Herrera, Leonor F. 1981. "Relaciones entre ocupaciones préhispánicas y suelos negros en la cuenca del Rio Caquetá en Colombia." *Revista CIAF* 6: 225–242.

Hilbert, Peter Paul. 1968. *Archäologische Untersuchungen am mittleren Amazonas: Beiträge zur Vorgeschichte des südamerikanischen Tieflandes*. Berlin: Reimer.

IBGE (Instituto Brasileiro de Geografia e Estatística). 2010. "Censo demográfico 2010." Rio de Janeiro: IBGE. Accessed June 29, 2013. http://www .ibge.gov.br/home/estatistica/populacao/censo2010.

Ioris, Edviges M. 2005. "A Forest of Disputes: Struggles over Spaces, Resources, and Social Identities in Amazonia." PhD diss., University of Florida.

Jackson, Wes. 2010. *Consulting the Genius of the Place: An Ecological Approach to a New Agriculture*. Berkeley: Counterpoint Press.

Jannsen, Raymond E. 1941. "Living Guide-Posts of the Past." *Scientific Monthly* 53.1:22–29.

Jeffery, Simon, Frank G. A. Verheijen, Martijn Van Der Velde, and Ana Catarina Bastos. 2011. "A Quantitative Review of the Effects of Biochar Application to Soils on Crop Productivity Using Meta-analysis." *Agriculture, Ecosystems, and Environment* 144.1:175–187.

Jordan, Elaine. 1997. *Indian Trail Trees*. Ellijay, GA: Jordan Ink.

Junk, Wolfgang J. 2001. "Appraisal of the Scientific Work of Harald Sioli." *Amazoniana* 16:285–297.

Junqueira, André B., Glenn J. Shepherd, and Charles R. Clement. 2010. "Secondary Forests on Anthropogenic Soils in Brazilian Amazon Conserve Agrobiodiversity." *Biodiversity Conservation* 19:1933–1961.

Kawa, Nicholas C. 2008. "Use and Management of Amazonian Dark Earth in Borba, Amazonas, Brazil." MA thesis, University of Florida.

———. 2011. "The Social Nature of Agrobiodiversity." PhD diss., University of Florida.

———. 2012. "Magic Plants of Amazonia and Their Contribution to Agrobiodiversity." *Human Organization* 71.3:225–233.

Kawa, Nicholas C., Christopher McCarty, and Charles R. Clement. 2013. "Manioc Varietal Diversity, Social Networks, and Distribution Constraints in Rural Amazonia." *Current Anthropology* 54.6:764–770.

Kawa, Nicholas C., and Augusto Oyuela-Caycedo. 2008. "Amazonian Dark Earth: A Model of Sustainable Agriculture of the Past and Future?" *International Journal of Environmental, Cultural, Economic, and Social Sustainability* 4.3:9–16.

Kawa, Nicholas C., Daniel Rodrigues, and Charles R. Clement. 2011. "Useful Species Richness, Proportion of Exotic Species, and Market Orientation on Amazonian Dark Earths and Oxisols." *Economic Botany* 65.2:169–177.

Keller, Franz. 1875. *The Amazon and Madeira Rivers*. London: Chapman and Hall.

Kelly, John D. 2014. "Introduction: The Ontological Turn in French Philosophical Anthropology." *HAU: Journal of Ethnographic Theory* 4.1: 259–269.

Kenny, Michael G. 2002. "A Darker Shade of Green: Medical Botany, Homeopathy, and Cultural Politics in Interwar Germany." *Social History of Medicine* 15.3:481–504.

Kim, Jong-Shik, Gerd Sparovek, Regina M. Longo, Wanderley Jose De Melo, and David Crowley. 2007. "Bacterial Diversity of Terra Preta and Pristine Forest Soil from the Western Amazon." *Soil Biology and Biochemistry* 39.2:684–690.

Kirksey, S. Eben, and Stefan Helmreich. 2010. "The Emergence of Multispecies Ethnography." *Cultural Anthropology* 25.4:545–576.

Kohn, Eduardo. 2007. "How Dogs Dream: Amazonian Natures and the Politics of Transspecies Engagement." *American Ethnologist* 34.1:3–24.

———. 2009. "A Conversation with Philippe Descola." *Tipití: Journal of the Society for the Anthropology of Lowland South America* 7.2:1.

———. 2013. *How Forests Think: Toward an Anthropology Beyond the Human*. Berkeley: University of California Press.

Kookana, Rai S., Ajit K. Sarmah, Lukas Van Zwieten, Evelyn Krull, and Balwant Singh. 2011. "Biochar Application to Soil: Agronomic and Environmental Benefits and Unintended Consequences." *Advances in Agronomy* 112:103–143.

Krulwich, Robert. 2012. "Cornstalks Everywhere but Nothing Else, Not Even a Bee." Accessed Nov. 15, 2012. http://www.npr.org/blogs/krulwich/2012/11/29/166156242/cornstalks-everywhere-but-nothing-else-not-even-a-bee.

Kurzweil, Ray. 2005. *The Singularity Is Near: When Humans Transcend Biology*. New York: Penguin.

Lal, Rattan. 2004a. "Soil Carbon Sequestration to Mitigate Climate Change." *Geoderma* 123.1–2:1–22.

———. 2004b. "Soil Carbon Sequestration Impacts on Global Climate Change and Food Security." *Science* 304 (5677): 1623–1627.

Latour, Bruno. 1993. *We Have Never Been Modern.* Cambridge, MA: Harvard University Press.

———. 1999. *Pandora's Hope: Essays on the Reality of Science Studies.* Cambridge, MA: Harvard University Press.

———. 2006. *The Politics of Nature: How to Bring the Sciences into Democracy.* Cambridge, MA: Harvard University Press.

———. 2007. *Reassembling the Social: An Introduction to Actor-Network-Theory.* New York: Oxford University Press.

———. 2012. "Waiting for Gaia: Composing the Common World through Arts and Politics." *Equilibri* 16.3:515–538.

———. 2014. "Another Way to Compose the Common World." *HAU: Journal of Ethnographic Theory* 4.1:301–307.

Leach, Melissa, James Fairhead, and James Fraser. 2012. "Green Grabs and Biochar: Revaluing African Soils and Farming in the New Carbon Economy." *Journal of Peasant Studies* 39.2:285–307.

Lehmann, Johannes, John Gaunt, and Marco Rondon. 2006. "Bio-char Sequestration in Terrestrial Ecosystems—A Review." *Mitigation and Adaptation Strategies for Global Change* 11:403–427.

Lehmann, Johannes, Dirse C. Kern, Bruno Glaser, and William I. Woods, eds. 2003. *Amazonian Dark Earths: Origin, Properties, Management.* Dordrecht: Kluwer.

Lehmann, Johannes, José Pereira da Silva Jr., Marco Rondon, Manoel da Silva Cravo, Jacqueline Greenwood, Thomas Nehls, Christoph Steiner, and Bruno Glaser. 2002. "Slash-and-Char: A Feasible Alternative for Soil Fertility Management in the Central Amazon?" In *Symposium 13: Organic Matter Management in the Humid Tropics,* ed. Bernard Vanlauwe. 17th World Congress of Soil Science, paper no. 449. Bangkok, Thailand. CD-ROM.

Lehmann, Johannes, José Pereira da Silva Jr., Christoph Steiner, Thomas Nehls, Wolfgang Zech, and Bruno Glaser. 2003. "Nutrient Availability and Leaching in an Archaeological Anthrosol and a Ferralsol of the Central Amazon Basin: Fertilizer, Manure, and Charcoal Amendments." *Plant and Soil* 249.2:343–357.

Leite, Serafim. 1943. *História da Companhia de Jesus no Brasil,* vol. 3. Rio de Janeiro: Instituto Nacional do Livro.

Levis, Carolina, Priscila Figueira de Souza, Juliana Schietti, Thaise Emilio, José Luiz Purri da Veiga Pinto, Charles R. Clement, and Flavia R. C. Costa. 2012. "Historical Human Footprint on Modern Tree Species Composition in the Purus–Madeira Interfluve, Central Amazonia." *PloS One* 7.11:e48559.

Lévi-Strauss, Claude. 1966. *The Savage Mind*. Chicago: University of Chicago Press.

Liittschwager, David. 2012. *A World in One Cubic Foot: Portraits of Biodiversity*. Chicago: University of Chicago Press.

Lima, Deborah de Magalhães. 1999. "A construção histórica do termo caboclo: Sobre estruturas e representações sociais no meio rural amazônico." *Novos Cadernos NAEA* 2.2:5–32.

Lima, Deborah, Angela Steward, and Bárbara T. Richers. 2012. "Trocas, experimentações e preferências: Um estudo sobre a dinâmica da diversidade da mandioca no médio Solimões, Amazonas." *Boletim do Museu Paraense Emílio Goeldi* 7.2:371–396.

Little, Paul E. 2001. *Amazonia: Territorial Struggles on Perennial Frontiers*. Baltimore, MD: Johns Hopkins University Press.

Lykiardopoulos, Amica. 1981. "The Evil Eye: Towards an Exhaustive Study." *Folklore* 92.2:221–230.

Macia, Manuel J., Emilia Garcia, and Prem Jai Vaiduarre. 2005. "An Ethnobotanical Survey of Medicinal Plants Commercialized in the Markets of La Paz and El Alto, Bolivia." *Journal of Ethnopharmacology* 97.2:337–350.

Major, Julie, Charles R. Clement, and Antonio DiTommaso. 2005. "Influence of Market Orientation on Food Plant Diversity of Farms Located on Amazonian Dark Earth in the Region of Manaus, Amazonas, Brazil." *Economic Botany* 59.1:77–86.

Mann, Charles C. 2002. "The Real Dirt on Rainforest Fertility." *Science* 297: 920–922.

———. 2011. *1493: Uncovering the New World Columbus Created*. New York: Vintage.

Marcoy, Paul. 2001. *Viagem pelo Rio Amazonas*. Manaus: Editora da Universidade do Amazonas.

Marris, Emma. 2006. "Putting the Carbon Back: Black Is the New Green." *Nature* 442:624–626.

Matthews, Duncan. 2011. *Intellectual Property, Human Rights, and Development: The Role of NGOs and Social Movements*. Northampton, MA: Edward Elgar.

Mauss, Marcel. 1979 [1935]. "Techniques of the Body." In *Sociology and Psychology: Essays*, 95–123. London: Routledge and Kegan Paul.

McHenry, Mark P. 2009. "Agricultural Bio-char Production, Renewable Energy Generation, and Farm Carbon Sequestration in Western Australia: Certainty, Uncertainty, and Risk." *Agriculture, Ecosystems, and Environment* 129.1–3:1–7.

McKenna, Dennis J., Luis Eduardo Luna, and G. H. Neil Towers. 1995. "Biodynamic Constituents in Ayahuasca Admixture Plants: An Uninvestigated Folk Pharmacopoeia." In *Ethnobotany: Evolution of a Discipline*, ed. Richard E. Schultes and Siri von Reis, 349–360. Portland: Timber.

McKey, Doyle, Timothy R. Cavagnarro, Julie Cliff, and Roslyn Gleadow. 2011. "Chemical Ecology in Coupled Human and Natural Systems: People, Manioc, Multitrophic Interactions and Global Change." *Chemoecology* 20.2:109–133.

McMichael, Crystal H., Mark B. Bush, Dolores R. Piperno, Miles R. Silman, Andrew R. Zimmerman, and Christina Anderson. 2012. "Spatial and Temporal Scales of Pre-Columbian Disturbance Associated with Western Amazonian Lakes." *The Holocene* 22.2:131–141.

Meggers, Betty J. 1954. "Environmental Limitation on the Development of Culture." *American Anthropologist* 56:801–824.

———. 1996 [1971]. *Amazonia: Man and Culture in a Counterfeit Paradise.* Rev. ed. Washington, DC: Smithsonian Institution Press.

Mitchell, John F. B., Jason Lowe, Richard A. Wood, and Michael Vellinga. 2006. "Extreme Events Due to Human-Induced Climate Change." *Philosophical Transactions of the Royal Society A: Mathematical, Physical, and Engineering Sciences* 364 (1845): 2117–2133.

Mitchell, Sean T. 2010. "Paranoid Styles of Nationalism after the Cold War: Notes from an Invasion of the Amazon." In *Anthropology and Global Insurgency*, ed. John D. Kelly, Beatrice Jauregui, Sean T. Mitchell, and Jeremy Walton, 89–104. Chicago: University of Chicago Press.

Mittermeier, Russell A., Gustavo A. B. da Fonseca, Anthony B. Rylands, and Katrina Brandon. 2005. "A Brief History of Conservation in Brazil." *Conservation Biology* 19.3:601–607.

Mora, Santiago. 2001. "Suelos negros y sociedad: Un sistema agrícola de entonces, ¿un sistema agrícola de ahora?" In *Desarrollo sostenible en la Amazonia*, ed. Mario Hiraoka and Santiago Mora, 31–45. Quito: Abya-Yala.

Moraes, Claide de Paula. 2010. "Sedentarismo e guerra no baixo Madeira pré-Colonial." Paper presented at the II Encontro Internacional de Arqueologia Amazônica, Manaus.

Moraes, Claide de Paula, and Eduardo G. Neves. 2012. "O ano 1000: Adensamento populacional, interação e conflito na Amazônia Central." *Amazônica: Revista de Antropologia* 4.1:122–148.

Moraes Bertho, Ângela Maria de. 2001. "As ciências humanas no Museu Paraense Emílio Goeldi em suas fases de formação e consolidação (1886–1914)." In *Conhecimento e fronteira: História da ciência na Amazônia,* ed. Priscila Faulhaber and Peter Mann de Toledo. Belém: Museu Paraense Emílio Goeldi.

Moran, Emilio. 1974. "The Adaptive System of the Amazonian Caboclo." In *Man in the Amazon*, ed. Charles Wagley, 36–159. Gainesville: University Press of Florida.

———. 1993a. *Through Amazonian Eyes: The Human Ecology of Amazonian Populations.* Iowa City: University of Iowa Press.

———. 1993b. "Deforestation and Land Use in the Brazilian Amazon." *Human Ecology* 21.1:1–21.

Morton, Timothy. 2007. *Ecology without Nature: Rethinking Environmental Aesthetics.* Cambridge, MA: Harvard University Press.

Muehlmann, Shaylih. 2012. "Rhizomes and Other Uncountables: The Malaise of Enumeration in Mexico's Colorado River Delta." *American Ethnologist* 39.2:339–353.

Mukewar, Anand M., Janaradhan S. Zope, Satish S. Narkhede, and Anant J. Deshmukh. 2006. "Hybridisation Studies in Jatropha—the Petro Crop." *New Agriculturist* 17.1–2:219–222.

Myers, Thomas P., William M. Denevan, Antoinette Winklerprins, and Antonio Porro. 2003. "Historical Perspectives on Amazonian Dark Earths." In *Amazonian Dark Earths: Origin, Properties, Management,* ed. Johannes Lehman, Dirse C. Kern, Bruno Glaser, and William I. Woods, 15–28. Dordrecht: Kluwer.

Nepstad, Daniel C., Claudia M. Stickler, Britaldo Soares-Filho, and Frank Merry. 2008. "Interactions among Amazon Land Use, Forests, and Climate: Prospects for a Near-Term Forest Tipping Point." *Philosophical Transactions of the Royal Society B: Biological Sciences* 363 (1498): 1737–1746.

Neves, Eduardo G., James B. Petersen, Robert N. Bartone, and Carlos Augusto da Silva. 2003. "The Historical and Socio-Cultural Origins of Amazonian Dark Earths." In *Amazonian Dark Earths: Origin, Properties, Management,* ed. Dirse C. Kern, Johannes Lehmann, Bruno Glaser, and William I. Woods, 29–49. Dordrecht: Kluwer.

Nimuendaju, Curt. 1927. "Streifzug vom Rio Jari zum Maracá." *Petermanns Geographische Mitteilungen* 73:356–358.

———. 1953 [1949]. "Os Tapajó." *Revista de Antropologia* 1.1:53–61.

———. 2004. *Pursuit of a Past Amazon: Archaeological Researches in the Brazilian Guyana and in the Amazon Region.* Etnologiska Studier 45. Göteborg: Världskulturmuseet.

Nugent, Stephen. 1990. *Big Mouth: The Amazon Speaks.* London: Fourth Estate.

———. 1993. *Amazonian Caboclo Society: An Essay on Invisibility and Peasant Economy.* Oxford: Berg.

Ogden, Laura. 2010. *Swamplife: People, Gators, and Mangroves Entangled in the Everglades.* Minneapolis: University of Minnesota Press.

Ortencio, W. Bariani. 1997. *Medicina popular do Centro-Oeste.* 2nd ed. Brasília: Thesaurus.

Oyuela-Caycedo, Augusto, and Nicholas C. Kawa. 2015. "A Deep History of Tobacco in Lowland South America." In *Master Plant: Tobacco in Lowland South America,* ed. Andrew Russell and Elizabeth Rahman, 27–44. London: Bloomsbury.

Pace, Richard. 1997. "The Amazon Caboclo: What's in a Name?" *Luso-Brazilian Review* 34.2:81–89.

———. 1998. *The Struggle for Amazon Town: Gurupá Revisited.* Boulder, CO: Lynne Rienner.

Padoch, Christine, and Wil de Jong. 1992. "Diversity, Variation, and Change in Ribereno Agriculture." In *Conservation of Neotropical Forests,* ed. Kent H. Redford and Christine Padoch, 158–174. New York: Columbia University Press.

Palmatary, Helen C. 1949. "Pottery of Marajo Island, Brazil." *Transactions of the American Philosophical Society* 39.3:261–470.

———. 1960. "The Archaeology of the Lower Tapajós Valley, Brazil." *Transactions of the American Philosophical Society* 50.3:1–243.

Parker, Eugene, ed. 1985. *Amazon Caboclo: Historical and Contemporary Perspectives.* Studies in Third World Societies 32. Williamsburg, VA: College of William and Mary.

Partap, Uma, Tej Partap, and He Yonghua. 2001. "Pollination Failure in Apple Crop and Farmers' Management Strategies in Hengduan Mountains, China." *ISHS Acta Horticulturae* 561:225–230.

Penna, Domingos Soares Ferreira. 1869. *A região occidental da província do Pará: Resenha estatísticas das comarcas de Obidos e Santarem.* Pará: Typographia do Diário de Belém.

Peres, Carlos A., Toby A. Gardner, Jos Barlow, Jansen Zuanon, Fernanda Michalski, Alexander C. Lees, Ima C. G. Vieira, Fatima M. S. Moreira, and Kenneth J. Freeley. 2010. "Biodiversity Conservation in Human-Modified Amazonian Forest Landscapes." *Biological Conservation* 143.10:2314–2627. doi:10.1016/j.biocon.2010.01.02.

Pickering, Andrew. 1995. *The Mangle of Practice: Time, Agency, and Science.* Chicago: University of Chicago Press.

———. 2008. "New Ontologies." In *The Mangle in Practice: Science, Society, and Becoming,* ed. Andrew Pickering and Keith Guzick, 1–16. Durham, NC: Duke University Press.

Pickett, Joseph P., ed. 2000. *The American Heritage Dictionary of the English Language.* Boston: Houghton Mifflin.

Pinedo-Vasquez, Miguel, Mauro L. Ruffino, Christine Padoch, and Eduardo S. Brondizio, eds. 2011. *The Amazon Varzea: The Decade Past and the Decade Ahead.* New York: Springer.

Pollio, Antonino, Antoniono De Natale, Emanuela Appetiti, Giovanni Aliotta, and Alain Touwaide. 2008. "Continuity and Change in the Mediterranean Medical Tradition: *Ruta* spp. (Rutaceae) in Hippocratic Medicine and Present Practices." *Journal of Ethnopharmacology* 116.3:469–482.

Posey, Darrell A. 1985. "Indigenous Management of Tropical Forest Ecosystems: The Case of the Kayapo Indians of the Brazilian Amazon." *Agroforestry Systems* 3.2:139–158.

———. 1992. "Interpreting the Reality of Indigenous Concepts." In *Conservation of Neotropical Forests: Working from Traditional Resource Use*, ed. Kent H. Redford and Christine Padoch, 21–34. New York: Columbia University Press.

Prentis, Peter J., Sathyamurthy Raghu, Kunjithapatham Dhileepan, and Andrew J. Lowe. 2008. "Worldwide Phylogeography of the Globally Invasive Plant: *Jatropha gossypiifolia*." *Proceedings of the 16th Australian Weeds Conference, North Queensland, Australia, 18–22 May*, 150–152. Queensland: Weed Society.

Prentis, Peter J., Dominique P. Sigg, Sathyamurthy Raghu, Kunjithapatham Dhileepan, Ana Pavasovic, and Andrew J. Lowe. 2009. "Understanding Invasion History: Genetic Structure and Diversity of Two Globally Invasive Plants and Implications for Their Management." *Diversity and Distributions* 15.5:822–830.

Prigogine, Ilya, and Isabelle Stengers. 1984. *Order Out of Chaos: Man's New Dialogue with Nature*. New York: Bantam Books.

———. 1997. *The End of Certainty*. New York: Free Press.

Rabelo, Genival. 1964. *Ocupação da Amazônia*. Rio de Janeiro: Empresa Journalística.

Raffles, Hugh. 2002. *In Amazonia: A Natural History*. Princeton, NJ: Princeton University Press.

———. 2010. *Insectopedia*. New York: Random House.

Rangel, Alberto. 2001 [1908]. *Inferno verde*. Coleção Resgate II. Manaus: Valer.

Ranzi, Alceu, Robert Feres, and Foster Brown. 2007. "Internet Software Programs Aid in the Search for Amazonian Geoglyphs." *Eos* 88.21:226.

Rebellato, Lilian, William I. Woods, and Eduardo G. Neves. 2009. "Pre-Columbian Settlement Dynamics in the Central Amazon." In Woods et al. 2009, 15–31.

Rebhun, Linda-Anne. 1994. "Swallowing Frogs: Anger and Illness in Northeast Brazil." *Medical Anthropology Quarterly* 8.4:360–382.

Redfield, Peter. 2000. *Space in the Tropics: From Convicts to Rockets in French Guiana*. Berkeley: University of California Press.

Roller, Heather F. 2010. "Colonial Collecting Expeditions and the Pursuit of Opportunities in the Amazonian Sertão, c. 1750–1800." *The Americas* 66.4:435–467.

Roosevelt, Anna C. 1991. *Moundbuilders of the Amazon: Geophysical Archaeology on Marajó Island, Brazil*. San Diego, CA: Academic Press.

———. 1993. "The Rise and Fall of the Amazon Chiefdoms." *L'Homme* 33 (126–128): 255–283.

———. 1995. "Early Pottery in the Amazon: Twenty Years of Scholarly Obscurity." In *The Emergence of Pottery: Technology and Innovation in An-*

cient Societies, ed. William K. Barnett and John W. Hoopes, 115–131. Washington, DC: Smithsonian Institution Press.

Roosevelt, Anna C., Rupert A. Housley, Maura Imazio da Silveira, Sílvia Maranca, and Richard Johnson. 1991. "Eighth Millennium Pottery from a Prehistoric Shell Midden in the Brazilian Amazon." *Science* 24:1621–1624.

Rose, Deborah Bird. 2009. "Introduction: Writing in the Anthropocene." *Australian Humanities Review* 49:87.

Rostain, Stéphen. 2008. "Agricultural Earthworks on the French Guiana Coast." In Silverman and Isbell 2008, 217–233.

———. 2010. "Pre-Columbian Earthworks in Coastal Amazonia." *Diversity* 2.3:331–352.

Ruddiman, William. 2013. "The Anthropocene." *Annual Review of Earth and Planetary Sciences* 41:45–68.

Runk, Julie Velásquez. 2009. "Social and River Networks for the Trees: Wounaan's Riverine Rhizomic Cosmos and Arboreal Conservation." *American Anthropologist* 111.4:456–467.

Sabandar, Carla W., Norizan Ahmat, Faridahanim Mohd Jaafar, and I. Sahidin. 2013. "Medicinal Property, Phytochemistry, and Pharmacology of Several *Jatropha* Species (Euphorbiaceae): A Review." *Phytochemistry* 85:7–29.

Sagan, Dorion. 2013. *Cosmic Apprentice: Dispatches from the Edges of Science*. Minneapolis: University of Minnesota Press.

Sandburg, Carl. 1900. *Incidentals*. Galesburg, IL: Asgard.

Santos, Boaventura de Sousa. 1992. "A Discourse on the Sciences." *Review* (Fernand Braudel Center) 15.1:9–47.

Santos, Francisco Jorge dos. 1999. *Além da Conquista: Guerras e rebeliões indígenas na Amazônia pombalina*. Manaus: Universidade do Amazonas.

Schaan, Denise P. 2004. "The Camutins Chiefdom: Rise and Development of Social Complexity on Marajo Island, Brazilian Amazon." PhD diss., University of Pittsburgh.

———. 2008. "The Non-agricultural Chiefdoms of Marajo Island." In Silverman and Isbell 2008, 339–357.

Schaan, Denise P., Martti Parssinen, Alceu Ranzi, and Jacó César Piccoli. 2007. "Geoglifos da Amazônia ocidental: Evidência de complexidade social entre povos da terra firme." *Revista de Arqueologia* 20:67–82.

Schmidt, Morgan J. 2010. "Reconstructing Tropical Nature: Prehistoric and Modern Anthrosols (Terra Preta) in the Amazon Rainforest, Upper Xingu River, Brazil." PhD diss., University of Florida.

Schmink, Marianne, and Charles Wood. 1992. *Contested Frontiers in Amazonia*. New York: Columbia University Press.

Searchinger, Timothy, Ralph Heimlich, Richard A. Houghton, Fengxia Dong, Amani Elobeid, Jacinto Fabiosa, Simla Tokgoz, Dermot Hayes, and Tun-

Hsiang Yu. 2008. "Use of US Croplands for Biofuels Increases Greenhouse Gases through Emissions from Land-Use Change." *Science* 319 (5867): 1238–1240.

Serres, Michel. 1995. *The Natural Contract.* Ann Arbor: University of Michigan Press.

Shepard, Glenn H., Jr., and Henri Ramirez. 2011. "'Made in Brazil': Human Dispersal of the Brazil Nut (*Bertholletia excelsa*, Lecythidaceae) in Ancient Amazonia." *Economic Botany* 65.1:44–65.

Silverman, Helaine, and William H. Isbell eds. 2008. *Handbook of South American Archaeology.* Berlin: Springer.

Simões, Mario F., and Daniel F. Lopes. 1987. "Pesquisas arqueológicas no baixo/médio Rio Madeira (Amazonas)." *Revista de Arqueologia* 4: 117–134.

Skrimshire, Stefan. 2010. "Eternal Return of Apocalypse." In *Future Ethics: Climate Change and Apocalyptic Imagination,* ed. Stefan Skrimshire, 219–241. London: Continuum.

Slater, Candace. 1996. "Amazonia as Edenic Narrative." In *Uncommon Ground: Rethinking the Human Place in Nature,* ed. William Cronon, 114–131. New York: Norton.

———. 2002. *Entangled Edens: Visions of the Amazon.* Berkeley: University of California Press.

Smith, Herbert H. 1879a. *Brazil: The Amazons and the Coast.* New York: Scribner's.

———. 1879b. "An American Home on the Amazons." *Scribner's Monthly: An Illustrated Magazine for the People* 18:692–704.

Smith, Nigel J. H. 1980. "Anthrosols and Human Carrying Capacity in Amazonia." *Annals of the Association of American Geographers* 70:553–566.

———. 1981. *Man, Fishes, and the Amazon.* New York: Columbia University Press.

———. 1996. *The Enchanted Amazon Rain Forest: Stories from a Vanishing World.* Gainesville: University Press of Florida.

Sombroek, Wim G. 1966. *Amazonian Soils: A Reconnaissance of the Soils of the Brazilian Amazon Region.* Wageningen: Centre for Agricultural Publication and Documentation.

Sombroek, Wim, Dirse C. Kern, Tarcício Rodrigues, Manoel da Silva Cravo, Tony Cunha Jarbas, William I. Woods, and Bruno Glaser. 2002. "Terra Preta and Terra Mulata: Pre-Columbian Amazon Kitchen Middens and Agricultural Fields, Their Sustainability, and Their Replication." Paper no. 1935. Symposium 18—Anthropogenic Factors of Soil Formation, 17th WCSS, Bangkok, Thailand, Aug. 14–21, 2002.

Stanfield, Michael E. 1998. *Red Rubber, Bleeding Trees: Violence, Slavery, and Empire in Northwest Amazônia, 1850–1933.* Albuquerque: University of New Mexico Press.

Steffen, Will, Paul J. Crutzen, and John R. McNeill. 2007. "The Anthropocene: Are Humans Now Overwhelming the Great Forces of Nature?" *Ambio* 36.8:614–621.

Stepp, J. Richard, and Daniel E. Moerman. 2001. "The Importance of Weeds in Ethnopharmacology." *Journal of Ethnopharmacology* 75.1:19–23.

Steward, Julian. 1946–1959. *Handbook of South American Indians.* 7 vols. Bureau of American Ethnology, Bulletin 143. Washington, DC: Smithsonian Institution.

Tang, Yi Shin. 2008. "Legal Frontiers in the Global Dissemination of Technology and Knowledge: The Significance of Three Case Studies for Economic Development." *Les Cahiers du CEDIMES* 2.2:8–25.

Taussig, Michael. 1984. "Culture of Terror—Space of Death: Roger Casement's Putumayo Report and the Explanation of Torture." *Comparative Studies in Society and History* 26.3:467–497.

Teixeira, Carlos Corrêa. 2009. *Servidão humana na selva: O aviamento e o barracão nos seringais da Amazônia.* Manaus: Valer.

Tilman, David. 1999. "Global Environmental Impacts of Agricultural Expansion: The Need for Sustainable and Efficient Practices." *Proceedings of the National Academy of Sciences* 9.11:5995–6000.

TNI. 2009. "Biochar, a Big New Threat to People, Land, and Ecosystems." Accessed July 21, 2014. www.tni.org/article/biochar-big-new-threat -people-land-and-ecosystems.

Tsai, Siu Mui, Brendan O'Neill, Fabiana S. Cannavan, Daniel Saito, Newton P. S. Falcao, Dirse C. Kern, Julie Grossman, and Janice Thies. 2009. "The Microbial World of Terra Preta." In Woods et al. 2009, 299–308.

Tscharntke, Teja, Alexandra M. Klein, Andreas Kruess, Ingolf Steffan-Dewenter, and Carsten Thies. 2005. "Landscape Perspectives on Agricultural Intensification and Biodiversity—Ecosystem Service Management." *Ecology Letters* 8.8:857–874.

Tsing, Anna. 2012. "Unruly Edges: Mushrooms as Companion Species." *Environmental Humanities* 1:141–154.

United States Census Bureau. 2013. "State and County Quick Facts." Available at http://quickfacts.census.gov/.

Vale, Mariana M., Maria Alice Alves, and Stuart L. Pimm. 2008. "Biopiracy: Conservationists Have to Rebuild Lost Trust." *Nature* 453 (7191): 26.

vanEngelsdorp, Dennis, Jay D. Evans, Claude Saegerman, Chris Mullin, Eric Haubruge, Bach Kim Nguyen, Maryann Frazier, Jim Frazier, Diana Cox-Foster, Yanping Chen, Robyn Underwood, David R. Tarpy, and Jeffrey S. Pettis. 2009. "Colony Collapse Disorder: A Descriptive Study." *PloS One* 4.8:e6481.

Viveiros de Castro, Eduardo. 1996. "Images of Nature and Society in Amazonian Ethnology." *Annual Review of Anthropology* 25:179–200.

———. 1998. "Cosmological Deixis and Amerindian Perspectivism." *Journal of the Royal Anthropological Institute* 4.3:469–488.

———. 2014. *Cannibal Metaphysics*. Minneapolis: University of Minnesota Press.

Viveiros de Castro, Eduardo, Morten Axel Pedersen, and Martin Holbraad. 2014. "The Politics of Ontology: Anthropological Positions." Fieldsights—Theorizing the Contemporary. *Cultural Anthropology* online. http://www.culanth.org/fieldsights/462-the-politics-of-ontology-anthropological-positions.

Voeks, Robert A. 1997. *Sacred Leaves of Candomblé: African Magic, Medicine, and Religion in Brazil*. Austin: University of Texas Press.

Wagley, Charles. 1976 [1953]. *Amazon Town: A Study of Man in the Tropics*. New York: Oxford University Press.

Walker, John H. 2008. "The Llanos de Mojos." In Silverman and Isbell 2008, 927–939.

Weinstein, Barbara. 1983. *The Amazon Rubber Boom: 1850–1920*. Stanford, CA: Stanford University Press.

———. 1985. "Persistence of Caboclo Culture in the Amazon: The Impact of the Rubber Trade, 1850–1920." In *The Amazon Caboclo: Historical and Contemporary Perspectives*, ed. Eugene Parker, 89–113. Williamsburg, VA: College of William and Mary.

Weismantel, Mary. 2001. *Cholas and Pishtacos: Stories of Race and Sex in the Andes*. Chicago: University of Chicago Press.

Woods, William I., Newton P. S. Falcao, and Wenceslau G. Teixeira. 2006. "Biochar Trials Aim to Enrich Soil for Smallholder." *Nature* 443:144.

Woods, William I., and Joseph M. McCann. 1999. "The Anthropogenic Origin and Persistence of Amazonian Dark Earths." Yearbook of the *Conference of Latin Americanist Geographers* 25:7–14.

Woods, William I., Wenceslau G. Teixeira, Johannes Lehmann, Christoph Steiner, Antoinette WinklerPrins, and Lilian Rebellato, eds. 2009. *Amazonian Dark Earths: Wim Sombroek's Vision*. Amsterdam: Springer.

Woolf, Dominic, James E. Amonette, F. Alaynes Street-Perrot, Johannes Lehmann, and Stephen Joseph. 2010. "Sustainable Biochar to Mitigate Global Climate Change." *Nature Communications* 1 (56): 1–9.

Zalasiewicz, Jan, Mark Williams, Will Steffen, and Paul J. Crutzen. 2010. "The New World of the Anthropocene." *Environmental Science and Technology* 44:2228–2231. DOI:10.1021/es903118j.

CPSIA information can be obtained
at www.ICGtesting.com
Printed in the USA
FSHW011838030821
83629FS